Persecuting Zeal

PERSECUTING ZEAL

A PORTRAIT OF IAN PAISLEY

DENNIS COOKE

BRANDON

First published in 1996 by
Brandon Book Publishers Ltd,
Dingle, Co. Kerry, Ireland

British Library Cataloguing in Publication Data
is available for this book.

ISBN 0 86322 222 6

Front cover photograph: Pacemaker
The publishers thank Trevor Gibson
for permission to use the photograph
of Ian Paisley at Crossgar.

Typeset by Koinonia, Bury, Lancashire
Cover designed by Peter Staunton,
the Design Gang, Tralee, Co. Kerry.

Printed by Redwood Books, Trowbridge, Wilts

To Joan
Jacqueline, Steve and Pete,
superb encouragers

and in memory of my parents

Contents

Acknowledgements

1. The Dilemma   *1*

2. The Noble Succession?   *9*

3. The Early Years   *23*

4. Anti-Catholicism   *41*

5. Apostate Protestants   *69*

6. Free Presbyterians   *103*

7. The Road to Stormont 1946–1970   *133*

8. Manoeuvring for Unionist Leadership 1970–1996   *167*

9. A Paisley Dynasty?   *217*

   Notes and References   *225*

List of photographs

1. On board the Clyde Valley in Larne in the 1960s
2. Ian Paisley at Crossgar, 1951; George Gibson is second from the right
3. Leaving the Ulster Workers' Council headquarters following an Action Council meeting, May 1977
4. The orator, July 1980
5. Staging one of many demonstrations outside the Presbyterian Assembly in Belfast, 1982
6. Marching, August 1985
7. Snipping the wire at the Stormont security fence, April 1987
8. With his flock
9. With his wife Eileen after winning the North Antrim election in 1992
10. With James Molyneaux
11. At Drumcree, July 1995
12. With Tony Blair, September 1995

Acknowledgements

My indebtedness is unbounded to those who have helped me towards the publication of this book: Andy Pollak and Ed Moloney granted access to their considerable research material which is in the keeping of the Linen Hall Library, Belfast; my colleague Revd Donald Kerr frequently gave the benefit of his scholarship regarding relevant New Testament passages; the Governors of Edgehill Theological College allowed a three months sabbatical; Irish church historian the Very Revd Professor Finlay Holmes kindly read my script, corrected mistakes, and made valuable suggestions to improve the text; Steve MacDonogh of Brandon was a pleasure to work with from beginning to end; above all my wife Joan, and Steve and Pete, gave endless encouragement.

The following libraries and resources were of immense help: Edgehill Theological Library; Linen Hall Library, Belfast; Union Theological Library, Belfast; the Library of the Queen's University, Belfast; the Public Record Office of Northern Ireland; Martyr's Memorial Church office and also the Recordings Office; the General Office of the Presbyterian Church in Ireland; and Belfast Public Library and especially its Lisburn Road branch.

Belfast, August 1996   Dennis Cooke

Chapter One

The Dilemma

ARTYRS' MEMORIAL FREE Presbyterian Church on the
Ravenhill Road in Belfast had a packed congregation at the
evening service on Sunday 17 November 1985. Two days
earlier at Hillsborough Castle in County Down the British prime minister, Margaret Thatcher, and the Irish taoiseach, Garret FitzGerald,
had signed the Anglo-Irish Agreement between the government of the
United Kingdom of Great Britain and Northern Ireland and the
government of Ireland. Feelings were running high among many in
the Unionist community as fears grew about the real significance of an
Inter-Governmental Conference to be set up to consider political,
security, legal and other matters within the province. From past
experience, people anticipated that Ian Paisley, MP, MEP, minister of
the church, moderator of the Free Presbyterian Church of Ulster and
leader of the Democratic Unionist Party, would have something to say
on the agreement, and they were not disappointed.

After the singing of two stanzas of the hymn, 'O God, our help in
ages past', Dr Paisley led in prayer. In his opening prayer at the morning service, he had already prayed, 'very solemnly right now we hand
Mrs Thatcher over to the devil that she might learn not to blaspheme',
and this was repeated in his opening prayer in the evening:

O God, defeat all our enemies. We call upon Thee. We pray this night that
Thou wouldst deal with the Prime Minister of our country. We remember
that the apostle Paul handed over the enemies of truth to the Devil that
they might learn not to blaspheme. In the Name of Thy Blessed Self,
Father, Son and Holy Ghost, we hand this woman Margaret Thatcher over
to the Devil that she might learn not to blaspheme. We pray that Thou
wouldst make her a monument of Thine Divine Vengeance; we pray that
the world will learn a lesson through the ignominy to which she shall be
brought. For wilt Thou not hear the cries of Thy people, and if Thou wilt
not hear their cry, we are confident that Thou wilt hear the cry of innocent
blood that comes from the soil of Ulster today. And O God in wrath take
vengeance upon this wicked, treacherous, lying woman. Take vengeance
upon her, O Lord. And grant that we shall see a demonstration of Thy
Power.[1]

Paisley reminded the congregation of the time he had prayed a similar prayer concerning Brian Faulkner, prime minister of Northern
Ireland prior to the prorogation of the Stormont Parliament in 1972
and chief executive in the brief power-sharing administration of 1974.
He told them that on that occasion his wife had said, 'Do you know
what you prayed?'

He answered, 'Yes.'

She said, 'That was an awful prayer.' But, he went on to recall,
'Brian Faulkner is no more. And it was at an entrance to a Free Presbyterian home that he died, the man that said that I was a doctor of
demons. The mills of God grind slow, but they grind exceedingly
small.'

The following Sunday evening Paisley told the congregation that
the press had telephoned him about his prayer of the previous week.
The Press Association had called it a 'terrible prayer'; the *Daily Mail*
and the *Daily Express* had commented on it, and their reporters were
now present in the congregation. He insisted that it had been a scriptural prayer, but he didn't expect journalists from these papers to
understand that. They didn't know the scriptures. Indeed one of the
writers was a Jew: 'He would be a rejector of the New Testament scriptures anyway, so he wouldn't have any idea what the New Testament
was about.'[2] Paisley claimed his authority lay in 1 Corinthians 5:3-5
and 1 Timothy 1:19-20, but made no reference to the fact that the
Apostle Paul had been speaking of people recently within the Christian
fellowship, a status which he, because of his Free Presbyterian separatist theology, could not have given to either Margaret Thatcher or
Brian Faulkner, regarding them instead as 'apostates'.

It is Paisley's custom, from time to time, to tell his congregation
about his political activities. As leader of the DUP he was involved in
the All-Party Talks in 1991 and 1992 between representatives of the
British and Irish governments and the Northern Ireland political parties. Strand Two of this process in the summer of 1992 focused on
north/south relationships. Conscious that there were those in his party
and congregation who were unhappy about his involvement in the
north/south talks, he assured the congregation on 5 July that he would
never surrender to the enemies of Ulster. He claimed that God had
given him great power as he addressed the representatives of the
British and Irish governments, that he had told the Irish foreign affairs
minister, David Andrews, that he was a malevolent and evil man
because of his attacks on the security forces in Northern Ireland. To
someone who had said to him, 'You're talking to them,' he had

replied, 'Yes, just the same way as David talked to Goliath and left him with a hole in his head,' which the Martyrs' Memorial congregation found very amusing.

Such verbal attacks have been characteristic of Paisley's preaching and writing for half a century, and age has not mellowed him. Politicians, clergy, former follow travellers have all been subjected to his scathing denunciations. He claims that in this he is simply continuing in the tradition of the apostles and Reformers, and even of Jesus Himself – 'Generation of vipers, how can you escape the damnation of hell?'

Particularly significant, given the troubled community relations in Northern Ireland, have been his criticisms of the Roman Catholic Church. Throughout his life he has repeatedly emphasised that the Roman Catholic Church is not a Christian church: 'Make no mistake. Romanism is as far removed from Christianity as Hell is from Heaven. Anyone who denies that is either ignorant of the Bible, or of Rome, or of both.'[3] His fury has been frequently directed at anyone who treats the Roman Catholic Church as a Christian church. 'My blood boils when I think of what the Church of Rome really believes, and how men can greet her as part of the Christian church. The Church of Rome has no part in Christianity whatsoever. The Church of Rome is baptised paganism, that is what it is. Her idolatries all come from the old idolatrous system of Nimrod. It is Nimrodism, not Christianity at all.'[4] In various ways he has alleged links between the Roman Catholic Church and the violence which was tearing the community apart. At the beginning of the Troubles, he declared: 'At night the murder gangs of the Roman Catholic Church and the Marxists are operating together.'[5] He described Tomás Ó Fiaich, Roman Catholic archbishop of Armagh (1977-1990), as 'the Sinn Féin Cardinal'.[6] In an article entitled 'Even Lourdes Could Not Heal Cardinal Thomas O'Fee', published on the cardinal's death in May 1990, Paisley's church magazine, *The Revivalist*, expressed surprise that when the cardinal was taken ill at Lourdes, the place so often spoken of as their 'healing mecca', he should have been rushed off to a hospital in Toulouse.[7]

Paisley's anti-Catholic views are well known in the north of Ireland and, to an extent, further afield. Gusty Spence, associated with the Ulster Volunteer Force (UVF) in the mid-1960s and imprisoned from 1966-1984, described knowledge of this side of Paisley's nature as commonplace: 'The dogs in the street were aware of Ian Paisley's anti-Catholicism.'[8] It forms one of the main emphases of his preaching and teaching. He believes that Catholicism has so blinded people to the

truth of Christ that it must be confronted and challenged. In October
1988, preaching in his church after protesting against an official visit
by the pope to the European Parliament at Strasbourg, he declared:
'This is the battle of the Ages which we are engaged in. This is no
Sunday School picnic, this is a battle for truth against the lie, the battle of Heaven against hell, the battle of Christ against the Antichrist.'[9]
He has passed on this anti-Catholic missionary zeal to his Free Presbyterian ministers and people, making it a force to be reckoned with in
the religious and political life of Ulster. There are those who see this
as part of the legacy of history, and Irish history in particular; as a
zeal which mirrors that found at various times in Protestantism since
the Reformation; as a characteristic which places him firmly within the
Reformation and evangelical tradition.

Protestant ministers and churches have also been targets of his
scorn and condemnation, especially those in any way connected with
the World Council of Churches (WCC). Scandalised by divisions
within Christianity which were thought to be contrary to the will of
Christ, representatives of 147 churches, mostly from Europe and
North America, met together at Amsterdam in 1948 to form the
World Council of Churches. It has since held seven World Assemblies,
the most recent being at Canberra in 1991, and its member churches
have grown in number to over 300, coming from about 100 countries
all over the world. Despite its basis of membership – 'The World
Council of Church is a fellowship of churches which confess the Lord
Jesus Christ as God and Saviour according to the Scriptures and
therefore seek to fulfil together their common calling to the glory of
the one God, Father, Son and Holy Spirit' – Paisley has accused the
WCC of apostasy and prophesied damnation for anyone connected
with it: 'Every soul that commits itself to the World Council of
Churches or to a Church connected with the World Council of
Churches will perish, and perish in the Judgment of Almighty God.'[10]
Hardly a Sunday goes by without some reference in his prayers or
sermon to the apostasy of the ecumenical movement. However, apostates can also be the object of fun. Speaking at a Bible conference held
in the Bob Jones University, South Carolina, he expressed interest in
the chancellor's gold-topped cane: 'I was going to suggest that he
could bring that cane back with him to Ulster the next time he comes
as there's a few apostates could do with a good clubbing over the
head!'[11] The conference erupted in laughter at the thought of it.

No church, or so it would appear, has come through unaffected by
Paisley's attacks. Even the Reformed Presbyterian Church of Ireland,

or 'the Covenanters' as they are more commonly known, which granted special permission for him to be a 'guest student' at their Theological Hall from 1942 to 1945, has received a public though mild rebuke. In an article in *The Revivalist* entitled 'Reformed Ecumenical Synod in WCC Parley', it was considered 'a most serious question' that the Synod, which included the Reformed Presbyterian Church in its membership, was 'joining a World Council consultation on church unity'.[12] Two months later the magazine welcomed and published a letter received from Knox Hyndman, clerk of the church, indicating the concern of the church at recent developments in the Reformed Ecumenical Synod and the strong likelihood of their withdrawal, which, in fact, took place within a year.

This belligerent and judgmental attitude so frequently evident in his treatment of those with whom he disagrees in religion or politics – and for Paisley the two are generally interrelated – is far from providing the complete picture of the man. He is known to many, particularly his family, but also people in his congregation, his church, his party, and occasionally his constituents, as a compassionate and caring person. His second eldest daughter, Rhonda, was concerned about what she felt was a false media image of her father and agreed to share her own reflections in a book entitled *Ian Paisley, My Father*. She has described her father, the head of their home, as 'one of the most compassionate men I have ever met'.[13] She can see nothing wrong in the manner in which he has acted towards religious and political opponents; indeed, she insists, 'he is a meek man – he is dynamite under control if you like'.[14]

There can be no doubt about the strength of the ties that bind the family together and especially the love between Ian Paisley and his wife, Eileen. As Rhonda has expressed it, 'Mum is the perfect partner for Dad.'[15] With the exception of Kyle, the eldest twin, who is a Free Presbyterian minister at Oulton Broad in East Anglia, the family all attend their father's church: Sharon, the eldest, married to John Huddleston, and their daughter Lydia; Rhonda; Cherith, married to Andrew Caldwell; and Ian, the younger twin, his wife Fiona and daughters Emily and Lucy Jane. Despite the vast amount of travelling he undertakes in Ireland and to various parts of the world, he has always made time to be with his family and to be available to them. When they were growing up they were conscious of the duties and obligations which often necessitated their father's absence, but they always knew that if they had a problem their father would be sensitive to it.

Kyle is indebted to his father for the help he received in his own spiritual pilgrimage. As a child he had made a commitment to Christ, but in his early teens he went through a difficult time of uncertainty regarding his salvation. His father and mother were both aware of his feelings. The help he received from his father is indelibly printed on his memory:

He pointed me to a verse, John 6:37, 'All that the Father giveth me shall come to me; and him that cometh to me I will in no wise cast out.' He pointed out to me simply, 'if you have come to Christ, you've got to take Christ at his word. Christ says, "him that cometh to me I will in no wise cast out": and if Christ says "in no wise" He must mean "in no wise". And if you've given your heart and your life to Him, and if you've asked Him to take away your sins and prayed that and meant it from your heart, and you've come to Him in that way, He has already said that He will in no wise cast you out. So you just have to take God at His word and rely upon His promise.' And as soon as I did that, just took the Lord at His word, the doubts disappeared.[16]

It is not surprising that there was a strong emphasis on family worship in the Paisley home. They would share worship as a family in the morning or evening, or sometimes at lunchtime, depending on when the whole family were together. Each member of the family participated. As Kyle recalls, 'Father would start, then my mother, and go from the oldest right to the youngest.'

While some among the general public in Northern Ireland refer to Paisley as 'the Big Man' – he is 6 feet 3 inches tall and weighs around sixteen and a half stones – his congregation at Martyrs' Memorial know him affectionately as 'the Doc'. They follow his travels, whether within the province, to Westminster, to the United States, or elsewhere, with great interest and prayer. When he is away for extended periods they can be sure they will receive reports on his health and the success of his engagements to date, knowing also that he himself will give a full account on his return. In their eyes he can do little wrong and his place in the annals of history as a political and religious leader is already guaranteed.

The Revd Eric Smyth, lord mayor of Belfast in 1995 and member of the Democratic Unionist Party, is full of appreciation for the help he received from Paisley. He was brought up on the east side of the city and was converted to Christ at the age of fourteen in the little Everton Drive Mission Hall off the Cregagh Road. While involved with the Mormons, he learned that Dr Paisley had challenged them to a debate on the scriptures and Mormon beliefs. It was around this time that he started going to Paisley's church on the Ravenhill Road and he continued going there for about twenty years. Paisley encouraged him in mission work and then became aware of his desire to engage in full-time Christian work. But there was a problem. Smyth was dyslexic, and because no one had understood his problem at school he was 'classed as a dunce and stupid'. Paisley knew he did not have the educational qualifications necessary to enter training for the Free Presbyterian ministry, so he put him in contact with Dr Peter Ng of Singapore, director of the Jesus Saves Mission organisation, who was looking for someone to do mission work among the poor in Belfast. Smyth was ordained by Ng in 1984 and is now minister of the Jesus Saves Mission Church at the corner of the Limestone Road and North Queen Street. He is unstinting in his praise for Paisley's generosity: 'Dr Paisley is a man that I love so dearly; and he's only a man, he makes mistakes like the rest of us, but he's a man with a big heart. I know of young men who were in difficulty financially. Dr Paisley put his hand in his pocket and helped them. He did it with me in my early days when I wasn't getting very much money. He's a man who encourages people along.'[17]

Paisley's political activities were a definite influence on him, as he felt he too had an obligation to get involved in politics 'to defend what is right'. In his opinion Paisley has been the right man in the right place at the right time: 'I believe Dr Paisley was called in the day of need in the political scene to stand up and be counted against what we would feel is the betrayal of the British government.'

Few members of Parliament have received such heartfelt expressions of gratitude as Paisley has from his constituents on Rathlin Island, part of the North Antrim constituency which he has represented at Westminster since 1970. For a long time the hundred or so islanders, said to be about 90 per cent Roman Catholic, had felt that nobody was interested in them. As Tommy Cecil of the Rathlin Island Community Association describes it, 'Rathlin was a forgotten island, a dying island. Nobody was concerned. Government officials didn't want to know about it.'[18] The association decided to write to Paisley and tell him their problems. To their surprise, for he hadn't told anyone he was coming, Paisley crossed the six and a half miles from Ballintoy in a small boat on 12 June 1973, well remembered as being a very stormy day. He promised that day he would do all in his power to get things done for the island and has been true to his word. Since he took an interest in Rathlin there has been a radical transformation, with the installation of a mains water supply, a main sewage system, electricity and telephone services, and a new harbour with a roll-on/roll-off ferry service. He has also been helpful in dealing with problems and concerns brought personally to him. Understandably, Cecil comments: 'People in Rathlin have a very high regard for him. He has a very caring attitude. Most of the islanders he knows personally.'

In addition to this side of Paisley's personality, his love and compassion for people, there is also another side to his preaching. Not all of it is condemnatory of other people's beliefs or actions. There are many who feel he is at his best when pointing people to Christ as Saviour. His preaching on the love of God, the need for forgiveness and commitment to Christ, and the devotional side of the Christian life, is very moving and convincing, especially as on these occasions he is seldom shouting and speaks more gently. His sermon, 'The First of all Firsts', based on 1 John 4:19, 'We love him because he first loved us', perhaps one of his best sermons, illustrates this appeal:

That is amazing, is it not? That is incomprehensible. Before God created He loved. Creation is the putting forth of God's power, but love is His nature. It is inherent to God to love. He cannot keep from loving, for God is love. I am afraid God's people have forgotten that. 'He first loved us.' What a loving that is! God's love manifested, revealed, unveiled, uncovered in the Person of His wonderful Son.[19]

These two sides to his nature, one which is aggressive, judgmental, gratuitously insulting at times, and the other which is warm, friendly, sympathetic and loving, indicate the complexity of his personality. 'I have often thought there are about six Paisleys,' Maurice Hayes, a former chairman of the Northern Ireland Community Relations Commission, suggests. 'Two of them are very nice people, two quite awful, and the other two could go either way.'[20] But the main dilemma is to understand how he reconciles his Christian profession with such continual caustic condemnation of others in the political and religious life of the country and how he can so dogmatically deny others, and their churches, the right to be called 'Christian', when they confess, as he does, the same personal faith in Christ. Rhonda Paisley's explanation is hardly adequate: 'Dad is a defender and contender for the faith he cherishes. This does not make him a rough man of war, nor an unreasonable man of attack.'[21] Those whom he fails to recognise as Christians would also believe they must contend for the faith, but this has not led them to deny his Christianity.

Chapter Two

The Noble Succession?

PAISLEYISM HAS ITS roots in the ethnic and religious aspects of Irish history. Since these factors were also related to the question of the ownership of land, the ingredients for suspicion and tension were always potentially present. It is vital, therefore, to pause and examine these various elements which form the background to the politics and theology of Ian Paisley.

The Mesolithic hunter-fisher people are thought to have been the earliest inhabitants of Ireland, possibly around 5,000 BC. Various other cultures existed between their arrival and that of the Gaels, who began to come from Gaul about the first century BC. The story of migrations, people arriving and sometimes people leaving, characterises much of the island's history. One such immigrant, Patrick, or others before him, brought Christianity in the fourth century, and by the mid-sixth century it was well established throughout most of the country. Irish monks like Columba, Columban, Aidan and Colman have made the evangelising commitment of Celtic spirituality famous by their missionary endeavours in Scotland, the north of England and west central Europe.

By the eleventh century, however, prompted by concern for the condition of the Irish church, which had been considerably weakened by the Norse wars of the previous two centuries, and wishing to bring it under greater papal control, Adrian IV (actually, Nicholas Breakspeare, the only Englishman ever to have been elected pope), by the bull 'Laudabiliter' commissioned Henry II of England in 1155 to establish lordship in Ireland so that its 'nurseries of vice' might be rooted out and each house required to pay an annual pension of a penny to the heir of St Peter. The bull, often regarded as one of the curiosities of history, reveals that Henry may already have had plans to extend his influence to Ireland:

If then you are resolved to carry the design you have conceived into effectual execution, study to form that nation to virtuous manners; and labour by yourself and others whom you shall judge meet for this work, in faith, word, and life, that the Church may be there adorned, that *the religion of the Christian faith may be planted and grow up,* and that all things pertaining to the honour of God and the salvation of souls be so ordered, that you may be entitled to the fulness of the eternal reward in God, and obtain a glorious renown on earth throughout all ages.[1]

J. C. Beckett has described Henry II's six-month visit in 1171 to establish lordship in Ireland as one which 'opened a new phase in Anglo-Irish relations', but has also pointed out that 'it is misleading to regard the events of these years as constituting an "English" conquest of Ireland. The invaders were Norman, Norman-Welsh and Flemish, rather than English, and their language and traditions were French.'[2] However, this English identity was well established by the time of Henry VIII's schism with Rome in 1534 and the Irish Parliament's conferment of the title 'king of Ireland' in 1541. Henry had now made it clear that his authority no longer depended on a papal grant.

The sixteenth-century Reformation which influenced England, Scotland and certain parts of Europe had little, if any, effect in Ireland. Patrick Corish, former professor of modern history at St Patrick's College, Maynooth, has acknowledged that 'By any standards, the old religion needed reform and revitalisation'.[3] But English monarchs were more intent on establishing military supremacy than enforcing Reformation beliefs and practices. Indeed, it was this very need, and the obvious benefits of having more loyal subjects, which led to the plantation policies of the sixteenth and seventeenth centuries. The enduring legacy of this policy was to introduce a religious divide between those inhabiting the island, a divide which eventually was seen as setting apart 'the ruling class' from 'the governed', 'the privileged' from 'the dispossessed'.

One of these policies, the Plantation of Ulster, is of particular relevance to any enquiry into the background and roots of Paisley. Following a period of war and suspicion between native Irish chiefs and the administration of Elisabeth I, the 'flight of the earls' in 1607 – the earls being Tyrone and Tyrconnel – was taken as an opportunity to introduce Scottish and English settlers into the region. The vast area over which the earls had exercised control, the six counties of Armagh, Cavan, Coleraine, Donegal, Fermanagh and Tyrone, were declared forfeit to the Crown, and the plantation arrangements for the new settlers followed closely on the model which had recently been operating in Antrim and Down. But the new lands were not entirely taken over by the incoming settlers because difficulties experienced in bringing in the Scots and English made the new owners prepared to ignore government instructions and accept former landlords as the new tenants. The pattern established, therefore, was one which deeply embedded the religious divide into Ulster society.

Presbyterianism in Ireland traces its beginnings to the settlers who came from the Lowlands of Scotland. Their first ministers, who had followed them to Ulster, found they had to come to some accomodation with the Episcopalian form of church government in the Church of Ireland. A fair amount of tolerance and understanding was exercised by both Episcopalians and those more inclined to Presbyterian structures, but this came to an abrupt end on the appointment of Thomas Wentworth as Lord Deputy in 1633. Strict conformity to the articles and canons of the Church of Ireland were now enforced, convincing some of the leading ministers to make an abortive attempt to sail to America where they expected they might enjoy a greater liberty of conscience. Blocked by rough seas, they returned to Ireland and eventually made their way to Scotland.

The circumstances leading to the formation of the first presbytery in Ulster were unusual, to say the least, but reflect something of the life-and-death struggle in which most were now inevitably caught up. The insurrection of the Irish in Ulster in 1641, mainly a reaction to their dispossession under the plantation system, had led to the formation of a Catholic confederacy at Kilkenny in 1642 and the murder of thousands of colonists. Professor Finlay Holmes explains the link between the rebellion and the formation of the presbytery: 'Their rising brought a Scottish army to Ulster in 1642 and it was the chaplains and officer-elders of the regiments of that army who formed the first Presbytery in Ulster and began the formal history of Irish Presbyterianism.'[4] Within twenty years the Presbyterian form of church government was organised throughout Ulster.

Irish resistance continued until 1652, but it was the ruthlessness and cruelty of Oliver Cromwell's campaigns from August 1649 to May 1650 which, Beckett reminds us, have left a memory that succeeding centuries have been unable to erase:

He came to Ireland not only as a parliamentary commander pursuing the royalist enemy to his latest stronghold, but also the avenger of blood, the minister (as he believed) of divine justice on those responsible for the cruelties which had been committed in the Ulster rising of 1641. It is this which explains not only the sack of Drogheda and of Wexford but even more the satisfaction that appears in Cromwell's reports. 'I am persuaded,' he writes from Drogheda, after describing how 2,000 men were put to the sword, 'that this is a righteous judgement of God upon those barbarous wretches, who have imbrued their hands in so much innocent blood.'[5]

The years 1688-1690 were very significant in Irish and British history. James II, crowned king in 1685, had introduced policies particularly favourable to Irish Roman Catholics: the army was purged of Protestants, Roman Catholics were admitted to the privy council, judiciary, and municipal corporations, and expectations were raised that the Cromwellian land settlement might be repealed and the previous proprietors restored to their estates. However, these and other factors cost James II the support of the English Parliament and he had to flee to France in December 1688.

William of Orange accepted Parliament's invitation to be the new monarch and was crowned king in February 1689. But James had not given up: he landed at Kinsale in March 1689, intending to use Ireland as a base to restore his power in England.

Meanwhile, on 16 September 1688, thirteen apprentices had closed the gates of Londonderry against the Earl of Antrim and his regiment. In April 1689 James set seige to the city, cutting off access from the sea by placing a boom across the River Foyle. We are told that the 30,000 within the walls were reduced to living on dogs, cats, mice, candles and leather until the seige was broken on 1 August 1689. The story of the seige, its eventual relief, and the subsequent victory of William III over James II at the Battle of the Boyne on 1 July 1690, are commemorated annually by the Apprentice Boys' Clubs and the Orange Order. Peter Robinson, deputy leader of the Democratic Unionist Party, and thereby a close associate of Ian Paisley, suggests there are lessons to be learned from the seige:

There are many, even though in the service of the Crown, who profess to support the Unionist cause, yet their every action betrays the principle they claim to uphold. There are those like Major-General Kirke who, though they possess the power to take action that would relieve suffering and distress, hesitate, waiting on their own convenience, before engaging the enemy. But, thank God, there are many, like the brave thirteen, like Baker, Michelburne and Murray, who have that indomitable spirit which refuses to accept anything short of an honourable outcome.[6]

Anti-Catholicism

Anti-Catholicism took two main forms in Ireland during the eighteenth century. On the one hand penal laws were enacted in the Irish Parliament after the Williamite victory and in the early eighteenth century to render Irish Roman Catholics impotent politically and economically. Later in the eighteenth century the evangelical movement, personified in John Wesley, the founder of Methodism, who undertook twenty-one preaching tours in Ireland during the period 1747-1789, intensified Protestant hostility to Roman Catholicism.

Patrick Corish has highlighted the potential threat to Catholicism posed by the penal laws: 'The penal code contained numerous provisions which if put into effect would have extinguished the Catholic church in Ireland.'[7] Its main concern was with property, particularly land held by the Catholic gentry. Land was seen as the key to political power and therefore every effort was made to limit still further the amount of land held in Catholic hands. At the end of the Cromwellian period, Catholic ownership of land had been reduced to 14 per cent but under the provisions of the penal code it fell to 5 per cent. Catholics were forbidden to purchase or inherit land from a Protestant; by the law of 'gavelkind' a Catholic proprietor's land was to be divided equally among his sons on his death, but should one of them become a Protestant he would inherit everything; Catholics could only lease land for a maximum of thirty-one years. Legislation also made it difficult for priests to fulfil their duties and the church to be properly administered. And Catholics were excluded from Parliament, the legal profession, the army and the civil service.

John Wesley (1703-1791), a Church of England minister convinced of the need to encourage a revival of true religion, spent much of his time and energy in pursuing this goal in Ireland. Historians have regarded him as the dominant figure within evangelicalism during the eighteenth century, but they have not always agreed regarding his attitude to Catholicism. Earlier biographers have concentrated on his more irenical writings, but recent scholars have insisted on a more comprehensive approach. An accurate judgement on this subject is particularly relevant as Paisley has frequently quoted Wesley in support of his own position.

In the complexity of his teaching Wesley appears to have been able to accommodate two quite different approaches to Catholicism. Most of the time he is dismissive of the Catholic religion, regarding it as so illiberal and erroneous that it fails to portray the essence of true Christianity. His 1745 publication, *A Word to a Protestant*,[8] set the tone for much of his later writing on Catholicism. He warned against errors established and legalised by the Council of Trent: 'their doctrine of seven sacraments; of transubstantiation; of communion in one kind only; of purgatory; and praying for the dead therein; of veneration of relics; and of indulgences, or pardons granted by the Pope, and to be bought for money'. These errors, he suggested, 'defile the purity of

Christianity', but three other doctrines were much more destructive of
true Christianity: 'these grand Popish doctrines of merit, idolatry, and
persecution, by destroying both faith, and the love of God and of our
neighbour, tend to banish true Christianity out of the world'.
Commenting on 2 Thessalonians 2:3 in his *Notes on the New Testament*, he suggests the title 'the man of sin' is applicable to the pope:
'*the man of sin, the son of perdition*, – Eminently so called, is not yet
come. However, in many respects, the Pope has an indisputable claim
to those titles. He is, in an emphatical sense, *the man of sin*, as he
increases all manner of sin above measure. And he is, too, properly
styled, *the son of perdition*, as he has caused the death of numberless
multitudes, both of his opposers and followers, destroyed innumerable
souls, and will himself perish everlastingly.'⁹ David Hempton suggests
that writings of this nature represent the general thrust of his teaching and concludes: 'Wesley's anti-Catholicism was one of his profound
and enduring legacies to the Wesleyan connexion.'¹⁰

Despite these criticisms of the Catholic Church, he still recognised
it as part of the Christian church.¹¹ In what is certainly his most
conciliatory writing, *Letter to a Roman Catholic*,¹² written in July 1749
after serious rioting in Cork involving threats and injury to Methodist
members and their property, he affirms that Protestants and Catholics
have the fundamentals of true Christian faith and practice in common
and suggests that differences of opinion in other matters should not
prevent them from encouraging each other to love and good works:
'let us resolve, First, not to hurt one another; to do nothing unkind
or unfriendly to each other.... Secondly, God being our helper, to
speak nothing harsh or unkind of each other.... Thirdly, to harbour no
unkind thought, no unfriendly temper towards each other.... Fourthly,
to help each other in whatever we are agreed leads to the kingdom.'

Republicans and Orangemen

Modern Irish Republicanism traces its origins from the formation of
the Society of United Irishmen in 1791. Traditionally associated with
the Church of Ireland barrister, Wolfe Tone, it has been shown by
A.T.Q. Stewart that its real founder was Dr William Drennan, the son
of a Presbyterian minister. Three factors influenced its formation:
firstly, the growth of radicalism among a section of the Presbyterian
population; secondly, the impact of the French Revolution of 1789;
thirdly, continuing Roman Catholic discontent.

Following their contribution to the Williamite victory of 1690,
Presbyterians were surprised and aggrieved to find themselves

disadvantaged, along with their Roman Catholic neighbours, by discriminatory legislation passed by the Irish Parliament. Episcopalians, particularly landed gentry who dominated the Parliament, were possibly concerned about the numerical strength of Presbyterians in the north, their virtual monopoly of trade, and the triumph of the Presbyterian form of church government in Scotland. This may have been behind the introduction of the sacramental test of 1704, which excluded from public office all who did not take the sacrament according to the Church of Ireland rite. Despite protests the test was not removed until 1780. Presbyterians were also annoyed that their marriages were not recognised in ecclesiastical courts and that the burial of their dead required the participation of Church of Ireland clergy. Their one consolation was the continuation of the *regium donum*, a payment to Presbyterian ministers first introduced by Charles II in 1672.

It was this sense of injustice which fostered a spirit of radicalism among some Presbyterians, eventually leading to their involvement with the United Irishmen. Indeed, all who attended the meeting of the first society in Belfast in 1791 were Presbyterians.

At first they intended to pursue their programme of reform and independence from England by constitutional means, but they were forced by circumstances and choices to resort to the use of physical force with French help. Republicans today often repeat Wolfe Tone's summary of their aims:

To subvert the tyranny of our execrable government, to break the connection with England, the never failing source of all our political evils, and to assert the independence of my country – these were my objects. To unite the whole people of Ireland, to abolish the memory of all past dissensions, and to substitute the common name of Irishmen in place of the denomination of Protestant, Catholic and Dissenter – these were my means.[13]

The formation of the Orange Order at Loughgall, County Armagh, was not a reaction to the United Irishmen, but to the challenge of Roman Catholic Defenders who were allies of the United Irishmen. The memory of the Williamite victory of 1690 had not faded and had been commemorated by Protestants, sometimes annually, often to the annoyance of their Roman Catholic neighbours. Tension also erupted over economic competition and tenancy of land, and paramilitary groups from both sides were often involved. It was after one such skirmish, known as the 'Battle of the Diamond', at Loughgall in September 1795, that Protestants met together and vowed 'to maintain the laws and peace of the country and the Protestant Constitution, and to defend the King and his heirs as long as they shall maintain the Protestant ascendancy'.[14]

The diversity within Presbyterianism at this time is evident in that some were involved in the United Irishmen, forming the main body of those who rebelled in 1798 in Antrim and Down, while others in mid-Ulster joined the Orange Order and rallied to the support of the government forces engaged in crushing the rebellion. But there can be no doubt where the majority sentiment lay. As early as 1793 the Synod of Ulster had supported reform by constitutional means but rejected 'with abhorrence every idea of popular tumult and foreign aid'.[15] Immediately after the failure of the rebellion, the Synod affirmed its loyalty to the king and apologised for the 'inexcusable crimes' of some of its members.[16]

The rebellion, short lived though it was, established a tradition of revolutionary violence which has remained with us ever since. In the nineteenth and twentieth centuries, some have pursued change by constitutional methods, but the physical force alternative has sometimes been used and has certainly never been far away. In the short term there were two significant results of the 1798 Rebellion: firstly, Britain was now convinced of the need for legislative union with Ireland; and, secondly, abhorrence at the sectarian nature of the uprising in Wexford reminded Protestants of the common danger which they all faced and thereby contributed to a 'closing of ranks' within their community. This was highlighted when the great Presbyterian leader, Dr Henry Cooke, published the banns of marriage between presbytery and prelacy at a huge Protestant demonstration at Hillsborough in 1834.

Evangelicals and Papal Catholics

A conversionist policy towards Roman Catholics became a more clearly defined tradition within Protestantism in Ireland during the nineteenth century, even though it was not always actively and enthusiastically pursued. At the beginning of the century it was anticipated in the evangelistic work of the Irish Methodist Mission, founded in 1799, particularly in the preaching of Gideon Ouseley, and later in the attitude of militant evangelical Anglican bishops like William Magee, archbishop of Dublin, 1822-1831, and Power le Poer Trench, archbishop of Tuam, 1813-1839. Trench was unapologetic in his approach:

We are proselytisers. We plead guilty to this terrific and unpardonable charge. Nay, if we are not proselytisers we could lay no claim to the name of Christians.... Am I to be told that for fear of offending an unscriptural church I am to join in league with its priesthood to close the pure simple unnoted book of inspiration, to withhold the book of God from his condemned and perishing creatures?[17]

Dr William Urwick's mid-century pamphlet, entitled *A Brief Sketch of the Religious State of Ireland*,[18] indicates the intensity of this interest in the conversion of Roman Catholics in the period immediately following the Great Famine, 1845-1849. In addition to providing statistics of membership, numbers of clergy and places of worship, for both Roman Catholics and Protestants in all four provinces of Ireland, and an extensive report on the success of missionary work among Roman Catholics, he lists the number of societies engaged in this work: General, 6; Church of Ireland, 13; Presbyterian, 2; Methodist (reflecting the schisms then existing), 3; Congregationalists, 1; Baptists, 1; United Brethren, 1; Others, 1. One of the Anglican societies listed by Urwick, the Society for Irish Church Missions to Roman Catholics, whose founder and main inspiration was Alexander Dallas, rector of Wonston, Hampshire, is generally portrayed as the most aggressive of all these groups. Supported mainly by English evangelicals, many of whom were in prominent positions in the Church of England, this and other societies inevitably drew strong condemnation from Cardinal Paul Cullen, the Roman Catholic primate, who described their work as 'the disgraceful and unchristian system of proselytism which is reprobated by all liberal and generous people of whatever denomination'.[19] Historians have suggested that these missions to Roman Catholics were counter-productive.[20] While reports in the early 1850s indicate that they initially met with some success, numbers of conversions dwindled and the divisive effects of the campaign on the community eventually made them unpopular among Protestant clergy serving in these areas. It has been suggested that the crusade policy actually assisted Cardinal Cullen in his re-organisation of the Irish Catholic Church along ultramontanist lines. (Ultramontanism means literally 'beyond the mountains', referring to the location of the papacy south across the Alps from French Roman Catholics, with whom the term originated.)

If evangelicalism characterised Irish Protestantism during the nineteenth century, this nineteenth-century renewal movement in the Catholic Church, exalting the role and authority of the papacy and emphasising such distinctively Roman dogma as the Immaculate Conception of the Virgin Mary (1854), was the main influence on the Irish Roman Catholic Church. The person chiefly responsible for this was Cardinal Paul Cullen (1803-1878), who had gone to Rome in 1820 to study for the priesthood and remained there in various posts until 1849, when he was appointed archbishop of Armagh and a short time later archbishop of Dublin. Corish suggests that ultramontanism may have had its faults: 'A genuinely more dedicated clergy was not alive to new intellectual developments, nor did it devise any notable new pastoral methods. By and large, it pinned its faith to the patterns thought up long ago at Trent.'[21] It did nevertheless contribute to a resurgence of confidence among Roman Catholics in Ireland. The organisation of the church was strengthened, attendance at worship improved, and the number of priests and nuns increased dramatically. In 1800 there had been about 120 nuns, but by 1900 the total had risen to 8,000.

As already mentioned, Cullen did not take kindly to evangelical Protestants who attempted to poach members from his flock, especially in the west of Ireland where the effects of the famine had been so devastating. Protestants, he believed, needed illumination:

We should entertain most expansive sentiments of charity towards Protestants but at the same time we should let them know that there is but one true Church and that they are strayed sheep from the one fold. We should let them know this; otherwise we might lull them into a false security in their errors and by doing so we should really violate charity.[22]

Despite the fervency of the crusade policy, evangelical leaders accepted the Roman Catholic Church as a Christian church. Even Dallas acknowledged that Anglicans and Roman Catholics both agreed that Christ had founded a church within which people would find salvation, and that both churches appealed to the authority of scripture.[23] A few years later at the time of the 1859 Revival in Ulster, when the General Assembly of the Presbyterian Church in Ireland discussed the validity of baptism of Roman Catholics who had joined Presbyterianism, Henry Cooke, perhaps the leading Presbyterian evangelical of the nineteenth century, defended the traditional reformed view that the Roman Catholic Church was part of the visible church, though, like all churches, in need of reformation under the word of God.[24] There had therefore developed a clear evangelical tradition, evident in Wesley during the eighteenth century, which held in balance, on the one hand, the right to criticise what they considered to be errors in Christian belief and deviations in Christian practice in the Roman Catholic Church, with, on the other hand, an acknowledgement that it is a Christian church.

Evangelicalism influenced Protestant political opinion to a remarkable degree during the nineteenth and early twentieth century. It never sought or considered any degree of accommodation with the majority Roman Catholic population. Any attempts to find common cause with Roman Catholics, like the radical Presbyterians among the United Irishmen, were seen to have ended in failure, and indeed the events of the '98 Rebellion had only served to underline their fears and suspicions regarding Catholic intentions in Ireland. In their organisation of mission societies, evangelicals had adopted an attitude of superiority to Roman Catholics, and it was this attitude throughout the nineteenth century which made them vigilant in preserving Protestant rights and privileges. Any measure concerned with or related to Catholic rights was interpreted as one which would endanger Protestant privileges. With predictable consistency and almost complete unanimity, Irish evangelicals opposed Catholic Emancipation (1829), O'Connell's repeal movement in the 1840s, the increase of the Maynooth grant (1845), disestablishment of the Church of Ireland, (1869), and the various Home Rule measures introduced between 1886 and 1912, all of which were perceived as concessions to 'Rome' and defeats for Irish Protestantism. In taking this negative approach they were not always in step with Protestant evangelical opinion in Britain, which was often divided in its attitude to Ireland. Evangelicals like C.H. Spurgeon tended to support Irish Protestants; more liberal Free Churchmen like R.F. Horton supported Gladstone and Home Rule.

The Path to Partition

The Catholic Association, founded in 1823 by Daniel O'Connell, a successful barrister, had led the agitation for Catholic Emancipation, which removed restrictions preventing Roman Catholics from becoming members of Parliament. The association relied considerably on the support of parish priests who acted as local agents, collecting the 'Catholic rent' of a penny a month and exercising a political influence over their membership. However, O'Connell was less successful with his next major campaign, the repeal movement, which sought to reverse the Act of Union. He could not raise the same volume of support in Ireland, where many bishops were not repealers, nor the same sympathy in liberal circles in Britain.

The formation of the Home Government Association in 1870 by Isaac Butt, a Protestant barrister and former Orangeman who had also been professor of political economy at Trinity College, Dublin, continued O'Connell's policy of seeking political change by constitutional methods. Relaunched as the Home Rule League in 1873, its chief aim was the establishment of an Irish Parliament subordinate to Westminster but having responsibility for Irish affairs. When the leadership passed to Charles Stuart Parnell, a Protestant landlord who had imbibed a strong hatred of England from his American mother, the movement adopted a more aggressive approach in the form of 'obstructionism' – lengthy speeches by its members in the House of Commons – which occasionally frustrated parliamentary business but brought Irish affairs to the attention of both the main political parties. While pursuing constitutional methods of change at Westminster, there is also evidence that Parnell was in contact with the American leaders of the Fenian Brotherhood, a movement founded in 1858 and dedicated to the swift and violent removal of British rule. While not abandoning their belief in physical force, they were prepared to give Parnell their tacit support.

As the Home Rule movement grew in momentum, so too did resistance, particularly in Ulster. Henry Cooke (1788-1868), the Presbyterian leader described as the 'Father of Ulster Unionism', had already encouraged Protestant unity as a necessary safeguard against encroachment on their interests. This solidarity now became evident when, apart from a few dissenting voices, Protestant opinion expressed itself strongly against the Home Rule proposals. In March 1886, at the time of the first Home Rule Bill, the General Assembly of the Presbyterian Church in Ireland warned that Home Rule would place the civil rights of minorites at risk:

.... a separate parliament in Ireland, or an elective National Council, or any legislation tending to imperil the legislative union between Great Britain and Ireland.... would in our judgment, lead to the ascendancy of one class and creed in matters pertaining to religion, education and civil administration. We do not believe that any guarantees, moral or material, could be devised which would safeguard the rights and privileges of minorities scattered throughout Ireland against encroachment of a majority vested with legislative and executive functions.[25]

The editorial of the *Christian Advocate*, a Methodist paper, was less guarded in its sentiment: 'Home Rule for Ireland means not only war against the Crown rights of England, but war against the Crown rights of Christ.... its inspiration is religious antipathy, its methods plunder, its object Protestant annihilation.'[26] Many Protestants expressed it even more succinctly: 'Home Rule is Rome Rule.' Economic reasons were also given against Home Rule, especially in relation to its effects in Ulster. Ireland's economy, it was argued, was not independent of Britain but complementary to it. Industries in the north would face

ruin due to difficulties in obtaining essential supplies and the possibility of being cut off from the markets of the British Empire.

Though Home Rule had failed to gain full parliamentary approval
in 1886 and 1893, the likelihood of its success in 1911 and 1912 led
to massive Unionist opposition under the leadership of Sir Edward
Carson (1854-1935), solicitor-general in Arthur Balfour's Tory administration in the first decade of the century. A provisional Ulster government was set up, a volunteer army was organised, and a series of
large demonstrations was held throughout the north, culminating at
the City Hall, Belfast, on 28 September 1912, with the signing of the
Ulster Covenant. Based on the seventeenth-century 'Solemn League
and Covenant', it pledged the signatories 'to stand by one another in
defending for ourselves and our children our cherished position of
equal citizenship in the United Kingdom and in using all means which
may be found necessary to defeat the present conspiracy to set up a
Home Rule Parliament in Ireland'. The clear commitment of the
Protestant churches to this course of action is illustrated by the list of
church representatives who signed immediately after Edward Carson
and Lord Londonderry at the City Hall gathering: Henry Montgomery, moderator of the General Assembly; Charles D'Arcy, then
bishop of Down and Connor and Dromore and later archbishop of
Armagh; Charles Grierson, dean of Belfast; James Lowry, general
secretary of the Presbyterian Church; George Wedgewood, president
of the Methodist Church in Ireland; and James Hanson, ex-chairman
of the Congregational Union. At various centres throughout the north,
218,206 men signed the Covenant and 228,991 women signed a similar 'Ulster Women's Declaration'.

Unionists, supported by representatives of the Protestant churches,
had indicated their intention to go beyond constitutional methods and
use physical force should the former prove inadequate in protecting
their interests. The Government of Ireland Act was passed on 18
September 1914, establishing an Irish Parliament with jurisdiction
over its own affairs, but the delay in its implementation until the First
World War should end, and further developments in the south, meant
that Unionist intentions were never put to the test.

The 1916 Easter Rising in Dublin which has been interpreted as a
'blood sacrifice' was intended and eventually succeeeded in drawing
many to Republicanism. It was essentially the work of the Irish
Republican Brotherhood, founded in 1858 but revived again at the
beginning of the century, which interacted with and at times infiltrat-
ed other organisations that had arisen. These included the labour

movement, which had generated considerable strength under the leadership of Jim Larkin and James Connolly; Sinn Féin, established in 1905 by Arthur Griffith; and, by 1914, the Sinn Féin Volunteers, a breakaway group from the Irish Volunteer army, formed as a reaction to the Volunteer army in the north. The Rising failed, but on Easter Monday at the General Post Office in O'Connell Street, Dublin, Patrick Pearse, poet and nationalist mystic, had read a proclamation of the new Republic of Ireland from the 'provisional government'; in communication with the British forces he had referred to himself as the 'Commandant General of the Irish Republican Army'.

The nature of the British reaction to the Rising, the execution of its leaders over a period of days, and hints that the 1914 Act would not be fully implemented, turned the rebels into martyrs and effectively made Sinn Féin the most popular political party in Ireland. Rather than attending Westminster, Sinn Féin MPs met as 'Dáil Éireann' ('Assembly of Ireland') under the presidency of Eamon de Valera, one of the surviving 1916 leaders. The British government now opted for partition, the alternative choice for the Unionists should they fail in their opposition to Home Rule. In 1920 the Westminster parliament passed the Government of Ireland Act, which provided for two Irish Parliaments, one in the north and one in the south, and for a Council of Ireland to link them. Violence in the south between the IRA and Crown forces made it evident that the Act was unacceptable to Sinn Féin. After a period of difficult and protracted negotiations, both sides eventually agreed to the treaty of December 1921, setting up the Irish Free State with dominion status and recognising the right of six northern counties to opt out. Nationalists believed that the 'Six Counties', as they called Northern Ireland, would not be able to survive and they began a campaign to destabilise the treaty with a policy of non-co-operation with the Stormont government.[27]

The Ireland in which Ian Paisley was born in 1926 was a country which had experienced centuries of bitter conflict going back to pre-Christian times. The conflict which characterised the early twentieth century had been occasionally erupting, but always simmering, for at least four hundred years. Religious and political factors had become interwoven within each of the communities involved in the conflict. Both sides identified themselves as Christians, followers of the 'Prince of Peace'. This was the land and these were the contexts in which Paisley was to grow up and to minister in the name of Christ.

Chapter Three

The Early Years

IAN RICHARD KYLE Paisley was born on 6 April 1926 in the small cathedral city of Armagh. He was the second son born to James Kyle Paisley, a Baptist pastor, and his wife Isabella. The Paisleys traced their origins back to the settlers who had come from the Lowlands of Scotland in the early seventeenth century and established themselves mainly as farmers in the hilly areas of Tyrone around Killeeshill, between Ballygawley and Dungannon, and further north near Sixmilecross. But they were Church of Ireland, not Presbyterian, as might have been expected from their Scottish background. The Paisleys were devout people, cherishing the use of the Bible in family worship and maintaining a strong interest in the activities of the church. And latterly they had been Orangemen with a strong tradition of providing leadership in the order.

It was at the homestead in Kilcam, Sixmilecross, that James Kyle Paisley was born in August 1891. After leaving school at the age of fifteen, he went to work in Anderson's drapery business in Omagh. During his second year in Omagh, while attending meetings in the Young Men's Christian Association (YMCA) conducted by a Presbyterian minister, David Russell, he was led to accept Christ as his personal Saviour. Soon after this he broke his links with the Church of Ireland and joined a small group of Baptists who worshipped in the Orange hall in Omagh. One frosty Sunday morning soon after, he was baptised in the river Strule. In later life he often remarked: 'I have been coming out of things all my life – always coming out.[1] In the years before the First World War, Kyle Paisley was deeply affected by the Home Rule Crisis. Like many of his co-religionists, he signed the Ulster Covenant in September 1912 and joined the Ulster Volunteer Force, which soon had 100,000 men enlisted who were prepared to resist any attempt to implement Home Rule. Many of these Volunteers served during the war in the British army, which suffered an enormous loss of life, most notably at the Battle of the Somme in 1916. Later in life Kyle instilled into his sons the fears and concerns which had led him to join the Volunteers. 'He taught my brother and me the principles of true patriotism and the principles of civil and religious liberty,' recalls Ian Paisley. 'He loved this country, he loved this land, and he wanted to see this land free from the power of Rome by the power of the Gospel.'[2]

Kyle Paisley moved to Dungannon for a period and then in 1915 to Armagh, long regarded as Ireland's ecclesiastical capital since it is thought St Patrick chose it as the centre for his work. Two cathedrals, Roman Catholic and Church of Ireland, standing on adjoining hills, dominate the landscape. Kyle had started preaching in various places and in 1918 he was asked to become the pastor of a newly formed Baptist assembly in the city. He needed training and soon became a part-time 'external' student at the Irish Baptist College in Dublin. Correspondence courses were available for students who were unable to come into residence, and while Kyle Paisley attended some classes in Dublin, most of his studies were completed under this arrangement. Possibly it was on one of his trips to the college that he met and was impressed by a Dublin pastor, Pierson Harrison, whom Kyle booked to conduct a two-week mission in Armagh in 1923. The local pastor demonstrated a flair for publicity by organising nightly marches around the city prior to the meeting. The *Christian Herald* of 23 December 1923 reported: 'souls were saved, and some who were saved at the mission have been baptized and added to the church'.[3]

Love blossomed when Kyle went to take a service in Lurgan Baptist Church and met Isabella Turnbull, originally from Kilsyth in Scotland but at that time working as governess to the children of a local doctor.[4] Free Presbyterian sources interpret the Kilsyth connection as signifying that she came from the 'Covenanting tradition', but this can only refer to the town's historical links with the Covenanters as there has never been a Covenanting church at Kilsyth. Kyle and Isabella were married in 1923 and had two sons: Harold Spurgeon, born in 1924 when they lived in Killylea, and Ian, born two years later when they had moved to Armagh.

Kyle Paisley had been with the Armagh assembly for ten years when he accepted a call to be pastor of Hill Street Baptist Church in Ballymena, a largely Presbyterian town, its history dating back to the arrival of settlers from the Lowlands of Scotland in the early seventeenth century. The congregation had been formed by the Revd John Galway McVicker at the time of the 1859 Revival in Ulster, a period of great spiritual awakening and renewal. He had been the Covenanting minister at Cullybackey, but when he began to have doubts about the scriptural authority for infant baptism, he left his

church and formed the nucleus of a new Baptist congregation at Hill
Street. Very soon after this his views changed again, this time on the
ordained ministry, and, much to the consternation of his new congregation, he left to form the first Brethren assembly in the town.[5]

The Hill Street site will always have a special significance for Ian
Paisley as it was here as a boy of six – on 29 May 1932 – that he heard
and responded to the call of Christ when his mother was speaking
about Jesus the Good Shepherd at her weekly children's meeting:

As I passed up Mount Street tonight, and I passed my eye over to Hill
Street Baptist Church, I thought of a second pew on the right hand side
as you go in at the doorway. I thought of a little boy kneeling many years
ago at the second pew. That little boy was me. I found Jesus at that pew,
that memorable day. I found the pearl of greatest price. I found the greatest
Friend that a boy could find. I found God in Christ. I found pardon. I
found peace. I found glorious liberty. I found it in Jesus Christ. I tell you
I have let Him down many a time. I have failed Him on many occasions.
He has never failed me. I have got his promise, and some day I will be
with Him forever.[6]

Kyle Paisley was pastor of Hill Street for just five and a half years,
from May 1928 to November 1933. It was a time of continuous turmoil
and friction. Very soon the congregation was split into two factions:
on the one hand, the pastor and his wife with a few of the deacons
and members who had recently joined the church; on the other, the
majority of deacons along with the older and longer-established members. William McKillen's unpublished history of Ballymena Baptist
Church explains how the division arose.[7] Kyle's predecessor, Richard
Hodgett, had been a much-loved and highly esteemed pastor. His
death in hospital after only five years' service with the congregation
was keenly felt by everyone. As often happens, comparisons were
made between the two pastors, and Kyle's forthright and forceful style
of evangelism was not appreciated as much as Hodgett's skills as an
expository preacher and teacher – they regarded him as 'a giant' in
that particular sphere – and his reserved and unassuming manner outside the pulpit. They recognised Kyle's untiring evangelistic work in
mission halls, barns, farmhouses and tents loaned by the Northern
Baptist Association, and admired his extraordinary gifts as a communicator. 'He was a most eloquent preacher, we can safely say he was
an orator. He had a strong clear voice, spoke slowly and distinctly, and
was possessed of the ability to grip the attention of the members of
his audience from the moment he rose until he brought his message
to a close.' Such preaching attracted people to the services. Despite

these positive factors, it took many of the members a long time to adapt to such a radical change of ministry.

Two issues in particular split the congregation. Pearson Harrison, whom Kyle had already brought to Armagh when he was pastor there, was one of a number of preachers and evangelists invited to Hill Street. However, many felt he was advocating a standard of Christian living that was 'so near sinless perfection as to be impractical'. When Harrison left, Kyle Paisley continued this emphasis in his own preaching. Another issue of contention was the church's membership of the Baptist Union of Great Britain and Ireland. Concern was expressed about the 'modernistic' tendencies of some of the English pastors in the union, and division arose on the method of dealing with it. Kyle Paisley and the new members wanted to withdraw the church's membership, but the senior members thought this would be running away from the problem and advocated staying within the union to maintain the fundamentalist witness. Besides, they felt a great debt of gratitude to the English members of the union who had generously supported the congregation from the time of its foundation. A strong and genuine filial relationship bound them to the union.

The issue of contention therefore was not whether the local church was for or against fundamentalism. Both groups in the dispute supported the fundamentalist position. The question on which they differed was the method to be adopted in supporting the fundamentalist witness: stay in the union and strive for orthodoxy or take the separatist position and withdraw from the union.

The roots of fundamentalism are found in the American millenarian movement of the mid-nineteenth century which emphasised the imminent Second Coming of Christ and an ensuing thousand years of peace (the 'millennium'). William Miller's unfulfilled prediction that the Second Coming would occur in or before 1843 did not destroy the movement, but did make its leaders more cautious about fixing dates. Emphasis on the imminent return of Christ continued to be one of special interest. Millenarian theology was soon influential in Britain, and it was the millenarians of North America and Britain who were in the vanguard of opposition to the methods of biblical criticism which some scholars were using from the middle of the nineteenth century onwards. Basically the same critical tools and methods which had been used in the study of secular literature since the eighteenth century were now being applied in the study of the Bible. For example, questions were asked regarding the historical circumstances out of which the biblical books developed and the literary forms in which they were written. Fundamentalists interpreted this approach as an attack on the authority of scripture and affirmed its inerrancy with little or no attempt to understand the method of enquiry.

Fundamentalists had five common aims. Firstly, the defence of what they perceived to be the fundamentals of the Christian faith: the Trinity and unity of the Godhead, the virgin birth of Christ, the miracle-working power of Christ, the substitutionary theory of the atonement, and Christ's bodily resurrection. Secondly, an emphasis on the verbal inspiration and inerrancy of scripture. Thirdly, millenarianism. Fourthly, exorcism of modernism and all its associated demons. And fifthly, opposition to unitive movements within Christianity. While they usually agreed on these five aims, fundamentalists differed on the action to be taken should the perceived spiritual decline persist. This was the point on which the two groups at Hill Street differed.

Confusingly, while Kyle Paisley persistently worked for withdrawal during the major part of his pastorate, for some unexplained reason he changed his mind at the church meeting of 20 March 1933, and proposed that the church should remain in the union. His motion was carried unanimously.

There were also some 'unseemly occurrences' which caused friction during his pastorate, but McKillen purposely omits the details. He refers to a rift between the Paisleys and the church treasurer, but delights in adding that after a few years they became close friends, so much so that Kyle visited his shop regularly and the two could be seen standing at the door of the premises chatting like old friends. What then were the other matters which he alludes to but does not explain? Maloney and Pollak, in their 1986 biography, *Paisley*, refer to disputes which Mrs Paisley had with members of the choir, and one in particular over hairstyles.[8] She apparently objected to girls whose hair was 'bobbed' as being guilty of ignoring scriptural guidelines (1 Cor. 11:6). In these disputes she displayed a 'tempestuous nature', which her husband was 'totally unable to curb'. 'They should have thrown a bucket of water over her' was the comment heard from Frank Forbes, Kyle's successor at Hill Street.[9]

The situation must have deteriorated considerably, because news filtered through to the Baptist Union of Ireland, who suggested sending a deputation to advise on how the breach between the two parties might be healed. A high-powered deputation, including the union secretary, Pastor J.W.S. Fraser, and three others, listened to the points of difference and grievances at a specially convened church meeting in Ballymena and left in the belief that reconciliation had been achieved.

But it was not long before the old hurts and divisions once again appeared. Then suddenly, without warning, Kyle Paisley announced at the morning service on Sunday, 3 November 1933, that he was terminating his pastorate at Hill Street after the evening service. After initial relief at this announcement, some members of the congregation were soon shocked to learn that he did not just intend to resign his position. He had also made plans to take a section of the membership with him to establish an independent 'Regular Baptist' assembly in the town in opposition to Hill Street. This reminded them of the traumatic events in the early days of the congregation when J.G. McVicker resigned the pastorate and founded a Brethren assembly with members who had left with him. For the second time in their history, they were to experience schism from their congregation. On this occasion Kyle Paisley took a few of the original members with him, but for the most part the exodus consisted of new members added during his ministry.

Kyle Paisley's departure is interpreted by Free Presbyterian sources as being the result of the same separatist causes which later led to the founding of their church. Kyle's action is perceived as a protest against declining moral standards in the church and the development of modernistic tendencies in the Baptist Union in England. This reading of the 1933 schism at Hill Street may represent simply an explanation in retrospect; more likely, it reflects Kyle Paisley's own interpretation of the circumstances of his separatist action. But why did Kyle Paisley not acknowledge that he had actually proposed staying within the union? It is quite possible that this act of separation, and the explanations that went with it, had a moulding and determining influence on both sons, and particularly the younger.

McKillen believes that the schism could have been avoided. While apportioning blame on both parties, he suggests: 'Had pastor and deacons exercised a little more restraint, been a little more flexible and less positive and dogmatic and talked less about being uncompromising, the eventual outcome could have been very different.'

Kyle Paisley knew there were precedents for the drastic action he had taken. His hero Charles Hadden Spurgeon (1834-1891), for many years the pastor of the Metropolitan Tabernacle in London and regarded as one of the greatest preachers of the nineteenth century, had severed his links with the Baptist Union at the time of the 'Downgrade Controversy'. Though unwilling to give names, Spurgeon had charged the union with having pastors who were abandoning biblical doctrines and standards of behaviour. Three doctrines in particular, he said, were being threatened: biblical infallibility, substitutionary atonement, and the finality of judgment for those who died outside Christ.

Paisley would also have been aware of another controversy which had recently rocked the Presbyterian Church in Ireland. In 1927, Professor Ernest Davey, one of the teaching staff at Assembly's College, Belfast, had been accused of heresy at the presbytery of Belfast, acquitted, and then on appeal the case was brought to the General Assembly. Davey, later to become principal of the college and moderator of the General Assembly, was one of the outstanding scholars of his day. When the college was presented with a coat of arms in 1955, the inscription to the principal read 'the Reverend Professor James Ernest Davey, MA, DD, sometime fellow of King's College, Cambridge, Doctor of Divinity of the Universities of Dublin, St Andrew's, Edinburgh and Belfast'. The charges against him related to his views on the person and work of Christ, the Trinity, the doctrine of sin, and the inspiration of the scriptures. By a large majority, 707 to 82, the assembly found him not guilty of the charges and dismissed the appeal against the decision of the Presbytery.

Free Presbyterian interest in the findings of the heresy trial has continued unabated. Ian Paisley has been adamant that Davey was guilty of apostasy: 'Professor Davey's body is today eaten by the skin worms; his soul is in Hell in the torments of the damned.'[10] In light of these criticisms, two of Davey's statements at the trial on the divinity of Christ and the meaning of the cross are of particular interest:

I believe in the Divinity of Christ in the full sense of Deity as set forth in the Trinitarian Doctrine; I believe in Christ as very God of very God, as being of one substance with the Father, as taught in the Scriptures, the ancient ecumenical creeds and the subordinate standards of our Church.[11]
I fully accept the catechism definition of justification with its salvation by the imputed righteousness of our Lord Jesus Christ, and I hold as my own faith the doctrine of his substitutionary atonement.[12]

Kyle Paisley, like Davey's accusers in the Presbyterian Church, now clearly adopted a strong fundamentalist position. He invited one of North America's leading fundamentalists, Dr T.T. Shields of Jarvis Street Baptist Church in Toronto, to lay the foundation stone of the new building, the 'Gospel Tabernacle'. He drew up a covenant in which the congregation pledged themselves 'in a day of apostasy, declension and compromise' to stand with Christ and maintain a testimony to 'the supernaturalism of Christianity against the anti-supernaturalism of modernism and the formality of a dead and defunct orthodoxy'. But perhaps the most significant part of the covenant was the opening call to separatism: 'As God providentially raised up Elijah, we believe He is now calling out a faithful remnant to maintain a testimony, free from compromise against every opposition of the enemy.'[13] Kyle Paisley threw himself into the new work with great determination and enthusiasm. As in Hill Street, people enjoyed his preaching and regarded him as a good communicator. His strong voice was an asset to him in his open-air preaching. He did not feel restricted to Ballymena but took preaching engagements and missions in various places, sometimes travelling to England, Scotland and Wales.

How successful was the work at Waveney Road? R.J. Beggs' account of Kyle Paisley's ministry and the separatist cause in Ballymena, *Great is Thy Faithfulness*,[14] concentrates on the separatist issues but is strangely silent on the response to Paisley's thirty-three year ministry at Waveney Road. Beggs had married Margaret, the youngest member of the Paisley family, and taken over responsibility for the work at Waveney Road after Kyle's retirement in 1966, and was therefore in a position to be well informed on his father-in-law's ministry. McKillen states that initially there was spectacular progress. Then, gradually, for one reason or another, a number of the original members who had seceded drifted back and asked to be readmitted to membership at Hill Street. It appears that the Independent Baptist membership actually dwindled over the years, but this and its subsequent history as part of the Free Presbyterian Church of Ulster is a story for another chapter. (See chapter six.)

From an early age Ian Paisley took a deep interest in his father's work. On Sunday mornings he always accompanied him to the little room above the vestry where prayer was offered for that day's worship. In the services his mother played the organ and sang as she played. It was not uncommon to hear people shouting 'Hallelujah' during the service. Both younger son and mother accompanied the father to the open-air services. There was a marked contrast at this stage between Harold, the older brother, and Ian. Finlay Holmes, whose father was the principal of the Model School attended by the Paisley boys, remembers the difference between them.[15] Harold was a 'well-built athletic chap who participated in games and school life generally', whereas Ian was 'a gangling unco-ordinated boy, always a bit of a loner and outsider'. He didn't get involved in organised school games or watch films, even educational films arranged by the school. Holmes recalls Ian's nervousness when the teacher asked a question. 'He would tremble and find it difficult to give an answer, which is very strange, considering his repartee and oratory in later days'.

Conflicting stories are told about the reputation of the Paisley brothers as schoolboy fighters. Ian has suggested that disputes at the Model were eventually settled at the back of the Court House: 'That's where we all fought, at the back of the Court House. The school came round to see the fight.'[16] While Holmes may not have been one of these spectators, he does recall the older Paisley brother: 'I never remember Ian Paisley involved in a fight in the schoolyard, but I do remember Harold being involved.'

Between twelve and fourteen was generally the age at which pupils left the Model. Some went on to grammar school, some like Ian to technical college, and a few like Harold stayed on in a matriculation class specially arranged by the principal for those who hadn't managed to get to grammar school but wanted to improve their chances of further education at a later stage. Harold opted out of this stream when he was sixteen, enlisted in the RAF after pretending he was seventeen, was withdrawn when his father revealed he had faked his age, joined the merchant navy for a time and then the police. It was a period which gave his father and mother great concern and they prayed earnestly for the return of the prodigal. Holmes, who kept in contact with Harold for a long time, was in the Gospel Tabernacle when he first spoke publicly about his conversion:

His father had prayed most fervently, giving thanks for 'this brand plucked from the burning'. Then Harold got up to speak. He was wearing a double-breasted dark suit, a fine figure of a man. He stood there for a full minute without saying anything. You could just feel the tension rising. He said nothing at all. Then he threw back his head and began to sing when we were expecting him to give his testimony. He sang 'I'd rather have Jesus than silver or gold' and when he had finished the Hallelujahs were going up. Then he said, 'Last Saturday night I was singing with a dance band in Enniskillen and tonight I'm singing for Jesus.' And the roof nearly went off the little hall at this.

Harold went on to become a Brethren evangelist, eventually emigrating to Canada. Like his father, and soon his younger brother, he was known as a gifted communicator with strong fundamentalist convictions.

When he was sixteen Ian Paisley was accepted for a year's training at the Barry School of Evangelism, a fundamentalist college near Cardiff in South Wales. In 1950 it was renamed the South Wales Bible College and in 1985 it became the Evangelical Movement of Wales College and relocated at Bridgend. It was really as a favour to his father, who was friendly with the principal, Mr S.B. Fidler, that he was admitted at such a young age. In war-time the enrolment was small, about a dozen students. Ian got on well with the other students, who were embarrassed, and perhaps a little envious, that the younger student built up such a reputation as a preacher and received personal invitations for outside engagements while they had to rely on the normal routine appointments arranged by the principal. Although he had often stood with his father in open-air meetings, his experience now, preaching in Barry Island and Cardiff docks with Ted Sherwood, a former welter-weight boxing champion, proved invaluable training for him in the art of communication.

While he was at Barry, Ian became convinced that God wanted him to be a preacher. He had been thinking about it for some time and was concerned to know if this was the right course for him. One day in his prayers he said, 'Lord, I want to be dead-on sure, absolutely certain that I'm called to preach the Word of God, and if I'm not sure I'm quitting, not going to stay on and be a failure. And just like a flash the text "And I will make you to become fishers of men" came into my mind.' As the same text kept on reappearing at other times that day, he became convinced that this was God speaking to him, providing confirmation and demanding commitment, which he unhesitatingly gave. 'I said, "Lord, forgive me my unbelief. I see it now. You've called me. I'm to follow and you will make me a fisher of men."'[17]

His colleagues of those days recall a frequent saying of his, 'He's a shocking fellow,' jokingly used about themselves and others. And even at this early stage he gave the impression that one day he would plough his own furrow. 'He was a man who was going to walk his own road,' said Ivor Colman, who went on to train as a Baptist pastor after leaving Barry.[18] However, it is significant that Paisley has kept in contact with his Barry companions, phoning them up at times of illness or bereavement. Actions like these have obviously meant a lot to them, especially when Paisley became a national personality.

Now that Ian had decided on his life's vocation, it was recognised that he needed training to be a full-time Christian minister. However, he was still only seventeen. Once again his father's influence and intervention played a major part in deciding where his son should be trained. Kyle Paisley apparently didn't want his son to go to the Baptist College in Dublin. There would obviously have been difficulties to overcome because of the circumstances of his departure from Hill Street and his subsequent separatist work at Waveney Road. There was also the problem of Ian's age. But even if these had been surmountable, there was yet another obstacle. It appears that the real reason why the Baptist College was not approached was the fact that Kyle Paisley simply didn't like the principal, Harold Spurgeon, grandson of his hero Charles Haddon Spurgeon. Why this was so is not known. Perhaps it was because Spurgeon, like his grandfather, smoked a pipe! Baptist links between Britain and Ireland should not have been a factor because Harold Spurgeon, despite being principal, had little time for the union because of his grandfather's experience in the 'Downgrade Controversy'.

Kyle Paisley's preference was for his son to study in the Theological Hall of the Reformed Presbyterian Church in Ireland. In this he was undoubtedly influenced by the history and principles of Reformed Presbyterianism, the 'Covenanters'.

A presbyterial form of church government was never permanently established in Scotland during the sixteenth and seventeenth centuries. Struggle and uncertainty marked its implementation. One of the most memorable dates in the ongoing saga of that struggle was 1643, the date of Solemn League and Covenant drawn up between Scottish Presbyterians and the English Parliament during their struggle against the despotism of Charles I. By the terms of the Covenant, they pledged themselves 'to preserve the Reformed religion in Scotland and to work for the Reformation of religion in the three kingdoms in doctrine, worship, discipline and government according to the Word of God'.[19] The English, however, did not understand that this meant Presbyterianism, and after the restoration of the monarchy in 1660, attempts were made to reimpose episcopacy on the unwilling Scots. It was resisted fiercely by men like Richard Cameron and James Renwick, who believed they were justified in using physical force to defend their liberty and freedom of religious conscience. By the 1680s their resistance, which often resulted in martyrdom, represented only a minority of Presbyterians, but they felt vindicated in their stand when in 1689 the crown was transferred from James II to his son-in-law William of Orange, thereby signifying the people's right to dethrone a monarch who was understood to be subverting the constitution.

Their pleasure, however, was short-lived; they were dissatisfied with the terms of the 1690 Scottish church settlement. While many accepted that it sufficiently restored Presbyterianism in Scotland, the strict followers of Cameron and Renwick opposed it on the grounds that the power of convening and dissolving assemblies remained in civil hands, thereby giving it the appearance of a 'state church' without a reciprocal commitment on the part of the monarchy to implement religious orthodoxy as laid down in the earlier covenants. This small group of dissidents separated from the national church and by the eighteenth century had formed themselves into the Reformed Presbyterian Church. While the political situation in Ulster was different from Scotland, ministers and congregations in agreement with their principles gradually established themselves in different parts of the province.

Kyle Paisley may have felt there were parallels between his own separatist stand in Ballymena and the historical separation of the Covenanters from the national Church of Scotland. Both claimed to be uncompromising in the pursuit of their principles. While there is no evidence to suggest that Ian had any wish to be trained as a Covenanting minister, his father now decided to explore the possibility of his son's being permitted to enrol as a student at their Theological Hall on the Grosvenor Road, Belfast. So Kyle Paisley asked the Revd Lynas, a friend who was the Reformed Presbyterian minister at Cullybackey and also a member of the College Committee of Superintendence, if Ian could be allowed to study at the college. Lynas took it to the committee and permission was given in October 1943 for Ian to enter as a 'guest student'.[20] The committee minutes of the Theological Hall state: 'The Convener reported that an application for admission to the hall had been received from Mr Ian Paisley of the Baptist Church. The Committee cordially agreed to admit Mr Paisley.'[21] As a guest student he was never under the same discipline as those accepted for ministerial training.

The Theological Hall, now relocated on the Lisburn Road, used premises adjoining the Reformed Presbyterian church on the Grosvenor Road. It was always a small college, its enrolment never more than five while Ian was there. It had three professors, all part time, as each also had pastoral responsibility for a congregation: Thomas B. McFarlane, church history and pastoral theology; John McIlmoyle, systematic theology; John Ramsey, Hebrew, biblical criticism and New Testament Greek. The subjects taught by the professors give some idea of the course followed. As a guest student no questions were asked of Ian about his academic qualifications at the time of entry, although the other ministerial students were required to have a university degree. Some students had already studied languages, including Greek, at school and university, so in this area he was at a disadvantage and required classes on his own. But he possessed a first-class knowledge of the English Bible and a keen interest in church history. He was regarded as a 'good' student, in that he applied himself earnestly to his studies and won prizes in each year of his course. His relations with the other, and inevitably older, students were good, and they recognised his earnestness and spirituality.

The war years brought both hardship and prosperity to Northern Ireland. Its society still experienced divided loyalties on the parts of the unionist/Protestant majority and the nationalist/Catholic minority. The neutrality of the Free State in the south, the opposition of northern Catholic bishops to conscription in 1939 and the IRA campaigns of 1940 and 1942-1944 had confirmed unionist attitudes and perceptions of the southern state and the Catholic community in the north. On the other hand, nationalists and Republicans could see no possibility of fulfilling their political aspirations in a state with a built-in unionist majority and government. The 1941 Blitz of Belfast and the sacrifice in human life of many who had enlisted added to the sense of hardship in both communities. But the war years had also brought increased prosperity. The need for food in Britain had rejuvenated agriculture in the province, and war-related industries like ship-building, aviation and engineering had improved the economy and decreased unemployment. At the outbreak of war, income per head of population had been three-fifths that of Britain, but had risen to three-quarters by 1945.[22]

By the spring of 1946, the end of the college lecture year, Ian Paisley had completed almost three years of theological training and had just turned twenty. His colleagues in the Theological Hall went on to become ministers of the Reformed Presbyterian Church, but for a short period he was a free spirit in that he could take preaching engagements and missions as and when invitations arrived. Indeed, he had already begun this while in college. Most of the invitations came from the ministers and congregations of the Irish Evangelical Church, which had broken away from Irish Presbyterianism at the time of the Davey heresy trial.[23] One of its leaders, the Revd W.J. Grier, befriended and helped Paisley financially, but there is no suggestion that he gave any thought to joining Grier's church.

In December 1945 he had been invited to preach in the Ravenhill Evangelical Mission Church, a small building at the corner of Glentoran Street and the Ravenhill Road in Belfast, and in the summer of 1946 was asked to become the pastor. The church had been formed in 1935 as a breakaway from the Ravenhill Presbyterian Church. Some members of the kirk session had complained to their minister, Revd Ross, that ladies whose hair was 'bobbed' (again see 1 Corinthians 11:6) were unsuitable to be Sunday school teachers or choir members. In a conflict which recalls the circumstances in the

Baptist Church in Ballymena when his mother was organist, the commission appointed by the presbytery to deal with the dispute suggested that the objectors were not always consistent in their literal application of the scriptures, and ruled that 'no law of the Church nor any law of God raises the question as to whether persons deemed suitable by Christian fellowship at the Lord's Table can be excluded from any form of Christian work for which they have the required capabilities'.[24] The objectors rejected the presbytery ruling and left to form the new congregation close by. Within a year Mr Ross, who was certainly no liberal, noted that harmony and oneness had been restored and that 'the work has become an increasing delight'.

Four ministers took part in Ian Paisley's ordination service on 1 August 1946: Professor T. B. McFarlane, who had taught him at the Reformed Presbyterian Theological Hall, offered prayer; Revd Thomas Rowan, a Presbyterian minister, gave the exhortation and charge to the congregation; Revd W.J. Grier's sermon called on the young ordinand to be faithful in contending for the faith; and Kyle Paisley laid hands on his son in the solemn act of ordination. Only one minister took part in the actual act of ordination because it was felt that they represented four different denominations and therefore could not have a united approach. Paisley claims that W. P. Nicholson, a noted evangelist,[25] attended the mission hall on the first Sunday morning after his ordination and, addressing both himself and the congregation, declared: 'I have one prayer for this young man, that God will give him a tongue like an old cow. Young man, go into a butcher's shop and try and run your hand along a cow's tongue; it's as sharp as a file. Please God this man will have a tongue that shall be as sharp as a file in the heart of the enemies of the king.'[26] Paisley believes that God answered that prayer.

Evangelism, 'contending for the faith', political agitation, prayer meetings, and congregational and personal squabbles characterised Paisley's work in those early days on the Ravenhill Road. Evangelism started within the church. John Douglas, now principal of Whitefield College of the Bible, the theological training college of the Free Presbyterian Church, was his first convert. He was a young teenager at the time, attending the afternoon Sunday school of the church. The family lived in the Ravenhill area and were members of Megain Memorial Presbyterian Church on the Newtownards Road. While they walked regularly to church, the Ravenhill Mission Sunday school was near by, and Douglas's friends went there too. One Sunday he stopped a teacher at the close of one particular session and indicated that he wanted to follow Christ. However, it was Mr Paisley who came to counsel and explain from the scriptures the way of salvation. This was Douglas's first introduction to Paisley. 'He led me to the Lord. I knew that day that I was born of God.' Paisley than asked what at the time appeared a shocking question: 'Will you now confess Christ as your Saviour?'[27] But Douglas is grateful now for that question. He told his family about his decision, and this proved a great means of strengthening him in the faith. Understandably, John Douglas is deeply appreciative of Paisley's gifts.

Attempts were made to reach out to the wider community. Paisley organised open-air meetings, tent missions and Friday evening meetings in the church for men invited in from the local pubs. He recalls 200 or 300 men attending the Friday night meetings, leaving their bottles outside on the window-sills of the church and singing heartily some of the simple choruses they had learnt as children in Sunday school. The tall young preacher's boundless energy was never spared in the task of declaring the good news of Jesus Christ. His gifts in communicating this message have been widely recognised, and many feel that he should have dedicated all his time and talents to this alone. The Reformed Presbyterian Church historian, Adam Loughridge, has assessed Paisley as 'the most effective preacher to the masses since W.P. Nicholson. And my own view is this, and I've said it when I'm questioned on radio programmes in the United States, that if he had pursued his role as an evangelist, he would have had a tremendous use. But I felt once he became embroiled in politics, he took a wrong turning.'

Paisley saw a number of other concerns as related to his evangelistic work. Like his father, 'contending for the faith' was one of his chief passions. His father's warnings of Rome's treachery and deviousness, his carefully selected reading of historical instances of religious persecution and his imbibing of the anti-Catholic sentiment often prevalent in the Ulster Protestant community all gelled together to make him a formidable crusader against Catholicism. Similarly, he regarded himself as a prophet warning against 'Protestant apostasy'. The formation of the World Council of Churches in 1948 and the involvement of Irish Protestant churches in its activities were perceived as clear evidence of Protestant spiritual decline. He advertised sermons on Reformation themes, teaching that a great difference existed between the church of the twentieth century and the church of the Reformers.

He was also deeply interested in politics. Ian loved to discuss political issues and was eager to be involved. He joined the Orange Order, helped form the National Union of Protestants in Ireland, working

vigorously on its behalf, and showed undoubted skills as a campaign-
er on behalf of unionist politicians. If some saw a conflict between his
religion and politics, he did not.

All these concerns and activities were backed up by prayer.
Frequently church prayer meetings would last into the early hours of
the morning. Only a few would attend, but neighbours could hear
their fervent supplications and sometimes thought the noise was louder than reasonable at that time of the night. One weekend of prayer is
particularly remembered by Paisley and Douglas as a time of great
blessing. The former describes it as 'one whole day and one whole
night and the remainder of another night'.[28] He refers to the blessing
experienced as a high point in his life. 'God filled me with His blessed
Spirit and that was the beginning of a great work of God.' Douglas
was still only in his middle teens at the time, but he recalls that the
growth in the church was remarkable from that point onwards.

But there was also considerable friction within the Ravenhill
Mission Church in those early days. Some of it was due to squabbling
between individual members, but other instances were understood by
Paisley as opposition to his preaching of the gospel. One Sunday he
was rebuked by a prominent lady in the congregation for the sermon
he had preached on hell. She didn't want her 'unsaved' father alarmed
by such preaching. 'Man, I've met the devil in a pair of trousers, but
I met him in a skirt that day,' said Paisley. Threatened with his dismissal, he retorted, 'Madam, *you're* fired!' That week he called a meeting of the elders of the church and asked them to choose between the
woman and the preacher. They said, 'We're choosing the preacher.'[29]

The absence of choirs in Free Presbyterianism is probably due to
Paisley's experience of in-fighting which occurred between two ladies,
each of whom had a daughter in the choir, though some would say it
goes back to the incident of his mother's confrontation with girls in
the choir at Hill Street Baptist. His account of this later squabble also
illustrates his undoubted gift for story-telling.

Two women in the church, one I would call Mrs Self-Opinionated and the
other I would call Madam Domineering, had two daughters. These daughters were members of the choir. The daughter of Mrs Self-Opinionated I
would call Miss Pert, and the daughter of Madam Domineering I would
call Miss Prim.

Now of course, when Miss Pert and Miss Prim came to the choir on
the Sabbath Day they each sought to outdo one another in regard to dress.
Mrs Self-Opinionated thought that no one knew how to dress like herself,
and, of course, she dressed her daughter according to her taste. The dress

was not to be characterised by modesty or by decency or by subjection to the Scriptures or holiness, but rather to make an impression. Madam Domineering was not to be outdone by Mrs Self-Opinionated, so when Miss Prim turned up at the church she also, to use an Ulster colloquialism, was 'dressed to kill'. Well, it was not only the matter of a fashion parade at the choir each Sabbath between Miss Pert and Miss Prim, but it was the comments that were made by both mothers concerning how the daughter of each of them dressed. Mrs Self-Opinionated was sarcastic in her criticisms of the dress of Miss Prim, and Madam Domineering was equally sarcastic about the dress of Miss Pert.

Paisley goes on to say how both mothers also disagreed about which daughter was the better singer and that the argument spilled over to involve others in the choir and the congregation. His solution to the problem was drastic.

So the preacher was faced with the need to take the little fox – the little fox of envy that had grown into a wolf of jealousy and a tiger of hatred, to take that little fox and choke it to death. At the end of the day the choir was abolished. Every member joined the new choir which consisted of the whole congregation.[30]

The immediate area of the church was, and remains, a working-class area, but most of the people attracted by his sensational style of preaching came from outside the area. Gordon McMullan, Church of Ireland bishop of Down and Dromore, whose family lived in St Kilda's Street, remembers clearly the beginning of Paisley's ministry on the Ravenhill Road. The family were members of Willowfield parish church, but like John Douglas he had enjoyed going to the mission church Sunday school. The teachers were serious-minded and subdued but kindly people. 'You would never have felt threatened by them.' As a boy he was struck by the difference in style between Paisley and other clergy whom he knew: 'He was a man of considerable physical presence. He seemed to me as a child in a working-class area as being rather loud and somewhat uncouth for a cleric, because one's knowledge of clergymen was such that they were rather quiet, pastorally aware people. Most working-class Protestants were not into high-profile preachers, were not into extravagant, embarrassing religious evangelism and therefore the presence of that kind of clergyman really didn't cut a great deal of ice.'[31] At about twelve years of age McMullan joined the Boys' Brigade in another church, and Sunday morning Bible class replaced the afternoon Sunday school. However, he was living in the area until his late twenties and although no longer in contact with the mission church was very aware of Paisley's presence and especially, as he perceived it, his forceful personality. 'He seemed to be a person, as I looked on, who needed to be the dominant person in what was happening, who had a rather heavy-handed type of humour; it could easily be used to put people down.'

Chapter Four
Anti-Catholicism

Compulsive preacher, large, and loud of voice
in octaves of abuse, invective, hate;
a Samson self-ordained, his strength destroys
whatever justified our canting state,
since his chief skill is to articulate
the smouldering terrors and the prejudice
that makes our heritage a dubious freight
which, now exposed, is seen for what it is.

John Hewitt, 'Demagogue'[1]

TWO THEMES HAVE been central to Ian Paisley's teaching and preaching on the Roman Catholic Church: firstly, and very simply, the Roman Catholic Church is not a Christian Church; and secondly, Roman Catholicism is an instigator of persecution and revolution throughout the world and has been behind the 'Troubles' in Northern Ireland.

'As a Protestant I could not accept that the Church of Rome is a Christian Church,' Ian Paisley wrote to Dean Samuel Crooks when protesting against Cardinal Leon Suenens' visit to St Anne's Cathedral during the Week of Prayer for Christian Unity in January 1986.[2] In August the same year, the World Congress of Fundamentalists, of which Paisley and his friend Dr Bob Jones, chancellor of the Bob Jones University, Greenville, South Carolina, are co-chairmen, affirmed its negative attitude to the Roman Catholic Church: 'Recognising the Church of Rome as revealed in Scripture as the "mother of harlots and abominations of the earth" [Revelation 17:5], we maintain our total resistance to every attempt to accept that system as a Christian church.'[3] Paisley has held this opinion right through his ministry. In February 1956, reflecting on the effects in Ireland of the 1954 Second Assembly of the World Council of Churches meeting in Evanston, USA, he complained that Irish Protestant church leaders were accepting the Roman Catholic Church as part of the

Christian Church.[4] On another occasion he lamented that it was not just church leaders but rank and file Protestant ministers who were 'going about this country preaching Rome is a Christian church'.[5] He regards Roman Catholicism as a system of satanic deception[6] which has never changed over the centuries and will certainly never change in the future.[7]

As in other matters Paisley has passed on this teaching to his followers. His preachers, a determined group of men whom he keeps under strict control, have accepted his analysis, and they in turn pass it on to their congregations. Speaking at a mission in Martyrs' Memorial Church in October 1995, David Fletcher, Free Presbyterian minister in Calgary, Alberta, shared his concern that Canadian evangelical churches like the Baptists, Pentecostalists and Brethren should have absolutely no difficulty in having fellowship with the Roman Catholic Church as a sister Christian church.[8] The Free Presbyterian hymnal illustrates the degree to which this anti-Catholic invective has permeated every aspect of their life and worship:

Hymn 757

1. Our Fathers knew thee, Rome of old,
And evil is thy fame;
Thy fond embrace, the galling chain;
Thy kiss, the blazing flame.

2. Thy blessing, fierce anathema;
Thy honeyed words, deceit;
Thy worship, base idolatry;
Thy sacrament, a cheat.

3. The Mystery of Wickedness,
Right surely is thy name,
The Harlot in the Bride's attire,
As all thy ways proclaim.

4. No peace with Rome shall be our cry,
While Rome abides the same;
We'll let her know that Protestants
Will not disgrace their name.

6. Long hast thou sat in Queen's attire,
Of purple, pearls and gold;
O soon shalt thou be stripped of all –
Thrown down be thy stronghold.

7. Thy sentence dread is now pronounced,
Soon shalt thou pass away.

> O soon shall earth have rest and peace –
> Good Lord, haste Thou that day.[9]

Why does Paisley hold so tenaciously to this position? His writings indicate that he is fully aware that Pope John Paul II affirms the central doctrines of the historic Christian faith.[10] Indeed in the October 1983 issue of *The Revivalist*, he included the complete text of the same pope's letter of Christian greeting to delegates attending the Sixth World Council of Churches Assembly at Vancouver. The letter clearly indicates John Paul II's emphasis on the centrality of Christ:

I am pleased that for this important meeting in the service of the ecumenical movement, you have decided that the central theme would be: 'Jesus Christ the life of the world'. In doing this, you have reached out to Christians everywhere, to all who confess faith in Jesus Christ, believing that 'there is salvation in no one else, for there is no other name under heaven given among men by which we must be saved' [Acts 4:12]. You have confirmed our common belief that Jesus is the crucified Saviour, the Redeemer of all, the Lord of life who was 'designated the Son of God in power according to the Spirit of holiness by his Resurrection from the dead' [Rom.1:4], the Risen Christ whose oneness with us in all things but sin has firmly established the dignity and worth of every human being.[11]

Why have expressions of faith like this not been taken as genuine? It would appear that Paisley's conviction that the Roman Catholic Church is built on a system of deception precludes him from believing anything emanating from Rome or those in communion with Rome. The purest expression of faith or doctrine is regarded as tainted by Satanic deception. Nothing can convince him that the Roman Catholic Church is in any sense to be regarded as a Christian church.

If Paisley's analysis of the Roman Catholic Church is built on the assumption that it is a system of deceit, it is perhaps worth considering the degree of accuracy in the literature he has published against it. His *Concise Guide to Bible Christianity and Romanism*[12] has been considered by two Roman Catholic scholars: Michael Hurley, SJ, founder of the Irish School of Ecumenics in Dublin, and of the Columbanus Community for Reconciliation in Belfast, and Paul Fleming, lecturer in Old and New Testament at St Mary's Training College, Belfast.[13] They identified at least twelve incorrect or untrue statements in the document. Two examples illustrate the inaccuracy of his work.

Concise Guide, Number 25, states:

The Church of Rome claims that the Pope as the successor of St Peter is the Vicar of Christ on earth; the Supreme head and Infallible Teacher of the Church, *and those who do not believe this cannot be saved*.[Emphasis added.]

Hurley and Fleming refer to Vatican II's *Dogmatic Constitution of the Church* (*Lumen Gentium*), paragraph 15:

The Church knows that she is joined in many ways to the baptised who are honoured by the name Christian, but do not however profess the Catholic faith in its entirety or have not preserved unity or communion under the successor of Peter. For there are many who hold sacred scripture as a rule of faith and of life, who have a sincere religious zeal, who lovingly believe in God the Father Almighty and in Christ, the Son of God and the Saviour, who are sealed by baptism which unites them to Christ.

They also point to paragraph 16:

Those who, through no fault of their own, do not know the Gospel of Christ or his Church, but who nevertheless seek God with a sincere heart, and, moved by grace, try in their actions to do his will as they know it through the dictates of their conscience – those too may achieve eternal salvation.[14]

The Concise Guide to Bible Christianity and Romanism, Number 52, states:

Rome teaches that children dying unbaptised 'are born to eternal misery and perdition'.

Hurley and Fleming refer to the Roman Missal, which includes the text of the *Funeral Mass of a child who died before baptism*.[15] The opening prayer of this mass states:

May they [the parents of the child] find comfort in knowing that he/she [the child] is entrusted to your loving care.

Protests against the Roman Catholic Church in this 'Battle of the Ages' are a great source of amusement to Paisley and his colleagues. In reporting his exploits it is quite clear that the protester has enjoyed himself and expects his audience to be amused by his stories. The trip to Rome by Ian Paisley, John Wylie and John Douglas in October 1962 to 'mount a witness' at the opening sessions of Vatican II appears to have been a laugh a minute from beginning to end for all three.[16] At London Airport 'black-garbed clerics and nuns' seemed to be everywhere. John Wylie in particular relished the occasion: 'Walking alongside these black-coated specimens he would strike up a familiar tune like "The Auld Orange Flute" which he would whistle at full volume. When he finished the rendition he would loudly declare, "Thank God to be delivered from popery!"' When they arrived in Rome they had difficulty in finding their way to St Peter's. All their enquiries in English seemed to bring them no nearer their destinaton.

Wylie decided that the next time Paisley asked for directions he would add his own input.

"'St Peter's. Where is St Peter's? We have come to see St Peter's," said Paisley.

"'What my friend means," Wylie butted in, " is that we have come to see the Antichrist. You know, the Beast. We have come to dung him out!'"

As the narrator summed it up, 'Paisley and Wylie were having a ball.' Considering the numerous protests of this nature which he has organised in Ireland and other countries during the past fifty years, it is a fair assumption that this has been perhaps one of his chief methods of relaxation and amusement.

Paisley makes no apology for having such a rollicking time when protesting against what he understands as apostasy. He regards Elijah's mocking of the priests of Baal on Mount Carmel as an appropriate scriptural guideline for his protests and preaching against Catholicism: 'Elijah mocked them! I believe in mocking Popery. It is about time that we had a few more men who knew how to mock Popery.'[17] It is right, he believes, to laugh at Catholicism: 'I have found this, that when people laugh at a thing they will not worship it. If people laugh at a thing they will not go a-whoring after it.' Free Presbyterians have never been short of a good laugh when Paisley has addressed them. Making fun of the Roman Catholic Church – 'there's a sniff of Popery in these verses' is one of his favourite phrases – the Protestant churches, or some politician, is always guaranteed to elicit a few ripples of laughter in the congregation.

In the Steps of the Reformers and Evangelicals?

In all this Paisley sees himself as following in the traditon of the sixteenth-century Protestant Reformers and the evangelical leaders of the eighteenth and nineteenth centuries. He repeatedly says that he is the one who stands in the true Reformation and Evangelical tradition.

Using his undoubted powers of persuasion, he has certainly convinced Free Presbyterians of this. Indeed, even beyond his church fold, some scholars have accepted Paisley's self-analysis. Professor Steve Bruce, a sociologist, whose biography of Paisley, *God Save Ulster! The Religion and Politics of Paisleyism*,[18] has been hailed by one reviewer as 'the first serious analysis of his religious and political careers',[19] suggested that from the 1950s onwards, a time which he describes as one of growing apostasy in the main Protestant churches, it was Paisley's preaching which represented the reformed and evangelical tradition.

'What had changed,' wrote Bruce, 'between the world of the late twenties and thirties, and Paisley's world of the fifties was the degree of "apostasy" in the Irish Presbyterian Church.'[20] The purpose of his book, therefore, was to consider 'those things which distinguished the conservative evangelical views of men like Paisley from the mainstream of Protestant teaching and practice'.[21]

Perhaps the greatest similarity between the Reformers and Paisley lies in his assertion that the pope is the antichrist referred to in Scripture (2 Thessalonians 2:3-4, 8-9; 2 John 1:7; Revelation 13:6). In *Antichrist*[22] and *No Pope Here*[23] he notes the names of the Reformers and others who referred to the papacy as the antichrist, the clear implication being that by his emphasis on this theme he represents the true Reformation tradition. Anyone entering into discussion with him on the Roman Catholic Church will be guaranteed to hear quotation after quotation from the Reformers' comments on the pope as antichrist.

In this respect he is correct, for on the subject of the antichrist he stands within the tradition of the Reformers. However, the Reformers were not the first to speak in this way. Professor John Barkley pinpoints the beginning of the practice to the fourteenth century and explains that in the first six centuries of the church the antichrist was generally viewed as a false Messiah and leader of a Jewish movement: 'He was one of the Jewish false Messiahs who appeared from time to time. No one ever thought that he would rise out of the Christian Church. He would be foreign to it and hostile. Far from calling himself Christian, he would ostentatiously profess his Judaism.'[24]

Apart from this common identification of the papacy as the antichrist, it is difficult to find further distinct similarities between Paisley and the Reformers. While the Reformers preached and wrote strongly against errors they perceived in the doctrine, worship and practice of the sixteenth-century papal church, they were also prepared to sit down with its representatives and discuss points of difference between them. This is something which Paisley refuses to do. He labels as 'traitors' and 'apostates' those who enter into dialogue with the representatives of the Roman Catholic Church. Yet he is aware of the 'colloquies', or conferences, in which the Reformers met with representatives of the papacy, and he mentions the Colloquy of Poissy (1561) in *The Massacre of St Bartholomew*.[25] His enthusiasm for this period of church history would suggest that he also knows about the three other colloquies at Hagenau, Worms and Regensberg in the years 1540-1541, when John Calvin, Philip Melanchton (representing Martin Luther), Martin Bucer and Pistorius met with the Roman representatives Giovanni Morone, Johann Gropper, Johann von Pflug and Johann Eck.

For whatever reason, Paisley either overlooks or misses the real significance of these colloquies: namely, that despite the difficult circumstances in which they met – the harsh things which had been said on both sides, the genuine doctrinal differences between the parties – despite all these factors, they were willing to meet each other in an endeavour to reach some measure of agreement. At the opening session of the colloquy at Poissy, Theodore Beza (1519-1605) indicated the hopeful and prayerful spirit in which he attended: 'I would to God that without further ado, instead of disputations and arguments, we could all with one voice sing a canticle to our Lord, and take each others' hands, as sometimes happened even among infidels, while their armies were already ranged against each other and the battle lines drawn.'[26] That the colloquies failed to secure a resolution to the religious conflict, sad as this certainly was, does not in any way diminish or detract from their significance: two conflicting Christian parties willing to have dialogue in an attempt at reconciliation. Paisley, however, fails to see this at Poissy and interprets it only as a triumph for Protestantism: 'The colloquy demonstrated that the Reformers were able to rout their opponents in debate and that the doctrines of the Reformation could stand up to the whole scholarship of the Roman church.'

The spirit behind the colloquies underlines the gulf between Ian Paisley and the Reformers. He has never recognised in even the minutest measure that the Roman Catholic Church is a Christian church while the Reformers, without exception, took the position that it was. In addition to the colloquies, other statements indicate this attitude. Martin Luther (1483-1546), the figure most clearly associated with the 'birth' of the Reformation, despite his many scathing criticisms of the papal church, when faced with demands from the Anabaptist movements for severance from all of the developments since New Testament times, was able to identify good features in the Roman Catholic Church.

We confess there is much that is Christian and good under the papacy; indeed, everything that is Christian and good is to be found there and has come to us from this source. We confess that in the papal Church there are the true holy Scriptures, true baptism, the true sacrament of the altar, the true keys to the forgiveness of sins, the true office of the ministry, the true catechism in the form of the Lord's Prayer, the Ten Commandments, and the articles of the Creed... I contend that in the papacy there is true Christianity, and many great and devoted saints.[27]

John Calvin (1509-1564), the 'father' of Presbyterianism, was also prepared, with considerable caution, to recognise the Roman Catholic Church as a Christian church. In August 1539, while ministering to a congregation of French exiles in Strasbourg, he received a request from Geneva, from which he had recently been expelled, to answer a letter received from Cardinal Jacopo Sadoleto (1477-1547), the bishop of Carpentras, who was attempting to persuade the Genevois to return to the papal fold.[28] The situation forced Calvin to wrestle with the question of how he really regarded the Roman church. While personally courteous to Sadoleto, he made it quite clear that under the papacy the church had suffered serious damage: 'The truth of Prophetical and Evangelical doctrine, on which the Church ought to be founded, has not only in a great measure perished in your Church, but is violently driven away by fire and sword.'[29] However, despite this and other severe criticisms of the Communion to which Sadoleto was endeavouring to woo the Genevois, he referred to it as 'your Church', as 'your faction of a Church', and he acknowledged that: 'We, indeed, Sadoleto, deny not that those over which you preside are Churches of Christ.'[30]

Calvin in his *Institutes*, Book IV, Chapter II, again discussed the position – or his view of the position – of the Roman Catholic Church:

We deny not to the Papists those vestiges of a Church which the Lord has allowed to remain among them amid the dissipation. Later – He, in order that His covenant might remain inviolable, first preserved baptism there as an evidence of the covenant.... baptism, which, consecrated by his lips, retains its power in spite of human depravity; secondly, He provided by His providence that there should be other remains also to prevent the Church from utterly perishing.

Therefore, while we are unwilling simply to concede the name of Church to the papists, we do not deny that there are churches among them....

In one word, I call them churches, inasmuch as the Lord there wondrously preserves some remains of his people, though miserably torn and scattered, and inasmuch as some symbols of the Church still remain – symbols especially whose efficacy neither the craft of the devil nor human depravity can destroy.[31]

What then of Paisley's claim to stand within the tradition of the Reformers? And what now is the significance of the busts of Luther and Calvin prominently placed over the main inside entrance door to the sanctuary in Martyrs' Memorial Church? The truth is that both Reformers, in common with the other Reformers, combined radical and sustained criticism of the papal church with a willingness to recognise it as part, however defective, of the universal Church of Christ. The corruption and error which they believed had developed within the Roman church prevented them from giving it their obedience and assent, but it did not cause them to deny its existence as a Church in need of reformation. In addition, they were willing to enter into dialogue with the Roman church, or, in Luther's case, send a representative. Both attitudes and actions are contrary – we could accurately say 'anathema' – to everything Paisley has preached and taught for half a century. How can he reconcile his statements with their position?

Paisley's occasional references to two evangelicals, John Wesley in the eighteenth century and Charles Hodge in the nineteenth century, while not entirely solving the mystery, do provide some clues to the way he approaches the topic of evangelical attitudes to the Roman Catholic Church.

The most charitable explanation of Dr Paisley's handling of the writings of these two evangelicals, and indeed the writings of the Reformers and other evangelical leaders, is that he interprets severe criticism of the Roman Catholic Church to be equivalent to his personal conviction that it is not a Christian church, and that he either fails to understand or chooses to ignore clear, unequivocal statements to the contrary. Paisley's pamphlet *John Wesley's Letter to the Church of Rome*,[32] one of a series of 'Fighting Pamphlets from the Past', indicates how he deals with Wesley's attitude to the Roman Catholic Church. Basically he is selective in the quotations used. There is certainly no scarcity of anti-Catholic polemic in Wesley's writings. However, even in the writings selected, there is no evidence that Wesley denied Catholicism's position as a Christian Church. But Paisley presents the comments of Wesley and others in such a way that it seems as if Wesley shared his view of the Roman Catholic Church. For example, in referring to Michael Hurley's edited publication of Wesley's *Letter to a Roman Catholic*, he ridicules Stanley Worrall's statement to the 1966 World Methodist Conference about people who believe that the Roman Catholic Church is not part of the Christian body and immediately comments: 'As a matter of fact, this was John Wesley's own view on popery – an insidious conspiracy of the devil and no part of the Christian Church.' The reader is left with the implied suggestion that Wesley denied that the Roman Catholic Church was part of the Christian church because he regarded the papacy as having no part in the church. Was this really Paisley's understanding of Wesley's position: that denial of the Roman Catholic Church as a Christian Church inevitably followed on from dismissal of the papacy as part of the Church? Or was he being mischievous?

In his complex theology Wesley was quite prepared to limit and qualify what is regarded as the classical Protestant understanding of the church as stated in Article 19 of the 39 Articles of the Church of England: 'The visible Church of Christ is a congregation of faithful people, in which the pure Word of God is preached, and the sacraments duly ministered according to Christ's ordinance...' Wesley believed that this definition placed limitations on the sovereignty of Christ and was not inclusive enough when considering the nature of the universal church. Consequently, in his sermon *Of The Church* he set out his own attitude:

I dare not exclude from the catholid Church all those congregations in which any unscriptural doctrines, which cannot be affirmed to be 'the pure word of God,' are sometimes, yea, frequently preached; neither all those congregations in which the sacraments are not 'duly administered.' Certainly if these things are so, the Church of Rome is not so much as a part of the catholic Church; seeing therein neither is 'the pure word of God' preached, nor the sacraments 'duly administered.' Whoever they are that have 'one Spirit, one hope, one Lord, one faith, one God and Father of all,' I can easily bear with their holding wrong opinions, yea, and superstitious modes of worship: Nor would I, on these accounts, scruple still to include them within the pale of the catholic Church; neither would I have any objection to receive them, if they desired it, as members of the Church of England.[33]

While he undoubtedly had his failings, Wesley always insisted that the love of God and the love of neighbour lay at the heart of true religion. One of his brother Charles's *Hymns of a Protestant*, published in 1745, illustrates how he knew these two great commandments of Christ had implications regarding his attitude to the Roman Catholic Church:

> 4. The spirit of my foes I caught,
> The angry bitter zeal;
> And fierce for my own party fought,
> And breathed the fire of hell.

> 13. Lord, I at last recant, reject,
> The fiery spirit unclean,
> The persecuting zeal impure,
> The sin-opposing sin.

> 18. Heathen and Jews and Turks, may I,

> And heretics embrace;
> Nor e'en to Rome the love deny
> I owe to all the race.   Hymn III[34]

This more irenical and inclusive side to Wesley's theology is not mentioned in Paisley's pamphlet, or in any of his other publications. His attack on Hurley – he accused him of 'atrocious libel' and called him 'a pedlar of lies' – indicates that he is familiar with Wesley's *Letter to a Roman Catholic* but chose not to quote from it. He may also have known his sermon *Of The Church* and perhaps Charles Wesley's *Hymns of a Protestant*. Yet he omits any reference to these documents and fails to give a more comprehensive report on Wesley's inclusiveness.

Charles Hodge (1797-1878) is another evangelical and reformed scholar whose writings feature prominently in Free Presbyterian literature; indeed, much more so than the writings of Wesley. Hodge taught at Princeton Theological Seminary for most of his life, wrote extensively in the area of systematic theology, constitutional church history and New Testament, and is thought by many to have been one of the greatest of American reformed theologians. Little wonder that Paisley would want to be regarded as following in the tradition of such an esteemed Presbyterian teacher. However, once again, he is selective, and omits any reference to Hodge's view that the Roman Catholic Church is a Christian church, argued in the section 'Validity of Romish Baptism' – twenty-four pages in length – included in one of his best-known books, *The Church and Its Polity*.[35]

Hodge explains why he had been prompted to write on the subject. He had just returned from a session of the General Assembly of the Presbyterian Church in the USA (*c.* 1845), where the Assembly had voted 169 to 8 against recognising the validity of baptism as administered by a Roman Catholic priest. It was his custom to comment on assembly decisions in the *Princeton Review*, and these were later collected and published in book form. Hodge was horrified by the Assembly decision: 'What stern necessity has induced the Assembly to pronounce Calvin, Luther, and all the men of that generation.... to have lived and died unbaptised?'[36] He regretted that the assembly voted without properly considering the matter. After offering various reasons in favour of recognising the validity of baptism administered by a Roman Catholic priest he then discussed what he regarded as the more basic question: is the Roman Catholic church a Christian church? The scriptures, he declares, indicate that two things are necessary to the being of a Church: firstly, 'The Bible teaches that whosoever is a true worshipper of Christ, no matter how ignorant or how erroneous he may be, is a true Christian. "Whosoever believeth that Jesus is the Son of God, is born of God." Such is the explicit declaration of the Bible. Whoever, therefore, professes to be a worshipper of Christ, i.e. to love, reverence and serve him as God, does thereby profess to be a Christian; and any body consisting of those who profess to worship Christ, is a body of professed Christians, that is, a Church.'[37] Secondly, argued Hodge, the standards of the church teach that there is no salvation outside the church. Protestant theologians have held this opinion which is similar to scriptural teaching that there is no salvation outside of Christ. It follows then 'that any religious body in communion with which men may be saved is a part of the visible Church; otherwise men may be saved out of that Church'.[38] Hodge then asked: does the Roman Catholic Church retain sufficient truth so that people can be saved?

We do not understand how it is possible for any Christian man to answer this question in the negative. They retain the doctrine of the Incarnation, which we know, from the infallible word of God, is a life-giving doctrine. They retain the whole doctrine of the Trinity. They teach the doctrine of the atonement far more fully and accurately than multitudes of professedly orthodox Protestants. They hold a much higher doctrine, as to the necessity of divine influence, than prevails among many whom we recognize as Christians. They believe in the forgiveness of sins, the resurrection of the body, and in eternal life and judgment. These doctrines are in their creeds, and however they may be perverted and overlaid, still as general propositions they are affirmed. And it must be remembered, that it is the truth presented in general propositions, and not with subtle distinctions, that save the soul.[39]

Hodge warned of the sin of rejecting genuine followers of Christ as reprobates and of viewing their Christian communion in the same manner as 'Pagans and Mohammedans'. He concluded by underlining how far the decision of the assembly had departed from both scriptural and Presbyterian teaching:

We are, therefore, constrained to regard the decision of the Assembly as in direct conflict with our standards, and with the word of God; and as incompatible with Protestant principles, as well as with the practice of the whole Protestant world. We have no scruples in saying this. For in protesting against the decision of one hundred and sixty-nine members of the Assembly, we can hide ourselves in the crowd of 169,000,000 of faithful men who, since the Reformation, have maintained the opposite and more catholic doctrine.[40]

Needless to say, the assembly soon reversed its decision and followed Hodge's appeal to base their practice on scriptural, Presbyterian and Protestant principles. There exists a major difference between Paisley's attitude to the Roman Catholic Church and that of the Reformers and evangelicals before him. Paisley's denial that the Roman Catholic Church is a Christian church and his ridiculing of Protestants who have accepted it as part of the visible church – though, like all churches, in need of reformation under the Word of God – represents the reversal of much that Protestantism stands for and is contrary, as Hodge declared, to 'the practice of the whole Protestant world'.

The Question of Dialogue

Unlike the Reformers who discussed Christian doctrine with representatives of the Roman Catholic Church in the colloquies of the 1540s and 1561, Paisley has resolutely refused offers of dialogue with Roman Catholics. When Tomás Ó Fiaich was appointed archbishop of Armagh in 1977, he made it known that he would like to meet Protestants and get to know them better. Many responded to this open invitation and came to appreciate his openness, friendliness and sense of merriment. They liked his genuineness. They may not have agreed with his politics, but they knew that behind it all he bore no malice. He was a very human person who wanted to reach out to people irrespective of their politics or denomination. It was natural, therefore, for Ó Fiaich to express a desire to meet Paisley, but the request was turned down because 'In ecumenical dialogue those taking part recognised the Christianity of the other'.[41] As an alternative Paisley suggested a televised debate on topics like the papacy and the priesthood: 'I am sure that the Television authorities would be happy to provide the facilities for such a disputation.'[42]

He always relishes the chance to have public debates with Roman Catholic priests and distinguished laity or Protestant ministers, and the story of his life is full of such challenges to debate. Such suggestions have usually been declined on the basis that he never really intended to have a genuine debate – there was guaranteed to be considerable shouting and cheering during the proceedings – and also because it was felt that his main aim was to gain the maximum publicity possible. Coupled with his suggestion to Ó Fiaich of a public debate was a fierce condemnation of the Roman Catholic Church: 'Today, as Elias stood on Carmel and cried out against the priests of Baal, so would I. I count no words too severe. If my every speech would be a thunderbolt, and every word a lightning flash, it would not be too strong to protest against the accursed system which once degraded the whole earth to kiss the Pope's foot.' Ó Fiaich thanked Paisley for his letter, regretted he could not engage in dialogue with him, and declined the idea of a public debate as he thought it would be divisive and possibly dangerous in its effects on the community: 'Against the background of so much sectarian violence in recent years it could be positively dangerous. You may not agree with this assessment of the position – and that is of course your right. But my own assessment of it precludes me from taking part in any programme which would run the slightest risk of deepening still further the divisions which unfortunately separate Christians in this country.'[43]

Ó Fiaich's invitation to dialogue and the manner in which he declined the suggestion of a televised debate indicates that he accepted Paisley as a Christian. Roman Catholics had travelled a long way in their attitude to Protestants since the sixteenth century. Then it was a matter of outright condemnation of the Reformers and all that they represented. Johannes Cochlaeus, a Catholic reformer and contemporary of Luther, did not have a very high regard for the Wittenberg professor:

Luther is a child of the devil, possessed by the devil, full of falsehood and vainglory... he lusts after wine and women, is without conscience, and approves any means to gain his end... he is a liar and a hypocrite, cowardly and quarrelsome.[44]

Finlay Holmes has shown that Roman Catholic opinions of Luther varied little from that of Cochlaeus until after the First World War. Then Catholic scholars started seriously to study his writings and a more sympathetic appreciation developed. By 1940 Joseph Lortz was suggesting that the Roman Curia was just as much to blame as Luther for the sixteenth-century schism. But this more sensitive approach by scholars to the Reformers and Protestants in general took a while to permeate the hierarchy of the church. In 1931 Cardinal Joseph McRory, archbishop of Armagh, 1928-1945, had declared that the Protestant churches were 'not even a part of the Church of Christ'.[45] However, the shift in official Roman Catholic evaluation and policy eventually came in the 1950s. The papal letter *Ecclesia Sancta* (20 December 1949) described those involved in the ecumenical movement as 'among those who are dissident from the Catholic Church' and 'believe in Christ the Lord'.[46] By 1964 Vatican II in its *Decree on Ecumenism* was referring to other Christian communions as 'separated Churches', their members as 'separated brethren', and was encouraging Catholics to be informed of their outlook and opinions so that they could engage in ecumenical dialogue 'with love for the truth, with charity, and with humility'.[47] It was in this spirit that Ó Fiaich had suggested a meeting with Paisley.

Paisley's unwillingness to recognise the Roman Catholic Church as being in any sense a Christian church and his refusal to enter into dialogue or discussion with its representatives runs contrary to the position taken by various world confessional bodies – Anglican, Baptist, Disciples, Lutheran, Methodist, Pentecostals, Reformed and Orthodox – which have each engaged in dialogue or conversations with it. Most of these international meetings commenced soon after the conclusion of the Second Vatican Council, some as early as 1967. The most recent were the international conversations between the Baptist World Alliance and the Roman Catholic Church which started in 1984. Topics discussed in these inter-confessional dialogues have varied, but most have included: evangelism; justification by faith; tradition and scripture; church, ministry and sacraments; the papacy; and the role of Mary. Participants have usually noted areas of agreement and disagreement. The first Baptist-Roman Catholic Church report (1988) referred to 'our common witness' based on shared faith in the centrality of Christ as revelation of God and sole mediator between God and humankind.[48] In penitence they acknowledged that competition and bitterness among missionaries had acted as a stumbling-block for those to whom the gospel is proclaimed. The Lutheran–Roman Catholic Church report on *Justification by Faith* (1983) included an agreed common statement: 'Our entire hope of justification and salvation rests on Christ Jesus and on the gospel whereby the good news of God's merciful action in Christ is made known; we do not place our ultimate trust in anything other than God's promise and saving work in Christ.'[49] One of the main obstacles to reconciliation between the Anglicans and the Roman Catholic Church appears to be their different attitudes to the ordination of women, but had Ian Paisley been 'a fly on the wall' during these discussions he would have found himself more in agreement with the Roman Catholic Church than the Anglicans.

Evangelicals associated with the Lausanne Committee for World Evangelisation also entered into dialogue with the Roman Catholic Church. 'The Evangelical–Roman Catholic Dialogue on Mission, 1977-1984: A Report'[50] considered topics similar to those which arose in the inter-confessional dialogues. Particularly significant, especially in relation to Paisley's attitude to the Roman Catholic Church and his claim to represent the historic evangelical tradition, is the fact that they suggested areas in which Catholics and evangelicals might share in common witness: Bible translation and publishing, use of the media, community service, social thought and action, dialogue, and common praise and prayer. Although the participants were aware that in some parts of the world Catholics and evangelicals have shared together in evangelism they thought that this was premature as substantial agreement on the nature of the gospel still eluded them.

Despite its problems, Ireland did not lose out on this improvement in Roman Catholic–Protestant relationships at international level. Signs of dialogue and co-operation could also be found in Ireland from the 1960s onwards. Such ventures were more easily planned in the south of Ireland than in the north, where nothing could be arranged without incurring fierce protests from Paisley and his aides. Obviously there were Catholics and Protestants, both clerical and lay, who experienced close friendships long before the sixties. However, the Glenstal, County Limerick, and Greenhills, Drogheda, annual conferences, which began in 1964 and 1966 respectively, were the first organised but unofficial points of contact between Catholic and Protestant clergy. Papers were presented and discussed and the participants usually shared in short acts of worship. For many it was a new and enriching experience.

Official contact between Roman Catholic and Protestant churches really started with the 'Ballymascanlon' inter-church meeting in September 1973, organised by the Roman Catholic hierarchy and the Irish Council of Churches. The talks, which continue to be held from time to time, were named Ballymascanlon after the hotel outside Dundalk where the meetings were held. Eric Gallagher and Stanley Worrall, in *Christians in Ulster 1968-1980*, have conveyed something of the drama which surrounded the first meeting. The members attending were immediately faced with two difficulties: journalists, who thought they had come to report on a 'peace conference', and Ian Paisley, who wanted to protest that the meeting was being held at all. On this occasion Paisley's protest appears to have been kept under control:

Dr Paisley threatened to disrupt the conference, but when the day came he contented himself with a picket of about 100 people. These gathered at the hotel gates and sought entry. When the police explained that the hotel management objected to a demonstration inside the grounds, Dr Paisley carried a letter of protest up the quarter-mile long drive and returned to his group outside. Within minutes the conference organisers made a public statement that the protest was based on a misunderstanding: the talks were not secret, the press being invited to attend; and they were not aimed at church union.[51]

Progress at the inter-church meeting, and the working parties it appointed, has been slow and often difficult, particularly in matters relating to doctrine. But agreement in areas of social concern have at times been outstanding, most notably in the 1976 report *Violence in Ireland.*[52]

Reconciliation groups have also been points of contact between Catholics and Protestants: Corrymeela Community was the first to be formed, followed by Protestant and Catholic Encounter (PACE), Glencree Centre for Reconciliation, the Peace People, Women Together, Columbanus Community for Reconciliation, Cornerstone Community, Co-operation North, and others. Catholics and Protestants have shared together in various ways at local level: inter-church services, Bible study and prayer groups, and matters of common social concern. Ministerial and lay theological students from different seminaries have met on various occasions for day conferences, common worship and sometimes even football. Inter-schools projects and integrated schooling have encouraged better community understanding for children and youth. Whether undertaken in response to the challenge to be constructive in the face of community violence or under the influence of improved inter-church relationships in other parts of the world, the fact is that opportunities for cross-community dialogue and contact have increased rather than diminished in Ireland in the last three decades.

'Rome is Behind the Troubles'

One of the saddest days ever experienced in Belfast during the twenty-five years of community violence was 21 July 1972. Twenty-two bombs set off by the IRA in the city killed nine people and injured many more. Because of the scenes of terrible carnage, it went into history as 'Bloody Friday'. Paisley's response was to mock as 'ecumenical stunts' the memorial services later held in the open air at the sites where the bombs had devastated so many lives. But he had another message: 'Rome is behind the troubles – that is an indisputable fact.'[53] This has been one of his main accusations against the Roman Catholic Church. As well as denying that it is a Christian church, he has repeatedly charged it with being an instigator of persecution and revolution throughout the world and the inspiration behind the 'Troubles' in Northern Ireland.

Five months after 'Bloody Friday' the pastoral visits of various Catholic clergy – including Dr McQuaid, the former archbishop of Dublin and Dermot Ryan, the archbishop in office at the time – to Seán Mac Stiofáin, IRA chief-of-staff, while he was on hunger and thirst strike in Mountjoy Prison in Dublin, led Paisley to assert: 'The

Provisional IRA is in reality the armed wing of the Roman Catholic Church. Its real aim is to annihilate Protestantism.'[54] Was Paisley's charge against the Roman Catholic Church just a knee-jerk reaction to the attention Mac Stiofáin was receiving from the Roman Catholic hierarchy? He would have been aware of the history of consultation existing between the Republican movement and the hierarchy, especially during the early decades of the century, but no one at that time had gone so far as to describe the IRA as 'the armed wing of the Roman Catholic Church'. It was strange that Mac Stiofáin received such a degree of prominent clerical concern. But Paisley was a Christian minister whose first obligation one might expect in such circumstances would have been concern for the person irrespective of class, creed, politics, meritorious deeds or lack of them. He must have given some thought to the personal crisis Mac Stiofáin was in and some reflection on the possible repercussions his death in prison might have had in the country.

It was not the first time that priests had shown concern for the souls of Republican prisoners in Mountjoy Jail. Cardinal John Heenan, a former archbishop of Westminster, described in his autobiography, *Not the Whole Truth*, the considerable pastoral concern shown for Joseph Brady, one of the 'Invincibles' who had stabbed Lord Cavendish and Mr Burke, the two British officials then responsible for Ireland, to death in 1882. After the ghastly incident, known as the 'Phoenix Park Murders', Brady had been apprehended by the authorities through information received from an informer. Imprisoned in Mountjoy and under sentence of death, Brady would not make his peace with God because he could not find it in his heart to forgive Carey, the informer. The prison chaplain, we are told, brought in many good priests who talked and prayed with him in an effort to persuade him to forgive Carey, but it was all to no avail. Eventually a nun asked if she could see Brady and permission was given only because she said she held the secret to Brady's heart. Heenan describes the encounter between Brady and the nun:

Entering Brady's cell the Sister apologised for the intrusion but said that she was in desperate need of help. As one about to face God Brady would be the most likely man in the world to give her the right advice. She explained that she hated a certain person with all her heart. It had become an obsession with her. She now asked Brady if she should throw off the veil and leave the religious life. Brady replied without hesitation: "For God's sake, Sister, don't do that. Try to forgive." "Very well, Mr Brady," the nun replied, "I forgive you for killing Burke in Phoenix Park. He was my brother." Brady, of course, begged her pardon, forgave Carey, made his confession and received Holy Communion the next morning before he was hanged.[55]

In one sense it is strange that Paisley did not comment on the pastoral concern the priests would have had for Mac Stiofáin. On the other hand, his conviction that the Roman Catholic Church was often guilty of satanic deception accounts for his political interpretation of the visits from the archbishops. And his comments were consistent with similar statements he had made in the past and regrettably similar sentiments he would voice in the future.

Just two months after the Ulster Workers' Council Strike of May 1974, Paisley was describing the Roman Catholic Church as 'Ulster's implacable foe' and accusing it of supporting the IRA in the hope of achieving a clear victory: 'What Rome failed to achieve in 1641, 1689, 1690, 1798, 1916 and 1968, she is pushing now for complete victory.'[56] Such comments continued unabated. A leading article in the *Protestant Telegraph* in February 1975 declared, 'It is hard to believe but Rome still claims the right to kill Protestants.'[57]

He believes that the IRA and the Roman Catholic Church are in fact to be viewed together. In one of his many comments on Tomás Ó Fiaich, he said, 'His flock has murdered many hundreds of Protestants, maimed for life many hundreds more and done millions of pounds worth of damage to Protestant properties.'[58] In September 1988 he said it was the 'Roman Catholic Irish Republican Army' who were responsible for the death of eight soldiers from the 1st Battalion Light Infantry when their bus was blown up on 20 August by a 200 pound landmine hidden in a drainage culvert outside Ballygawley, County Tyrone.[59] Earlier that year, on 19 March, millions across the world had witnessed on television the moments when two army corporals, Derek Wood and David Howes, had driven their car at the funeral procession on the Andersonstown Road for Kevin Brady, an IRA man murdered three days earlier at Milltown cemetry by a loyalist, Michael Stone. While viewers only saw the corporals being savagely dragged out of their car, it was later revealed they had been taken across the road into Casement Park, brutally beaten and dropped twenty feet over a wall, from where they were then driven a short distance and shot.

Paisley laid the blame at the feet of the Roman Catholic Church: 'Is it any wonder that they carved up two British Army Corporals on the Falls Road because that is the direct fruit of the very system in which they were brought up. If you teach people from infancy error, that error one day will surface and there will be diabolical fruit from that rotten root which was planted in their hearts.'[60] It is significant that Paisley made no reference to the influences which might have led Stone to murder the Republican mourners in Milltown cemetry. If, as he suggests, IRA terrorism is the fruit of a Roman Catholic upbringing, what about the UVF and UDA terrorists? Were people like Michael Stone and the 'Shankill Butchers' what they were as a result of their upbringing – anti-Catholicism? However, Paisley did not see it this way. In his eyes the root cause of all Ulster's ills is the Roman Catholic church. There is no need for tribunals or enquiries into the problems of Northern Ireland. He has always held that the Roman Catholic Church, which he is convinced is not really a Christian Church, is responsible for unrest and turmoil in the community: 'The Roman Catholic Church lies at the heart of the problem in Northern Ireland. She has indoctrinated her people against everything that is Protestant.'[61]

Rome's alleged encouragement of armed revolution in Ireland in the twentieth century is, in Paisley's opinion, simply a continuation of its practice in the past in other parts of the world. The *Protestant Telegraph* (and its successor, the *New Protestant Telegraph*) and *The Revivalist*, continually refer to historical events when the Roman Catholic Church is said to have persecuted Protestants and others because they dared to dissent from the official teaching of the papacy. Examples from the sixteenth century are particularly common. Addressing a public meeting (at which 1,650 people were present according to Paisley) on 'Irish Roman Catholic Priests Challenged And Answered' in the Ulster Hall, Belfast, on 13 December 1953, he asserted:'The darkest, bloodiest and most shameful pages of history are the dark records of the intolerance, bigotry and butchery carried out with the blessing of Rome.'[62] Most people are aware that religious wars, and wars in which Christian churches were identified with one side or the other, are sadly part of history and European history in particular. But these terrible events in the past do not indicate the involvement of only one church, the Roman Catholic Church, but other churches too. Paisley highlights only Roman Catholic persecution and violence, ignoring examples of Protestant intolerance and rapacity. The omission of such accounts poses the inevitable question: what purpose is served by such selectivity? The truth appears to be that Paisley decided in his late teens that the Roman Catholic Church was not a Christian church but rather a pernicious system whose goal was world domination; in order to convince others of his opinion, he has since been prepared to select from history only those events which appear to support this analysis.

The manner in which he selects sources to support his arguments and omits other sources which could contradict his case poses another question. Paisley lectures in church history in his own theological college, Whitefield College of the Bible, near Gilford, County Armagh. It is not surprising that the students find his lectures interesting and amusing. Indeed, some would say that these lectures – that is, when he is able to attend – are the most enjoyable on the course. His gifts in communication greatly assist his task as a lecturer; 'sniffs of popery' and tales from his travels would naturally delight students accepted for training in his church. But in his lectures he provides little in the way of source material. We have already observed that in relation to the Reformers, the Evangelical tradition, and now the subject of persecution and intolerance in church history, he only presents sources and information which support his case. We have also noted that even after carefully selecting his material and ignoring other sources, he is particularly adept at presenting his sources in such a way that they give the impression of supporting his analysis. His methods of historical research would certainly not satisfy normal academic standards, and his teaching is more a matter of indoctrination than of education.

When advising people how to respond to the 'enemies of Ulster's Protestantism' – a term he has often used to describe the Roman Catholic Church – he has sometimes distinguished between individual Roman Catholics and those involved in the official structures of the Roman Catholic Church – that is, the papacy, the hierarchy and the priesthood. He regards individual Roman Catholics as living in spiritual darkness, the victims of a corrupted system. They are really to be pitied rather than blamed. He believes it is the priesthood who have deluded them. He has said he has nothing against individual Roman Catholics. At an Oxford Union Debate on the motion 'The Roman Catholic Church has no place in the twentieth century', at which he described the mass as a 'blasphemous fable' and the priesthood as 'repugnant to the Christian faith', he began: 'I'd like to say first of all that anything I say here tonight is not said to insult any individual Roman Catholic.'[63] At the funeral service in Hillsborough Free Presbyterian Church on 2 March 1985 for Reserve Constable Kenneth Campbell, one of nine RUC personnel murdered in an attack on the Newry police station, he welcomed 'most heartily' the sincere sympathy expressed by the Roman Catholic population. 'We have no individual bias against our fellow Roman Catholics,' he insisted. 'We wish all men in this province to live at peace and enjoy a prosperity that comes through the benefits of civil and religious liberty for all men.'[64]

Such sentiments are certainly to be welcomed, but how consistent are they with his vulgar descriptions of Roman Catholics as 'pope-heads', Roman Catholic women as 'incubators for Rome', or Wylie's insults to priests and nuns at London airport? These, after all, are also people, not a system.

His distinction between individual Roman Catholics and the Roman Catholic hierarchy is blurred somewhat by his more frequent references to the 'Roman Catholic Irish Republican Army'. It is not always clear to whom he is referring when he urges resistance against the Roman Catholic Church. Sometimes distinctions are drawn, sometimes not. This uncertainty about who is to be resisted – the IRA yes, but how are we always to know who are good individual Roman Catholics? – also applies to the nature of the resistance suggested. His message in political and religious circles has always been basically the same: first, there is the warning of the subtle conspiracies of the Roman Catholic Church; then, an emphasis on the need for constant vigilance in the face of this threat; finally, the responsibility to resist the conspiracy. In July 1956, after warning about various alleged Roman Catholic tactics in the area of education, calling for vigilance in case Ulster Protestants might be 'sold down the river', he urged militant action:

Actions speak louder than words, and it is action – aggressive, militant, uncompromising action – which alone can save us from Egyptian slavery under the taskmasters of a thoroughgoing R.C. State. 'Oh, for the sword of Gideon to slay the apostates and rid the land of tyrants' should be the fervent prayer of every true born free son of the glorious Reformation. Let God arise, we cry, and let our enemies be scattered.[65]

Similar cries of rousing rhetoric have come from his lips ever since, and one must wonder what effect it has had on those who have heard it. He has travelled tirelessly across Northern Ireland for five decades, exhorting his audiences to be alert and ready for action. It would not be surprising if some may have taken literally his exhortations to wield 'the sword of Gideon to slay the apostates and rid the land of tyrants'.

The Roman Catholic Church and Paramilitarism

While Paisley has accused the Roman Catholic Church of being in cahoots with the IRA, the truth is that the Irish Catholic hierarchy has continually condemned IRA violence. In January 1956, five months before Paisley's call for militant action, the hierarchy had declared that 'it is a mortal sin for a Catholic to become or remain a member of an organisation or society, which arrogates to itself the right to bear arms or to use them against its own or another state; that it is also sinful for a Catholic to co-operate with, express approval of, or otherwise assist any such organisation or society, and that, if the co-operation or assistance be notable, the sin committed is mortal'.[66]

In 1979, after ten years of community violence in which some of the most horrific crimes imaginable had been committed, it was hoped that Pope John Paul II's visit to Ireland might have some effect on the Provisonal IRA. Paisley had warned the pope to keep out of Northern Ireland: 'this visit is not on – full stop. The pope is anti-Christ, the man of sin in the Church. Pope Benedict blessed the 1916 rebels... from that has flowed the IRA.'[67] Once again Paisley had got his facts wrong. In the first place the IRA stands in a tradition which is much older than 1916, which can be traced back to the Invincibles, the Fenians and the United Irishmen. Also, Pope Benedict XV had been informed by the Irish Republican Brotherhood (the Fenians) of their intention to hold a rebellion in Ireland and their emissary, Count Plunkett, had had the audacity to ask for the pope's blessing, but his reaction was one of 'great perturbation'. There is no record of the IRB receiving his blessing.[68]

When in 1979 Pope John Paul II did come to Ireland and visited Drogheda, the town which Cromwell had attacked with such ferocity, he addressed himself to the paramilitaries. His message was plain and direct:

Peace cannot be established by violence, peace can never flourish in a climate of terror, intimidation and death.... I pray with you that nobody may ever call murder by any other name than murder... let us remember that the word remains for ever: 'All who take the sword shall perish by the sword.' I appeal to you in language of passionate pleading. On my knees I beg you to turn away from the paths of violence and to return to the ways of peace. You may claim to seek justice. I too believe in justice and seek justice. But violence only delays the day of justice.[69]

Regrettably the pope's words were not heeded by the Provisional IRA or other paramilitaries. The violence and human suffering continued. And John Paul's words also failed to convince Paisley. In 1971 he had published an extract from Avro Manhattan's book, *Religious Terror in Ireland*, which claimed that the Roman Catholic Church could, if it really wanted, 'immobilise – indeed paralyse – the Roman Catholic promoters of violence throughout Ireland on both sides of the Border, any day it suited her to do so'. The article went on to suggest that the only reason for the continuation of the violence was that it was in the interests of the Roman Catholic Church for the war to continue.[70] The sentiments expressed in the article continued to be Paisley's attitude and message: if the Roman Catholic Church were resolute in their determination to stop violence, it would cease overnight.

It has been obvious for some time that the Roman Catholic Church has been fighting a battle with Republicans for the soul of the people in areas like West Belfast and has been exerting less and less influence on its members. Paisley appears to have chosen to ignore this reality in favour of information and allegations, accurate or otherwise, of Roman Catholic priests who seemed to be sympathetic to paramilitary violence. Tim Pat Coogan in his preface to *The Troubles* refers to 'a well-known priest who went to the IRA Army Council and asked that the IRA assassinate Paisley'.[71] Such stories – for example, of priests who insisted on the IRA's giving them the name of each new commander appointed in their parish – have influenced Paisley's judgment. He would not appear to have accepted that there may be 'rotten eggs in every basket' and that no church is immune from imperfections in its clergy.

Condemnations of IRA violence by the Roman Catholic Church hierarchy continued. In the summer of 1986 the IRA warned that civilians associated in any way, business or otherwise, with the army or police would be 'treated as collaborators' and 'must expect to suffer the consequences'. When they put their threats into action, Edward Daly, bishop of Derry, condemned them for living totally contrary to the teaching of Christ: 'If you wish to choose the Devil rather than Christ, be honest with yourselves and declare yourselves to be no longer Catholics or Christians because your lives and your actions are utterly inconsistent with Catholicism. If you cannot accept Christ's words and teachings or utterly reject them, then leave Him; leave Christ.'[72]

Rejection and condemnation of the IRA did not preclude the hierarchy from its understandable concern for social justice. Most Christians have understood their mission and purpose as including a deep interest in the conditions in which people live, and Ian Paisley is no exception. He has demonstrated this in his own particular way, combining the role of an ordained minister with being an elected politician. While none of the Irish Roman Catholic hierarchy ever tried to emulate Paisley's dual role – indeed, canon law prohibits them from seeking political office – they were rightly active in speaking out on issues of social justice. It is not the place now to consider the ways in which the Catholic hierarchy demonstrated this interest, but it is necessary to indicate that this too was their role. Their condemnation of violence was not in isolation from their concern for social justice.

Indeed, as John Paul had hinted, there was a relationship between the the two, not least the fact that paramilitary violence was hindering and delaying the implementation of social justice.

Cardinal Cathal Daly, archbishop of Armagh, who has occupied the episcopal office longer than most, has had a long and deep interest in removing obstacles to reconciliation in Ireland. Along with his other episcopal colleagues, he has clearly and unequivocally condemned paramilitary violence. But his views and opinions have been reached not in isolation in his own Catholic community but after sharing with and learning from members of the Protestant community. This was particularly evident in his joint chairmanship with Eric Gallagher, a former Methodist president, of the Working Party on Violence in Ireland set up by the Ballymascanlon Inter-Church Meeting. It was highly significant that Daly and the other members recommended that 'the Churches jointly remind their members that they have a *prima facie* moral obligation to support the currently constituted authorities in Ireland against all para-military forces'.[73] In the same report, issued at the time of the hunger strikes at the Maze Prison, they asked: 'Is Martyrdom the privilege of those who make an idol of their country and is it never to be expected of those who uphold justice or Christian standards of conduct?' They explained clearly that the churches and people in the community had serious questions to face: 'What is the ordinary man or woman to do when faced with demands for money, pressure to hide contraband material, and perhaps more commonly, the knowledge that to support authority, particularly by the release of information, would bring overwhelming retaliation?'

Daly's various personal statements on the situation have been collected in his book, *Price of Peace*.[74] During the violence he called on the Provisionals to examine their commitment to the principles of their heroes. Padraig Pearse, he reminded them, called off the 1916 Rising on the Saturday of Easter Week 'in order to prevent further slaughter of citizens' and the signatories of the Republican Proclamation of Easter Week said: 'We pray that no one who serves [the cause of the Irish Republic] will dishonour it by... inhumanity or rapine.'[75] Daly has repeated the message of his colleagues, namely, that the campaign is sinful and against the teaching of the Catholic Church: 'No faithful Catholic can claim that there is moral justification for the deeds of violence of these organisations.'[76] Furthermore, he suggested that the activities of the IRA were in fact killing, not only their victims, but also the souls of those involved in or actively supporting the organisation.

Roman Catholic Church and Paisley's Accusations

The Roman Catholic Church has never responded directly to Paisley's statements that it is not a Christian church, that it has been an instigator of persecution and war, and that it was behind the 'Troubles' in Northern Ireland.

The reason for the silence is possibly found in the exchange of letters between Ó Fiaich and Paisley. We recall that Ó Fiaich had made it known that he would like to meet Paisley. He wanted to see if some kind of friendship or at least better understanding could be formed between them. It was not an attempt to answer Paisley's already well documented comments on the Roman Catholic Church, but an attempt to break down barriers on a personal basis. If personal contact developed then that could form the basis for discussion on theological and social issues. As we know, Paisley refused the invitation to meet him informally and instead challenged him to a public debate. This Ó Fiaich declined because he felt, and with good reason, that a public debate could exacerbate tensions in the Northern Ireland community. And this surely provides the clue to the Roman Catholic Church position vis-à-vis Paisley: any public statements through the media in response to Paisley's charges could have hindered rather than helped the situation.

This silence as regards a public response to Paisley himself did not preclude general reflection on the kind of statements Paisley has made. His long public ministry has certainly influenced the views of Protestants beyond the Free Presbyterian fold. Consequently, the lengthy debate in the 'writeback' columns of the *Belfast Telegraph* during the late autumn and winter of 1995 on whether or not the Roman Catholic Church was a Christian church touched on one of the themes Paisley has continually emphasised. Patrick McCafferty, Roman Catholic curate in Holy Trinity, Lenadoon, Belfast, felt that a response was not inappropriate. Answering a correspondent whose letter had appeared on 14 December, McCafferty wrote: 'In his efforts to prove that Catholicism is not Christian he launches into a diatribe against Catholic beliefs and practices which he plainly does not understand... Nothing you can say will change the fact that countless Catholics have a real, living and personal relationship with Jesus their Saviour.'[77] Similarly, Cathal Daly did not mention Paisley by name but he may have had him in mind when he referred to the sectarian propaganda preached in some pulpits in Northen Ireland:

Sadly it must be added also that there are pulpits in this land of ours from which a weekly torrent of polluted propaganda is poured out against the Catholic Church. There are few places left in the Western world where any Christian pastors preach prejudice and lies and hatred in respect of their fellow Christians. All of us, Catholics and Protestants alike, must be deeply concerned that Northern Ireland is prominent among these very few places. We must pray and work, Catholics and Protestants together, to show that such behaviour has no place in our understanding of Christianity. As Christians, we cannot rest until this curse of sectarianism is banished from our land.[78]

Daly has been very aware of the deep-seated fear and suspicion of the Roman Catholic Church held by some Protestants. He believes that much of this fear is due to their ignorance of Catholic doctrines and practices, as McCafferty suggested. Daly is convinced that this fear contributes to community conflict and needs to be addressed: 'The persistent anti-Roman element in much popular Protestantism is an important factor in community conflict in the North.'[79] While he would like to see more informed education about the Roman Catholic Church among Protestants and increased Protestant–Catholic contacts and dialogue, he also knows that the Roman Catholic Church itself must take steps to combat the problem: 'Catholic bishops, clergy and laity must be particularly sensitive to this problem, and must do everything possible, in their words and by their lives, to bear witness to the true nature and authentic teaching of the Catholic Church.'

However, these general reflections on Protestant fears and anti-Roman propaganda have never mentioned Paisley by name. Roman Catholic Church leaders have studiously avoided personal confrontation with him.

Protestants have shown a marked reluctance to speak out in defence of the Roman Catholic Church when Paisley has made negative and damaging statments about it. Martin Luther, John Wesley, Charles Hodge and others in the past found that they could rally to its defence, while still reserving the right to call for its reformation; others within the universal Church of Christ in more recent times have generally refrained from challenging the accuracy of Paisley's statements.

Paisley's reasons for criticising the Roman Catholic Church have lacked credibility; his claims to follow in the steps of the sixteenth-century Protestant Reformers and the leaders of the evangelical tradition are groundless; his preaching and teaching have been the opposite of everything Protestantism stands for; yet Protestants have remained silent. Perhaps Protestants have felt that their actions spoke louder than words. Certainly, the reconciling spirit shown by Protestant leaders over the past twenty-five years has often been inspiring. Since Christmas 1974 the leaders of the four main churches have frequently been seen together – a powerful statement in itself of reconciliation. Was this practical demonstration of support for each other the most appropriate response to Paisley? Historians will in time make their own judgments, and possibly be as diverse in their findings on Northern Ireland as they have been in regard to other conflict situations elsewhere in the world.

Chapter Five

Apostate Protestants

There's a wideness in God's mercy
Like the wideness of the sea;
There's a kindness in his justice
Which is more than liberty.

For the love of God is broader
Than the measures of man's mind;
And the heart of the Eternal
Is most wonderfully kind.

But we make his love too narrow
By false limits of our own;
And we magnify his strictness
With a zeal he will not own.

Frederick William Faber (1814–1863)[1]

APOSTASY IS ONE of the most damning indictments that can be charged against any church or individual as it signifies the total abandonment of one's Christian faith. This is Ian Paisley's diagnosis on all the Protestant churches: 'The whole ecclesiastical setup of Protestantism has become corrupted, has become deProtestantised, has become apostate.'[2] Because, as he maintains, Protestantism has lost its spirituality, it is now 'defunct and dead and lifeless and useless'.[3] Giving the ordination charge in Martyrs' Memorial Church to Kyle, his eldest son, on 28 August 1991, he graphically described how he views the clergy of Protestant churches:

Apostate ministers are pimpled clergymen, pimpled with questionings, they are broken out in a rash of unbelief, they are covered in boils of scepticism, they are consumed with fevers of ecumenism, they are blackened with the blackness of popery and they are sick unto death with the cancer of blatant Bible-denials. These are the ministerial mongrels

– products of the College kennels of the apostate denominations.[4]

All the Protestant churches have been condemned at some stage in his ministry: Presbyterian (targeted more than any other church), Church of Ireland, Methodist, Baptist, Brethren, Elim Pentecostal; all have been condemned. His accusations against these churches and their clergy and preachers vary according to the denomination. The main charges include denial of the Deity of Christ, inadequate preaching on the atoning work of Christ, rejection of the Bible, abandonment of Reformation principles and tradition, ecumenical involvement, and links, however slender, with the Roman Catholic Church. Since so many churches have been attacked, he has never had difficulty in finding people to criticise: 'You could fire the gospel gun off anywhere and there's that many old apostates you're sure to hit one. They're around, they're everywhere, these apostates.'[5] The firing range is so wide that it now includes fundamentalists, or more accurately, as Paisley would define them, those who profess to be fundamentalist. That fundamentalists should have forsaken God and become involved in the destruction of His truth is sure evidence, he thinks, that 'the devil is at work'.[6]

The Ecumenical Movement

The ecumenical movement, and the World Council of Churches in particular, has been the focus of Paisley's attention right through his public ministry. He has frequently preached, written and protested against ecumenism, and hardly a Sunday goes by at 'Martyrs' without prayers that God will destroy it utterly. At various times he has called World Council of Churches assemblies 'the assembly of the ungodly', 'the great ecumenical assembly of Baalism' and 'a wicked chamber of corruption'. His denunciations of the World Council of Churches are similar to his condemnation of Protestants in Ireland. Christ, he declares, is denied and blasphemed: 'Where is the Lord Jesus Christ? He is not in the Vatican, He is not in Canterbury, He is not in the World Council of Churches – they hate Him, they fight Him, they defame Him and they reject Him.'[7] This lying system of the ecumenical movement, representing as he maintains 'the machinations of the devil', has presented a totally unscriptural picture of Christ: 'The Christ that is presented by the ecumenist and apostates is not the Christ of the New Testament. It is a Christ of their own importance. It is that other Jesus, the preaching and propagation of which the apostle condemned.'[8] He sees the movement as destroying the very essence of Protestantism and Christianity: 'In this hazy crazy day of ecumenism we have a race of preachers in the apostate Protestant denominations and their only concern is to evacuate Protestantism of its essential and distinctive doctrines, and to change the Bible and to change the gospel, and to change the whole of Scripture of the Protestant evangelical Church and the Protestant evangelical witness."[9]

So what is this movement which has drawn Paisley's wrath and condemnation over the years? The word 'ecumenism' comes from the Greek word for 'world'. In the New Testament it is used in two senses: one, as a geographical term to describe the whole inhabited earth; the other, as in Hebrews 2:5, where it describes the future redeemed and perfected society of the Kingdom of God. When these two usages are held together, the word is seen to convey a powerful hope and a vision that one day the whole inhabited earth will be evangelised and become the redeemed and perfected society of the Kingdom of God. The ecumenist, therefore, is one who has this vision of a world to be won for Christ and is committed in His name to working towards this goal.

Some date the beginning of the modern ecumenical movement to the World Missionary Conference held at Edinburgh in 1910, but others go back earlier for its origins to the vision of the great Baptist missionary, William Carey (1761-1834). Carey was never ashamed to tell people of his humble origins as the son of a cobbler in Northamptonshire. As a missionary in India for about forty years, he was sometimes invited to lavish functions hosted by colonial officials. On one such occasion the story is told of a British government official who wanted to humiliate Carey and let all and sundry know of his humble beginnings. In a loud voice he said, 'I hear Mr Carey, you are the son of a shoemaker!'

'No, your Lordship,' Carey replied, 'not a shoemaker; just a cobbler.'

Carey had been the inspiration behind the formation of the Baptist Missionary Society in 1792. He had listened to people praying for the evangelisation of the world and could not understand why they did nothing about it. His persistence in urging them to turn their prayers into action eventually resulted in the founding of the Missionary Society and his designation as a missionary to India. Until this time he had been earning his living as a shoemaker by night, serving as a school-teacher by day and acting as pastor of a church; and as if this weren't enough, he had also taught himself several languages: French, Dutch, Greek, Hebrew and Latin! It is understandable that a man as energetic and dedicated as this should have coined the famous watchword, 'Expect great things from God and attempt great things for God.' He went to India in 1793 and was soon deeply involved in mission work in villages in Bengal. He was appointed Professor of Sanskrit, Bengali and Marathi at Fort William College in Calcutta – a position that he held for thirty years – and immersed himself in the task of translating the scriptures. His achievements in this area were phenomenal: a translation of the whole Bible into Bengali, its translation in whole or part into twenty-four other languages and dialects, and the publication of grammars and dictionaries in Sanskrit, Marathi, Punjabi and Telegu.

Missionary work in India convinced Carey of the need for contact and co-operation between Christian missionaries in different parts of the world. In 1806, in a letter to his friend Andrew Fuller, secretary of the Baptist Missionary Society, he proposed that there should be convened 'a meeting of all denominations of Christians at the Cape of Good Hope somewhere about 1810', to be followed by a similar gathering once every ten years.[10] Fuller was not enthusiastic and commented, 'I consider this as one of Brother Carey's pleasing dreams.' Although his dream was not immediatley realised on a world scale, it was implemented on a regional basis. From Carey's day onwards gatherings of missionaries of various nationalities and denominations convened for the purpose of discussing mutual problems of missionary enterprise in India, China, Japan and Latin America. Commenting on one of these gatherings, Carey wrote: 'No shadow of bigotry falls on us here. It would have done your heart good to have joined us.... In these meetings the utmost harmony prevails and a union of hearts unknown between persons of different denominations in England.'[11]

International gatherings of Protestant missionaries as envisaged in Carey's dream were held in London and New York at various intervals from 1854 onwards, but it was the World Missionary Conference at Edinburgh in 1910 and its appointment of a Continuation Committee which provided the momentum and eventually the structures which were to lead to the formation of the World Council of Churches at Amsterdam in 1948. Three world bodies preceded its formation: the International Missionary Council, 1921; Life and Work, 1925; and Faith and Order, 1927. It was the drawing together of the second and third of these organisations which created the World Council of Churches in 1948, but it was joined by the first, the IMC, in 1961. The spirit and enthusiasm so evident in Carey characterised the work of many of the leaders involved in these events. Some examples illustrate this.

John R. Mott (1865-1955), an American Methodist layman, was one of the main figures in the ecumenical movement in the first half of the century. He had come to Christian faith through the preaching of C.T. Studd, one of the famous "Cambridge Seven" – a group of English undergraduate sportsmen who had dedicated their lives to foreign missionary service. Mott was a leader in the international work of the YMCA and the World's Student Christian Federation. His evangelistic vision – 'The evangelisation of the world in our generation' – was immense, but it was driven by a deep spirituality. 'Plan as if there was no such thing as prayer. Pray as if there was no such thing as planning.'[12] Mott was chairman at the World Missionary Conference at Edinburgh and was deeply involved in all the events and preparations leading to the formation of the World Council of Churches. He preached at the opening service in Amsterdam: 'We have entered the most exacting period in the history of the church. It will take all the statesmanship, all the churchmanship, all the self-forgetfulness of all of us. But to those who believe in the adequacy of Christ no doors are closed and boundless opportunities are open.'[13]

Perhaps none have done more for the ecumenical movement in this century than Willem A. Visser 't Hooft (1900-1985). Brought up in the Remonstrant Brotherhood Church in Holland, he entered the ordained ministry of the National Protestant Church of Geneva and the Netherlands Reformed Church. Groomed by Mott, he was the first secretary of the World Council of Churches, serving in this position for twenty years. One of his publications, *The Pressure of Our Common Calling*, underlines his belief in mission and unity as the primary objectives of the movement: 'The ecumenical movement does not owe its origin to a passion for unity alone. Its roots lie in a rediscovery of the nature and mission of the Church of Christ. Nothing less than that could have created the movement; nothing less than that can keep it going and growing.'[14]

The main opposition to the formation of the World Council of Churches in the 1930s was voiced by A.C. Headlam, bishop of Gloucester, a known supporter of Hitler's Third Reich who had been annoyed by Life and Work's criticism of Nazism. At its 1937 Oxford conference, Life and Work had repudiated the deification of any people or nation and declared the idea of racial superiority to be repugnant to God: 'Against racial pride or race antagonism the Church must set its face implacably as rebellion against God.... National egotism tending to the supression of other nationalities or of minorities is a sin against the Creator of all peoples and races.'[15] Long before Winston Churchill voiced his warnings about Hitler in the House of Commons at Westminster, the members of Life and Work were fully aware of the evils of Nazism through their contact with German Christians like Karl Barth and Dietrich Bonhoffer who had taken a clear stand against it.

Headlam, on the other hand, believed that National Socialism was not anti-Christian, and that the Third Reich was based upon positive orthodox Christianity. After the war it was disclosed the extent to which Headlam had collaborated with Bishop Heckel, the head of the Department of the Foreign Office of the German Evangelical Church, who had close relations with the Foreign Office of the Third Reich.

This outspoken criticism of Nazism by the Life and Work movement sets out the manner in which ecumenical bodies understood their mandate to make public statements and bring pressure to bear on national or international bodies when the issue was thought to go beyond mere party politics. In 1948 the World Council of Churches stated: 'We serve a Lord whose realm certainly includes politics but whose saving purpose cuts across all political alignments and embraces men of *all* parties, *all* lands.'[16] Later in the century the issue of apartheid in South Africa was similarly seen as a matter that went beyond party alignments, and statements were issued condemning it as a sin against God and humankind. However, in taking positions like this, the World Council of Churches never believed it was usurping the autonomy of its member churches and emphasised instead its purpose and role as an inter-church fellowship. The architects of the council knew there were no precedents in church history for what they were undertaking and they anticipated that some would misunderstand their plans. They were therefore at pains to emphasise that the World Council of Churches was not seeking to become 'a superchurch, a centre of ecclesiastical power, which will seek to control the churches adhering to it'.

Acknowledging the state of disunion of the visible churches and the need to move forward to the visible expression of their oneness in Christ, the members of the council set out its functions in clear and unmistakable terms at Amsterdam in 1948. It was in fact a manifesto which will remain timeless until the goal of visible unity is achieved:

We are a council of churches, not *the* Council of the one undivided Church. Our name indicates our weakness and our shame before God, for there can be and there *is* finally only one Church of Christ on earth. Our plurality is a deep anomaly. But our name indicates also that we are aware of that situation, that we do not accept it passively, that we would move forward towards the manifestation of the One Holy Church. Our Council represents therefore an emergency solution – a stage on the road – a body living between the time of complete isolation of the churches from each other and the time – on earth or in heaven – when it will be visibly true that there is one Shepherd and one flock.

The functions of the Council follow from this situation. We are a fellowship in which the churches after a long period of ignoring each other come to know each other. We are a fellowship in which the churches enter into serious and dynamic conversation with each other about their differences in faith, in message, in order. We are a fellowship in which Christian solidarity is practised, so that the churches aid their weak or needy sister churches. We are a fellowship in which common witness is rendered to the Lordship of Christ, in all matters on which a common word for the churches and for the world is given to us. We are above all a fellowship which seeks to express that unity in Christ already given to us and to prepare the way for a much fuller and much deeper expression of that unity.[17]

The World Council of Churches would have been remote from the local churches if National Councils of Churches had not already been in existence in many countries. In Ireland this national body, the United Council of Christian Churches and Religious Communions in Ireland, had been formed in 1922, changing its name to the Irish Council of Churches in 1966. Its membership includes: the Church of Ireland, the Lutheran Church in Ireland, the Methodist Church in Ireland, the Irish District of the Moravian Church, the Non-Subscribing Presbyterian Church of Ireland, the Presbyterian Church in Ireland, the Salvation Army (Ireland Division), and the Religious Society of Friends in Ireland. While member churches of the World Council of Churches had immediate and direct access to the headquarters at Geneva and sometimes were asked for their response to particular World Council of Churches reports, as happened in the case of the 1982 Lima document, *Baptism, Eucharist and Ministry*, its business was more likely to be discussed when representatives of the member churches met at the local level of the National Council of Churches.

Local councils of churches or clergy fellowships in towns and cities, where they exist, must also be regarded as examples of ecumenism. It is at this level that ecumenical activity is really significant, because if the principles of ecumenism are not accepted at the grass roots, there is very little value in representatives of the churches discussing them at national or international levels.

This, in brief, is the story behind the movement described as apostate by Paisley. Not surprisingly, he is against the ecumenical vision and places his own interpretation on one of the key scripture verses often quoted in ecumenical gatherings, the prayer of Jesus for his disciples recorded in John 17:21 'that all of them may be one, Father, just as you are in me and I am in you. May they also be in us so that the world may believe that you have sent me.' He explains the verse as follows:

This is the final unity of the church on the last great day of judgment, when before angels and devils and generations of lost men the church of Christ with Christ as its Head will stand forth as a partaker of the glory of God. Then and only then will the world of sinners believe that Christ is the Head of the church, and that the church is His body, the fullness of Him that filleth all in all. But that believing is not a saving believing, because the world then shall be judged and sent to the Hell which it deserves.[18]

Paisley, regrettably, has altered the meaning of the Greek verb *pisteuo*, to believe. Referring to Jesus' prayer 'that the world may believe', he suggests 'that believing is not a saving believing'. This interpretation of 'believing' is certainly not the meaning of '*pisteuo*' – the verb used – which clearly refers to a saving belief in Christ as, for example, in John 20:31: 'these are written that you may believe that Jesus is the Christ, the Son of God, and that by believing you may have life in His name'. Paisley's misinterpretation not only alters the intention in the words of Jesus but diverts attention from the earlier part of his prayer for the disciples 'that they may all be one'. The two parts are inextricably linked together as the oneness which he prays may be evident among his disciples is intended as a witness 'that the world may believe that you have sent me'.

Two specific areas of ecumenical activity have been condemned: evidence of contact with the Roman Catholic Church at international, national or local level; and secondly, alleged ecumenical involvement in terrorism. Churches or individuals who have formed some kind of contact with the Roman Catholic Church have been frequently criticised. His conviction that the Roman Catholic Church is not a Christian church precludes him from envisaging any kind of relationship between genuine Protestantism and the Roman Catholic Church: 'And there's no agreement between Protestantism and Popery, no agreement between the Gospel of Jesus Christ and the trash of the AntiChrist. Can't make them agree. And I'll not be taking half part with those who nailed my Saviour to the tree.'[19] He enjoys outlining what he perceives as the difference between his faith and that of the Roman Catholic and apostate Protestant: 'A Romanist and a defunct apostate Protestant has a religion, he is doing everything. I have a religion, Christ has done everything and I do nothing but believe in Him. That is it!'[20] It is noticeable that Paisley never refers to Roman Catholics as apostates. It is his practice only to refer to Protestants as apostates because, he believes, they come from churches that once were true to Christ but now have fallen into apostasy. Roman Catholics, on the other hand, were never in a true church and never had a real faith from which to fall, so they cannot be thought of as apostates. This, in Paisley's opinion, makes the apostate Protestant, who should know better, more deserving of condemnation than the Roman Catholic. 'We have no respect at all for the system of Romanism, and we have less respect for the system of apostate Protestantism.'[21]

Some examples of Paisley's wrath against Protestants who reach out to the Roman Catholic Church should be mentioned. In the late '80s many felt that a new and more comprehensive body with more appropriate structures should be created to succeed the British Council of Churches, the inter-church structure that had existed in Britain for about forty years. After various discussions and conferences on the matter, it was proposed in 1989 that a Council of Churches for Britain and Ireland (CCBI) be formed, which would include the Roman Catholic Church in England, Wales and Scotland in its membership, along with Anglican, Baptist, Black-led Pentecostal and Holiness Churches, Congregational, Lutheran, Methodist, Orthodox and Reformed Churches. Paisley in *Blu-Print Union with Rome* interpreted the proposal not only as another step toward union between the Protestant churches and Rome but as proof of Roman Catholic Church involvement in 'a grave conspiracy to overthrow the Protestant Constitution of our land'.[22] Following his practice of making fun of 'systems' or individuals he detests, he published in September 1989 a two-verse 'hymn' about the proposed new structure:

> Nearer my Pope to thee, Nearer to thee,
> Even though it be CCBI
> That raiseth me,
> Still all my sighing will be
> Nearer dear Pa, Pa, to thee,
> Nearer to thee.
>
> Though like an acolyte
> The candle burnt low,
> Sun moon and stars forgot,
> Into darkness I go
> Still in my filthy dreams* I'd be,
> Nearer dear Pa, Pa, to thee,
> Nearer to thee.
>   *Jude 8.[23]

Queen Elizabeth II's participation in an ecumenical service at Westminster Cathedral on 30 November 1995 was also seen as an attempt to undermine the Protestant Constitution. Paisley and his colleagues in the 'British Council of Protestant Christian Churches' –

a small group of fundamentalist churches which meets under his leadership – informed the queen that 'Roman Catholicism preaches another
gospel' and suggested that her attendance would 'undermine our
Protestant Throne and Constitution', but he held back from publicly
calling her an 'apostate Protestant', the normal indictment reserved for
Protestants involved in ecumenical services.[24] In a public statement
Buckingham Palace said they felt the queen's attendance was an appropriate way to celebrate the 100th anniversary of the cathedral and
indicated that she had already attended other ecumenical services,
including the annual Commonwealth observance at Westminster Abbey,
a service at Milton Keynes City Church in 1992, and more recently D-
Day, VE and VJ Day commemorations. Another change of tactics on
this occasion was Paisley's decision to restrict his protest to placing
pickets outside the cathedral. There were no reports of protesters within
the cathedral periodically disrupting the worship – a practice which he
and his colleagues have perfected to a fine art!

Earlier, away from the glare of publicity in London and in front of
an Ulster audience, he had been less cautious in his accusations against
the royal family, suggesting that they had turned away from God,
'flirted with Popery', and were suffering the consequences in the form
of the Roman Catholic Church's involvement in a conspiracy to break
up the marriage of the Prince and Princess of Wales. He revealed the
details of this plot to his congregation on 13 December 1992: 'Mrs
Camilla Parker-Bowles is a devout Romanist. One has only to read of
her interference in the Prince's life. One has only to read of the way
she has wormed herself between Diana and her husband to realise that
there is something very sinister here.' But others too are involved in
the plot! 'This young man James Gilbey, whose name has been
mentioned with the Princess of Wales, is also a very devout Romanist.'
And lest anyone should think he was scaremongering or suffering from
delusions, he declared: 'I am not given to exaggerating conspiracy
theories, but I believe we must face the facts.'[25]

Paisley's accusations of the World Council of Churches's involvement in terrorism is almost a carbon copy of his charge that the Roman
Catholic Church is a fomentor of revolution throughout the world.
Ecumenists, he declares, are supporting terrorists in different parts of
the world: 'We have often warned of the treachery of the ecumenical
movement. It is the ally of the terrorist movement throughout the
world. It supports them with money and provides religious cover for
their atrocities.'[26] He believes that the same spirit, the same deviousness, the same treachery, characterises both the ecumenists and the

Roman Catholic Church. Preaching on 'The Ecumenical Brew: Death In The Pot' in Jarvis Street Baptist Church, Toronto, on 22 October 1967, he declared: 'The spirit of Ecumenism, you know, is the same spirit that made the Inquisition.... If they had their way, friend, they would hang you up.'[27]

Irish Presbyterianism

No Protestant church has received more abuse and criticism from Paisley than the Presbyterian Church in Ireland. His ferocious attacks on its doctrinal orthodoxy and ecumenical tendencies have been unrelenting. Writing on 'The Apostasy of Irish Presbyterianism' in *The Revivalist* in June 1955 – an article which was to be reprinted many times – he declared:

How a Church founded by men of apostolic holiness and zeal, a Church born and bred in revival fire, a Church lifting high the banner of the cross in an island blighted with superstition and downtrodden by priestcraft, became a Church repudiating the doctrines of her founders, rejecting the Deity of the Son of God and rejoicing in the effort to renew fellowship with the Harlot Church of Rome [Revelations 17], surely is a record which must cause grief in the hearts of all who love the Lord's Zion, and who pray for the peace of Jerusalem. Alas, slothfulness led to silence, silence to compromise, compromise to betrayal, and betrayal to the great apostasy.[28]

Within a few months he was again writing: 'Irish Presbyterianism has repudiated the Scriptures of truth and the historic doctrines of the Westminster Standards in session and presbytery and in synod and General Assembly.'[29] And in the same article the leadership of the clerk of the assembly and others at Church House, Belfast, came in for particular criticism: 'The ecclesiastical hierarchy of Church House is as unbending as the Vatican, and ministers and elders fear the denominational biggies in the same cowardly manner in which the priests fear their superiors.' As he and his ministers enjoyed making fun of the Roman Catholic Church, so too they joked about the Protestant churches, particularly Presbyterianism. As usual, his lieutenant John Wylie was very adept at this. Alan Cairns, a Free Presbyterian minister at Greenville, South Carolina, USA, tells how on one occasion an Irish Presbyterian complained to Wylie that his language was often disrespectful to his church:

'I am not at all disrespectful to the Presbyterian Church,' replied John. 'In fact, I take my hat off every time I pass a Presbyterian church.'

His critic was somewhat mollified until John added, 'My mother always told me to raise my hat to the dead!'[30]

Paisley's attack on Presbyterianism is also coupled with a claim that he and his Free Presbyterian Church, and not the Presbyterian Church in Ireland, now stand in the true succession to historic Presbyterianism. Apostasy, he suggests, made its first inroads into Irish Presbyterianism in 1888 when Thomas Walker was appointed professor of Old Testament at Assembly's College, Belfast, the training college for students preparing for ordination in the Presbyterian Church. 'Many students imbibed his anti-biblical views,' he declares 'and so the poisoning of the Church commenced by the poisoning of the fountain head.'[31] The college, now Union Theological College, has often been the butt of Paisley's criticism ever since. Understandably, Paisley makes much of Henry Cooke (1783-1868), who was undoubtedly the leading figure in Presbyterianism in the nineteenth century. He highlights Cooke's stand for orthodoxy in the Arian controversy of the 1820s, with the clear implication that he himself is now seen to be following in Cooke's footsteps in his twentieth-century struggle for orthodox Trinitarian belief. Paisley's accusations of apostasy in Presbyterianism today are presented as a direct reflection of Cooke's struggle against Henry Montgomery and others: 'Championing the cause of historic Presbyterian orthodoxy, Cooke worked for the purity of the Synod and the ejection of the Unitarian or Arian interlopers. After a long and bitter struggle success attended his efforts with the withdrawal of the Unitarians from the Synod of Ulster.'[32]

In characteristic Paisley fashion, however, he only highlights those aspects of Cooke's teaching and ministry which suit him. While Paisley is quite happy to identify himself with Cooke's anti-Catholicism – 'Zeal against popery,' Cooke told his son, was one of the marks of a living Protestantism[33] – no mention is made of his recognition of baptism in the Roman Catholic Church. Similarly Paisley is mute regarding Cooke's appeals for tolerance and love between the Protestant churches, something he fervently believed was necessary for political reasons to counter what he perceived to be the increasing challenge to Protestant rights and interests by Catholic and nationalist Ireland. Cooke's speeches on this theme, had Paisley published them, would have contradicted his claim to stand in the line of succession to historic Presbyterianism. Cooke had urged: 'Let the Protestant Churches – and under the Scriptural name of Churches I include all Churches that avow and maintain evangelical truth, however differing in outward forms – let the Protestant Churches only learn to pray for one another; and they will not fail to love one another; and if they learn, as I know some have learned, or will soon be taught, to love together, I can fearlessly fortell that over superstitition and error they will soon become conquerors together.'[34]

Each year Paisley made it his practice to picket the General Assembly held in the first week of June. In 1966 he decided to add a little more drama to the occasion by arranging a march from his church on the Ravenhill Road to the assembly, which met in Church House in Belfast city centre. Possibly he had heard on the grapevine that the Orange Order were planning 'Twelfth of July' resolutions expressing concern about the ecumenical trend within the Protestant churches and he felt that this was an opportune time to heighten his level of protest. If his main aim had been to gain publicity for his own protests against Presbyterianism – and from his accounts of why he later chose to go to jail, this would appear the most likely explanation – he was not to be disappointed. His route to the city centre on 6 June took him past the Markets area situated on the west side of the River Lagan, close to the Albert Bridge and Cromac Square. Paisley's anti-Catholic and anti-Republican profile was already well known, so it was not surprising that a march of his placard-carrying supporters drew the interest of some of the local residents, leading unfortunately to skirmishes, mainly between the residents and police who cleared a way at Cromac Square for the march to pass.

Reaching the city centre, Paisley positioned his supporters on both sides of the ropeway erected by the police to allow access for the moderator, Dr Alfred Martin, and his guests – which on this occasion included the governor, Lord Erskine, and his wife – as they came out of the assembly to cross over Howard Street to the official reception in the Presbyterian Hostel. This was the setting for the second disturbance of the peace that day. The moderator's party was reportedly subjected to jeers, insults and abusive slogans from Paisleyites now pressing in from both sides of the ropeway. Dr Jack Weir, clerk of the assembly, recalls vividly the events of that afternoon:

I was leading out the governor, Lord Erskine, and Lady Erskine, and we came from the peaceful and inspiring meeting of the General Assembly into a turmoil of shouting. And I remember Ian Paisley standing by the door waving a fist with a Bible in it and briefly, in a sort of way, it seemed to me to give the feeling of 'Crucify! Crucify!' Now afterwards I know that he had been through riotous confrontation at the Cromac Square area and therefore he was in that confrontational mood. But the contrast between the worship service we had had was for us who came out, and of course for Lady Erskine, a real testing.[35]

Frank Pantridge, cardiologist at the Royal Victoria Hospital at the time, relates in his autobiography, *An Unquiet Life*, how, late in the afternoon, he received a request from the governor to come to Hillsborough to attend to his wife, who had become agitated and disturbed by the shouting, heckling and eggs hurled in their direction:

When I got to Hillsborough I was somewhat tired and hypoglycaemic [low blood sugar] – in those days there was not much time for lunch. I assured the Governor that Lady Erskine would suffer no permanent harm from the Paisley eggs, all of which had apparently missed their target. Lord Erskine demanded to know what should be done about Paisley. I said that if only I had a large Scotch I would be able to tell him exactly what to do. Erskine, in contrast to his successor, was notoriously mean. Bob Stephens, the Governor's private secretary, produced the necessary medicine for me and I explained that Paisley must be schizophrenic, since he waved the Union Jack one day and on the next day he threw eggs at the Queen's representative. I suggested that Lord Erskine demand that Paisley have psychiatric investigation. I said that it didn't much matter what the psychiatrist said. Headlines in the press to the effect that Paisley was under psychiatric investigation would be enough to stop him in his tracks. The Governor seemed to think that this was an excellent suggestion and sent for the DPP to demand action along the line suggested. Unfortunately the DPP was not available and the Deputy DPP declined to co-operate. Subsequently Paisley did get a jail sentence. I still feel that had a psychiatrist been brought in at the time, the whole history of Northern Ireland might have been quite different.[36]

Captain Terence O'Neill's unionist government at Stormont, already under fire from Paisley on other matters, took the matter seriously and sent R.W.B. McConnell, minister for home affairs, to the assembly to apologise for the fracas caused by the demonstration and to promise that steps would be taken to prevent any recurrence of these indignities in the future. O'Neill, speaking later in a Stormont debate, compared Paisley's street demonstrations to the terror struck by the Nazis in Germany in the thirties: 'To those of us who remember the Thirties, the pattern is horribly familiar. The contempt for established authority; the crude and unthinking intolerance; the emphasis upon monster processions and rallies; the appeal to a perverted form of patriotism; each and every one of these things has its parallel in the rise of the Nazis to power.'[37]

The General Assembly responded quickly to Paisley's accusations of apostasy by passing a series of resolutions which reaffirmed its Christian orthodoxy and carefully refuted various charges he had been making for at least seventeen years:

1. That we hold the Word of God, as set forth in the Scriptures of the Old and New Testaments, to be the only infallible rule of faith and practice and the supreme standard of the Church.

2. That we preach the doctrines of the Gospel, set forth in the Confession of Faith of this Church, especially the doctrines of the Trinity, of the deity and humanity of Christ, man's fallen condition, his recovery through the atonement of the Lord Jesus Christ, justification through faith in Christ, the deity, personality and work of the Holy Spirit, the Church and her missionary task, the sovereignty of Divine grace, the necessity of faith and repentance wrought in us by God's Spirit and, as a mark of our being in Christ, a life of practical godliness.[38]

Responding to Paisley's charge that their involvement in inter-church conversations and projects – at this time basically with other Protestant churches – was indicative of a 'Romeward trend' in which they were denying basic Christianity, they declared:

3. That we have no intention of accepting any doctrine or standard contrary to God's Word or beside it in matters of faith and worship; but rather, not refusing light from any quarter, under the guidance of the Spirit of God would seek to commend what we believe and preach to every man's conscience in the sight of God, whether it be in conversations with other Churches, in dealings with our fellow citizens in society, or in our missionary undertakings in Ireland and abroad.

And the assembly, which has always been vigilant in protecting the rights of the individual conscience, felt it was important to reaffirm its convictions on this subject and warn against any intolerance which would threaten its exercise and lead to sectarianism:

4. In keeping with our Presbyterian principles:
   A. We acknowledge that it is our Christian duty to respect the consciences of others and to defend the common liberties and civic rights of all men, without regard to colour, class or creed.
   B. We dissociate ourselves from any who would encourage political intolerance and sectarian strife, hatred and intimidation, misrepresentation and abuse of those with whom they disagree.

Departing from what seems to have been something of an unwritten rule among Protestant church leaders never to mention Paisley's name in church courts or publications, Dr S. J. Park, the outgoing moderator, declared: 'Some people may feel that this is aimed at the Revd Ian Paisley. We mention no names, but if this is true of Mr Paisley, if he is one who encourages political intolerance and sectarian strife, hatred and intimidation, misrepresentation and abuse of those with whom he disagrees, then we do dissociate ourselves from him and anyone else of the same ilk.'

On 18 and 19 July, Ian Paisley, John Wylie and Ivan Foster, another Free Presbyterian minister, appeared in court with others from his church charged with unlawful assembly in Howard Street, on the occasion of the General Assembly protest. It was not the first time Paisley had been charged in this manner, but in the past someone had always stepped in and paid the fines imposed by the courts. On this occasion Paisley and the others were all found guilty, fined and bound over to keep the peace or alternatively face a prison sentence of six months (which effectively meant three). Paisley, Wylie and Foster refused to give an assurance to keep the peace and consequently spent three months in Crumlin Road Prison.

Paisley's own explanation of why he chose to go to jail reveals something of the underlying principles and motivation which lay behind his ministry and political activities. 'As a clergyman, I refuse to be silenced. Error must be exposed and truth must be propagated. Warning must be given and the Gospel defended. Danger must be shown and true direction revealed. Darkness must be dispelled and the true light spread abroad.'[39] This was the religious motivation which fuelled his tremendous and seemingly endless energy. If he had read the resolutions of the Presbyterian General Assembly, he had certainly dismissed them. But this religious perspective was interwoven in his mind with politics. Clergy and politicians, he maintained, were conspiring together to betray Ulster: 'This has been an ecclesiastical plot, stemming from the World Council of Churches. It has been a political plot, devised by the Prime Minister and his lap-dogs.' He saw and portrayed himself as the upholder of justice, fighting against injustice and tyranny, and used arguments often similar to the rhetoric of nationalists and Republicans: 'We want to show that this is not a democratic country, but that it has been run by a group of dictators from Glengall Street. For years these men have tried to tell the Protestants of Ulster that they are loyal and true blues, but they are being found out now.' He gave no indication that he saw himself as the guilty party in the Howard Street confrontation. From his perspective, angry words, jostling, jeering and 'egg-throwing' were quite acceptable behaviour for a minister of Christ in the presence of the queen's representative. Indeed, he argued – and quite successfully, for his popularity from this time onwards began to soar quite dramatically – that he was the wronged party in the whole affair: 'Men may malign me, persecute me, speak evil against me, or even imprison me, but they cannot and will not silence me.'

Perhaps the most significant factor to emerge from the events surrounding the protest at the assembly was the revelation – unnoticed at the time – that Paisley was definitely planning a political career for himself. He saw himself as the champion of Protestantism and believed that this required a parliamentary role: 'By the grace of God and the help of the Protestants of Ulster, the day will come when I will be in Stormont – the only way true Protestant people can deal with the ruling junta of Lundies is to have someone there to root out the nest of traitors.' He had publicly mapped out his future, so it should have come as no surprise when three years later he took the first steps to achieve his political objectives.

No one could ever accuse Paisley of idleness, and Crumlin Road Prison did not noticeably affect his prodigious capacity for getting through mountains of work. He used the time to write a 191-page commentary on Romans for which he was later awarded a doctorate by his good friend Dr Bob Jones of Bob Jones University in South Carolina. Terence O'Neill's accusations that he had staged Nazi-type street demonstrations were possibly still ringing in his ears when he wrote on Romans 13:1-5, a passage which refers to the Christian's attitude to civil authorities: 'The chief magistrate is divinely ordained, the office is sacred, but a Hitler who usurps and abuses the office is not divinely ordained, neither are the laws of such a tyrant to be obeyed when they oppose the law of God.'[40]

Paisley's prison sentence did not in any way discourage him in his battle against Presbyterianism. Successive moderators of the General Assembly and its ministers were continually lambasted. Alfred Martin, moderator at the time of the 1966 protest, was described in various derisive terms: 'daft Alfie', 'clown-in-chief', 'little Lucifer' and 'perjurer'. His eternal destiny was prophesied in similar fashion to Ernest Davey's: 'Alfred Martin, we indict you as a perjurer at the bar of God. No words of man can describe the vileness of your sin in denying the very thing you have vowed to God to uphold. The Word of God says, "All liars shall have their part in the lake which burneth with fire and brimstone" (Revelation 21:8). Your part seems assured.'[41]

Donald Gillies was another regular victim of Paisley's sarcasm. When Gillies favoured Presbyterian withdrawal from the World Council of Churches, he was described as 'a saved man staying in apostasy' and was criticised for remaining a minister of the Presbyterian Church rather than separating from it. Choosing to emphasise Gillies' first name, Paisley, in a front page article headed 'Quack Doctor' in *The*

Revivalist, joked: 'Not everybody can be a successful quack. But one Irish Presbyterian minister is a past master at the art. To get to the "top of the bill" in his profession as a quack, he had to cultivate a close connection with the fowl which makes that noise so that now, when faced with any matter of importance (such as separation from apostasy) he can simply go "quack" and duck the issue.'[42] The criticism was intensified when Gillies changed his mind on the question of withdrawal from membership of the World Council of Churches. He had come to the conclusion that Irish Presbyterianism had a witness to offer within the fellowship of the World Council. On the eve of the 1978 General Assembly, Gillies and five other ministers – John Dunlop (elected moderator in 1992), Gordon Gray, David Lapsley, John Morrow and Ken Newell – published a document, *At Stake, Reformed Principle*, outlining their case for staying within the World Council of Churches. Paisley described the six ministers as 'deceivers and Devil-inspired agents' and their document as 'so blatantly false that it demonstrates the extent to which ecumenists will go in order to bolster up their dream of one World Church'.[43]

Presbyterian withdrawal of membership from the World Council of Churches in 1980 and its decision in 1989 against membership of the Council of Churches for Britain and Ireland made no difference to the scale of criticism coming from Paisley. Commenting on the vote (453-282) which kept the Presbyterians out of the Council of Churches for Britain and Ireland, Paisley said, 'The Irish Presbyterians, however, remain within the Irish Council of Churches and the Ballymascanlon Conference which includes the Irish Roman Catholic Church and is specially approved as a forum for ecumenical dialogue by the Swanwick Conference, the originators of the new church council. Alas, the Irish Presbyterian Church, weakened by apostasy from the Protestant Principles of its founding fathers, is today dialoguing with the Church of the Antichrist.'[44] Moderators who had been prominent in urging withdrawal of membership from the World Council of Churches in 1980 and later resisted the Council of Churches for Britain and Ireland proposal in 1989 were not spared the cutting remarks for which he was now well known. Possibly only one, William Craig – who was a friend of a friend (Pastor William Mullan) of his – got through his year of office without being insulted. In fact, Paisley actually praised him! 'The Pope came to Dublin and Dr Weir, the Clerk of the Assembly, went down to welcome him. Thank God they had a Moderator that year, Dr Craig of Portadown, who had enough strength of character and evangelical conviction to say, "No, I will not be there."'[45]

Robert Dickinson, the moderator from 1985 to 1986, had been one of the leaders of a group within Presbyterianism called the Campaign for Concerted Witness to Reformed Truth, drawn together for the purpose of persuading their church to withdraw from the World Council of Churches. One might have expected Dickinson's credentials to be almost impeccable as far as Paisley was concerned, but this was not the case. Paisley got wind of the fact that Dickinson had agreed to speak at a seminar in Fitzroy Presbyterian Church, Belfast, on 22 April 1986 on the theme, 'There is hope – in Christ', an appropriate theme considering the seventeen years of continuous violence which the community had then faced. But what particularly interested Paisley was the fact that Dickinson was only half the package for the evening, the other speaker being Cathal Daly, at that time the Roman Catholic bishop of Connor. Paisley publicised the event as Dickinson being 'in dialogue with Dr Daly', something which Dickinson had spent a lifetime publicly opposing. Paisley is bound to have known about Dickinson's opposition to dialogue but he pressed ahead regardless, placing his own interpretation on the evening's activities:

To bring Dr Daly into a Protestant Church, recognise him as a Christian Leader and Teacher and dialogue with him is:

1. An insult to the Lord Jesus whom he professes to create from a wafer every time he offers Mass.
2. A deception, for Dr Daly cannot direct anyone along a path of hope but rather along the path to hell.
3. A denial of all that historic Presbyterianism stands for.[46]

When Dickinson heard that Paisley was planning to picket the seminar at Fitzroy, he wrote to him 'As a brother in Christ, one who constantly remembers you at the throne of grace, praying for the wisdom, grace and blessing of God's Spirit on your behalf', and asked him 'in the interests of Christian honesty and integrity' to set the true facts of the situation before his congregation. Dickinson emphasised that he had been invited to go to Fitzroy to 'give a reason for the hope that is in me, AND to set forth the source of hope for mankind which I find alone in salvation by grace through faith alone in Christ Jesus'. Finally, he hoped that Paisley would use his influence 'to prevent actions which will do nothing other than bring the Name of Jesus Christ and the Gospel which you proclaim into disrepute before the eyes of unbelievers and of the world'.[47]

Dickinson's plea fell on deaf ears. Perhaps unknown to the moderator, Paisley had been hitting out at Dickinson from the moment he took office, and he had no intention of abandoning his story that this Fitzroy seminar was in fact an example of dialogue. He dragged out the story for three months and eventually concluded it by publishing Wylie's verses, entitled 'The Love Story of Dickinson and Daly':

> There was a little Dicky bird,
> He sat upon a wall
> Along came Cathal Daly
> And down did Dicky fall.
>
> But Daly picked him up and said,
> Come Dicky dear with me.
> We'll go along to Fitzroy Church,
> And have a jolly spree.
>
> So Dicky and the Antichrist
> Proceeded to the Church,
> To tell the mugs who'd gathered there
> For unity they did thirst
>
> Now Daly said to Dicky bird,
> I really love you so
> Just throw away your foolish Creed,
> And hand in hand we'll go.
>
> Wee Dicky smiled and sweetly said
> Dear Daly I love you so,
> My Creed is now old fashioned,
> I will surely let it go.
>
> They stood with tears in both their eyes,
> And held each other's hand,
> And Dicky said in Daly's ear,
> I feel just really grand.
>
> I'll never speak against your Church
> It's just as good as mine.
> Forgive me Brother Daly,
> For I cursed it many a time.
>
> Then Daly pressed wee Dicky's hand
> And smiled into his face,
> I'll pray 'His Gracious Holiness'
> To give you of his grace.
>
> So Dicky bird and Daly
> Are now the best of friends
> And are travelling on together
> To a dreadful journey's end.[48]

It is hard to avoid the conclusion that Paisley's campaign against Presbyterian involvement in the World Council of Churches had influenced to some extent the final decision to withdraw in 1980. Many of the arguments put forward by those favouring withdrawal were similar to Paisley's case, but were seldom presented with the same ruthless intent to rubbish everything connected with the World Council of Churches. For example, while a Presbyterian in favour of withdrawal might have argued that the basis of the World Council of Churches was inadequate, Paisley simply wrote the whole organisation off as the work of the Devil. Presbyterians wanting withdrawal might have said that they had nothing to learn from other member churches whose doctrinal basis and sacramental practice they regarded as suspect, while Paisley argued that Presbyterian involvement with apostate churches effectively made them apostate too. There was a clear difference in presentation of the case for withdrawal, and sometimes the Campaign for Concerted Witness to Reformed Truth may have been embarrassed in being classified as belonging to the same school of thought as the Free Presbyterians.

But perhaps the greatest similarity between Paisley and Presbyterians favouring withdrawal existed in their case against the World Council of Churches Programme to Combat Racism, set up in 1969. No arguments could convince either party that funds provided for humanitarian purposes to third world groups formed to combat racial injustice did not find its way eventually to the military wings of these movements. Evidence was never produced to prove that this was the case, but many living in a country ravaged by paramilitary violence did not need evidence, and they classified Patrick Mugabe and Joshua Nkomo's Patriotic Front in Rhodesia and Nelson Mandela's African National Congress in South Africa alongside the IRA in Ireland. It was argued that Mandela and Mugabe had tried all the democratic avenues available to further their civil rights before turning to violence, but apparent parallels with the Irish situation may well have been the deciding factor in the minds of those Presbyterians campaigning for withdrawal from the World Council of Churches.

The strongest evidence suggesting a Paisleyite influence in the Presbyterian decision to cut its links with the World Council of Churches is the 'graph of declining interest' in the World Council of Churches in inverse proportion to the length of Paisley's ministry. In the late forties when Paisley first emerged on the Ulster scene, Presbyterians were by far the most ecumenically minded of all the Protestant churches. Any comparison of the reports, minutes and magazines published by the various Protestant churches indicate that it was the Presbyterians who took the keenest interest in the formation of the World Council of Churches at Amsterdam in 1948 and made every effort to inform and encourage their membership about each new development. Presbyterians worldwide had been to the fore in the setting up of the council. When the first invitations went out in 1939 to churches throughout the world to join in the setting up of the council – the Second World War intervened and hence the postponement until 1948 – five of the thirteen signatories were Presbyterian/Reformed. This far outnumbered any Anglican, Lutheran, Baptist, Orthodox or Methodist involvement. Irish Presbyterian interest in the World Council of Churches and ecumenical developments at home, along with their traditional yet keen interest in foreign, home and Irish missions, continued right through the fifties and most of the sixties. It was only in the late sixties and seventies that the 'graph of declining interest' began to show a significant change in reporting World Council of Churches business, with equal space and effort being given instead to presenting both sides of the debate about whether to stay or leave the World Council of Churches. By the eighties the graph had almost reached zero level.

It is difficult to say exactly how much of this decline in interest in ecumenism was due to Ian Paisley's continous barracking and how much was due to the unsettled state of affairs in Northern Ireland – which some would say was also partly of his making. Whatever the reasons, there are many who would feel that the 1980 and 1989 decisions were disastrous for Irish Protestantism. The Protestant church with the largest membership in Northern Ireland, which had effectively given the lead in ecumenism, was now of its own decision largely a spectator on the stage of the world church. The Church of Ireland and the Methodist Church would remain within the World Council of Churches and the Council of Churches for Britain and Ireland, but the spiritual dynamism and theological experience of Irish Presbyterianism would be sorely missed.

The Black List

Paisley's attacks on Irish Presbyterians have been accompanied by similar criticisms of other Protestant churches. Anglican bishops and archbishops, Methodist ministers and presidents, some Baptist leaders – for example, D. P. Kingdon, principal of the Irish Baptist College in the sixties – and the Crescent Church (Brethren) in Belfast have all been targets in his campaign against apostasy. The arguments employed have often been similar, but his followers never seem to tire of its repetitiveness.

In March 1967 he introduced a new method of highlighting those whom he believed particularly guilty of apostasy. This he described as 'the first Black List of Ulster clergymen from all apostate denominations who in word and deed deny their vowed beliefs'.[49] Heading the list was Eric Gallagher, at that time superintendent minister of the Belfast Central Mission, and both secretary and president-designate of the Methodist Church in Ireland. Paisley had often sent some of his ministers and lay people to obstruct Gallagher when he preached in the open air on Sunday afternoons at the Customs House steps, even trying to make him inaudible by positioning a loudspeaker at his feet. Paisley criticised Gallagher for speaking of 'the barren irrelevant controversies that are tearing Northern Ireland limb from limb' and for his warning that 'the threat to the Christian faith today lies in paganism and immorality; in rapidly growing agnosticism and cynicism'. He advised Gallagher: 'If he would study the whole revealed counsel of God, he would realise the apostate Church is to join with the Roman Anti-Christ and this same paganism against the Lord Jesus Christ.' From Paisley's point of view it is clear that he was very perceptive in placing Gallagher at the top of his Black List, for Gallagher's leadership role, not only in Methodism – in which, among other things, he did much to prevent Paisley from making in-roads – but in the wider Christian church throughout Ireland, was already beginning to be recognised and was to continue and increase. Indeed, when historians come to write the history of Irish Christianity in the latter half of the twentieth century, it is more than likely that his role will be seen to have been the most significant.

Second in the Black List was Victor Griffin, rector of Christ Church, Londonderry, who was later to become dean of St Patrick's Cathedral in Dublin. Griffin was judged apostate for writing in his church magazine: 'Let us not forget that it was so-called religious people who crucified Christ. They saw in Christ one who was a threat to their vested interests, religious and political.' Griffin had gone on to speak of the Reformers' attitude to relationships with the Roman Catholic Church: 'The Reformers never closed the door to discussions with Rome – they welcomed it – it was Rome who opposed it.' Paisley incorrectly corrected Griffin: 'This is sheer, nigh-incredible, diabolical fantasy! Only the father of lies could spawn such a magnificent specimen.'

Billy Graham

The world-famous Baptist evangelist Billy Graham has been targeted continually by Paisley for over forty years. He has done all in his power to denigrate Graham's evangelistic work in the eyes of Irish Protestants, accusing his organisation, as he has so many others, of cunning deceit: 'The power of this Organisation, with its vast well-paid staff all geared to conceal unpalatable truths about compromising evangelism and armed with ready pens dipped in the ink of misrepresentation and falsehood, ranks second only to the World Council of Churches itself.'[50] However, Graham's greatest sin – in Paisley's eyes – has possibly been the abandoning of his early separatist fundamentalist position and his growing openness in sharing with other Christians who are willing to support his evangelistic outreach. Graham had studied for four months at Bob Jones University when it was located in Tennessee and acknowledged his debt to the college when broadcasting on his *Hour of Decision* radio programme in December 1951: 'Bob Jones University is a school which I went to fifteen years ago, and it was there that I first learned about evangelism. It was there that I first received my passion for the souls of men, and began to realise the desperate need of a world outside of Christ.' Cliff Barrows, the singer and choir leader who for a long time was Graham's number two, is also a graduate of Bob Jones University.[51] When, later, Graham became more open to other Christians who might not have shared all his fundamentalist convictions but who nevertheless convinced him of their commitment to evangelism, he rapidly lost the support of some of his former colleagues. Paisley refers to this new spirit of co-operation with other Christians as the 'downgrade of Billy Graham': 'Caught up in the wave of popularity which followed his evangelistic success Graham began, in the name of broadening his platform, to pitch his tent towards the apostasy of the modern Sodom of ecumenism.'[52]

Not unexpectedly, the goodwill shown by the Roman Catholic Church to Graham's evangelistic crusades was anathema to Paisley, especially when this goodwill was officially sanctioned in a two-hour meeting on 12 January 1981 between Graham and Pope John Paul II. Paisley commented, 'Now by his visit to the Pope his pilgrimage has culminated in his public identification of his form of Christianity with the Papal Antichrist; his apostasy is complete.'[53]

This Is the Lord's Battle

Paisley is convinced that everything he says and does against 'apostate Protestants' is divinely inspired and directed. He wants his followers to know that his protests over the course of fifty years have been anointed and blessed by God. He gives a holy sanction to his incessant denunciations of Protestantism by suggesting that they are all part of God's battle against apostasy: 'I'm glad this battle is not the battle of the Free Presbyterian Church. I'm glad this is the Lord's battle. Who is in the battle? The battle is not yours but God's. Those of you who are protesting against evil, the battle is not yours but the Lord's.'[54] Proof of this divine anointing, Paisley suggests, is evident in the comparative fortunes which follow or befall those who support or oppose him in this battle against apostasy. Addressing a large congregation of his followers in the King's Hall on 24 March 1991, the fortieth anniversary of the founding of the Free Presbyterian Church of Ulster, he told story after story of the dire consequences that befell their opponents over the years: 'I could give you the life story of twenty prominent personalities in Ulster, chiefs of police, businessmen, religious leaders, and they died in very strange circumstances. Every one of them hated and detested and worked against the Free Presbyterian Church.'[55]

Specific instances were recalled:

I could go on and on. I recall a Roman Catholic police officer, a head constable who loved to take a stick and beat up the Free Presbyterians as they protested. One day he was cursing us in Donegal Pass station and one of the fellow constables said, 'I would not curse those people, something could happen to you.' He laughed and in a moment he choked and fell down behind the counter and he was in God's eternity. He was meeting the God he defied.

In contrast, God is said to prosper those that support Paisley. He tells the story of a businessman who used to help him erect and move his tent when he was conducting missions. According to Paisley, the man and his workers found that every time he helped move the tent his business prospered! Reading the Bible – that is, the Authorised Version – can also bring prosperity: 'How do I know a man is reading the Book? I see the prosperity of his soul, and that prosperity runs out even into secular life.'[56]

Involvement in this battle against apostasy is said to be the mark of a true minister. He frequently reminds his ministers and students in training for the ordained ministry that this is an essential part of their ministry: 'I tell you we need preachers that will hit the bull's eye today.

We need preachers who will go after apostasy the way the prophets went after apostasy.'[57] He warns them that they could well be tempted to shirk this task and tone down their criticisms:

There will be *temptations*. The preacher will be tempted to compromise, to lower the flag a little, not to be so outspoken against damned black Popery and the accursed ecumenical system, not to denounce with prophetic and fiery language the apostates of our day – the World Council of Churches and the great whore of the Babylon of Revelation chapter 17. '*Just cool it, lower the flag a little, do not be so vehement in your protest and so strong in your separation stand,*' will be the cry.[58]

Paisley personalises his message by revealing from his own experience how these 'temptations' can come in the person of members of the congregation who might suggest a quieter, less outspoken type of protest against apostasy. He tells how on one occasion two 'prominent' men came to him after the prayer meeting one night and said they loved and admired him but felt he was going about things the wrong way. They suggested he was denouncing popery too much and antagonising too many people. Paisley relates how he responded: 'I had heard enough, so I stepped forward to the door and I opened it and said something like this, "Gentlemen, if you are gentlemen, you'd better leave now, for if you stay one moment longer my toe will assist you through the door." I meant it. They were emissaries from Hell, that is who they were, sent by Beelzebub, commissioned by Satan to tell the man of God to compromise.'[59]

John Wylie was always regarded as a good example of the determination and aggressiveness required in the battle against apostasy. Alan Cairns paints a picture of Wylie as the time approached for a major protest against apostasy: 'I well remember being in the home in Ballymoney just hours before one of the greatest protest witnesses against apostasy we ever had. John was to play a very prominent role, and he was full of nervous energy. Like a caged tiger that could not wait to get out after his prey, he paced the floor, rehearsing his planned speech to Ian Paisley and me. As a mere twenty-year-old I was fascinated.'[60]

'Fox-hunting' is another expression Paisley uses to describe the battle against apostasy. He says he became a fox-hunter in September 1949 after the lengthy weekend prayer meeting (referred to in chapter three) shared with John Douglas and Robert Scott: 'As a result of that time of prayer I became a fox-hunter, I became a seeker after those foxes that destroy the church of Jesus Christ, and that play havoc on the vines of the Lord's planting and on the grapes that come from those vines.'[61] This is authentic evidence of Paisley's own understanding of his attitude to the Protestant churches prior to the formation of Crossgar Free Presbyterian Church and the birth of the Free Presbyterian Church of Ulster. The date is significant as it means that he had already been waging war against what he perceived as the apostasy of Protestantism for at least two years prior to the events in Crossgar.

Concern has often been expressed about the intemperate language Paisley uses in his battle against apostasy. He is aware of this criticism and claims that his words are similar to those Jesus used in condemning apostasy: 'The vocabulary that I want in denouncing apostasy is the language of the Incarnate Son of God.'[62] It has to be acknowledged that Jesus did condemn the scribes and Pharisees in very strong terms, describing them as 'blind guides', 'hypocrites' and 'whitewashed tombs' (Matthew 23). But Paisley's attitude toward 'apostates' is one of unashamed hatred. He tells the story of how, on one of his many trips to Bob Jones University, the chancellor had a visit from 'an apostate'. Jones asked Paisley what he would have said to the visitor: 'I would have said to him, "Sir, you should be glad I am not Elijah for if I were Elijah your head would be coming off."'[63]

Hatred in fact is seen as a natural characteristic of the true Christian: 'This hatred is of the loyal servant who hates everything and everyone who hates his Lord.'[64] He has even gone so far as to make fun of any who criticise his references to hate: 'We live in an age when our educational hierarchy have decreed that our schools, colleges, and seminaries brainwash their students to believe that it isn't nice to speak of hating anything or anyone.'[65] This hatred of apostates is based on his interpretation of the words of the Psalmist, 'Do I not hate them that hate thee, O Lord?.... I hate them with a perfect hatred' (Psalms 139:21-22). This is why he regards apostates as his enemies:

Every enemy of my Lord is my enemy if I'm true to my principles. I will not compromise Christ's truth. I will not allow His person or His Passion to be vilified by the enemies of the Gospel and not make the most vehement of protests. I must, I will, stand up for Jesus. That's what I've got to do.... No words of mine can be too strong to condemn those who blaspheme my Lord and destroy His character and Cross. They are of the brood of Judas. They are of the offspring of Iscariot. They are the generation of that viper Satan.[66]

Is Paisley's attitude to those he regards as apostates at variance with Christ's explicit teaching on how we are to treat our neighbour and our enemies? Christ's two great commandments declare: 'You shall love the Lord your God with all your heart, and with all your soul, and with all your mind. This is the great and first commandment. And a second is

like it, You shall love your neighbour as yourself. On these two commandments depend all the law and the prophets' (Matthew 22:37-40).
Regarding one's enemies, Christ said: 'You have heard that it was said,
"You shall love your neighbour and hate your enemy." But I say to
you, Love your enemies and pray for those who persecute you, so that
you may be sons of your Father who is in heaven' (Matthew 5:43-45).

In an article, *Be Nice, Be Tolerant – Is it Scriptural?*[67] Paisley explains
what he thinks the commandments mean when they talk about loving:
'For a Christian to love is simply to desire with all the heart for everyone
to love and obey Christ Jesus.' For one who places such an emphasis
on the literal teaching of scripture, his comment seems extraordinary.
Significantly, the article omits the words of Christ's commandments,
only briefly and indirectly referring to them. Indeed, in all my reading
of Paisley's writings and on the scores of occasions I have heard him
preach, I cannot recall his ever mentioning these commandments other
than in this one slight indirect reference.

Paisley, however, is unapologetic about hating the apostate: 'So when
someone quotes the unscriptural folk saying, "Do not hate the sinner,
but the sin," take it with a grain of salt.' Ironically, in dismissing this
saying he is in fact dismissing the advice of his great hero Charles
Hadden Spurgeon, whose writings feature more frequently in *The
Revivalist* than those of any other preacher or theologian from the
Reformation or evangelical tradition. In October 1990 Paisley included
Spurgeon's sermon, *Righteous Hatred*, based on the text,'Ye that love
the Lord, hate evil' (Psalm 97:10).[68] Unfortunately, or so it seems,
Paisley had only read the title, assumed that Spurgeon thought the same
as himself on the subject, and included it in his magazine. If he had
taken the trouble to read the sermon, he would have left it out, because
it runs contrary to all he teaches about hating the apostate. In his sermon
Spurgeon immediately quotes Christ's teaching in Matthew 5:43-45,
quoted above, about loving our enemies. He underlines the teaching of
the Psalmist and Christ and demands, 'The word "hate" must be cut
out of the language of a Christian, except it be used with one meaning
and intention only, and that, the meaning of my text.' He continues:

Thou hast no right, O Christian, to tolerate within thy bosom, wrath,
malice, anger, harshness, or uncharitableness, towards any creature that
God's hands have made. When thou hatest the man's sins, thou art not
able to hate him, but to love the sinner, even as Christ loved sinners and
came to seek and save them. When thou hatest a man's false doctrine, thou
art still to love the man, and hate his doctrine even out of love to his soul,
with an earnest desire that he may be reclaimed from his error, and brought

into the way of truth. Thou hast no right to exercise thy hatred upon any creature, however fallen or debased, however much he may irritate thy temper, or injure thee in thy estate or reputation.

Nor did Spurgeon regard Psalm 139:21-22 (about hating God's enemies) as contrary to his text. He interpreted it as 'We are to love sinners, but we are to hate sin,' the very comment Paisley had dismissed.

Paisley's hesitancy regarding love for one's enemies is also evident in his teaching on forgiving others. He would have his followers believe that his attitude to forgiveness is that held by Christ: 'The Lord Jesus Christ has made it crystal clear that forgiveness can only be given to those who repent of their sins and crimes. There is no forgiveness nor offer of forgiveness to the unrepenting man.'[69] He was furious when he listened to the words of forgiveness spoken by Gordon Wilson after his daughter Marie's death as the result of an IRA bomb planted at the cenotaph in Enniskillen on Remembrance Day, Sunday, 8 November 1987. Interviewed by BBC reporter Mike Gaston on the Sunday night, Wilson had said, 'I bear no ill will, I bear no grudge. Dirty sort of talk is not going to bring her back to life. She was a great wee lassie. She loved her profession. She was a pet. She's dead. She's in Heaven, and we'll meet again.'[70] In his pulpit the following Sunday, Paisley set out to correct what he perceived as the damage done by Wilson's spontaneous words, which by this stage had been broadcast around the world. Paisley declared: 'When Mr Wilson says he has forgiven the murderer of the act which he did, in blowing up all those people and taking from him his daughter, he cannot, he cannot forgive the murderer.... There is absolutely no forgiveness, none whatsoever without repentance. Remember, this particular truth is also applicable to the offence which man does to man.'[71]

This question of the nature of God's forgiveness and its effect on the attitude of the forgiven person to other people brings us to the heart of the Christian gospel. Paisley's teaching in both areas appears to be seriously flawed. Firstly, it is true to say that our *experience* of God's forgiveness *is* dependent on our repentance; this is not being questioned, but this is different from teaching that God's act of forgiveness is dependent on our repentance. The prayer of Jesus on the cross, 'Father, forgive them, for they do not know what they are doing' (Luke 23:34), was not the consequence of an act of repentance by those responsible for crucifying him. The whole teaching of the Atonement, the work of Christ on the cross, is that God takes the initiative in redeeming humankind. The apostle Paul summed up his experience of God as, 'I live by faith in the Son of God, who loved me and gave Himself for me' (Galatians 2:20). In other words, it was God's reaching out in forgiveness to Paul which drew forth the response of faith in his life. Similarly, Jesus did not teach, and the New Testament never teaches, that we only forgive people when they come in repentance to us. Several passages make this abundantly clear:

1. Matthew 6:12, part of the Lord's Prayer: 'Forgive us our debts, as we also have forgiven our debtors.' 6:14-15, 'For if you forgive men when they sin against you, your heavenly Father will also forgive you. But if you do not forgive men their sins, your Father will not forgive your sins.' [The Lord's Prayer is seldom, if ever, used in worship at Martyrs'.]

2. Matthew 18:21-22 Peter asked Jesus how often he should forgive his brother. Jesus replied, 'I tell you, not seven times, but seventy times seven.'

3. Matthew 18:23-35, the parable of the unmerciful servant. The final verse reads in the words of Jesus: 'This is how my heavenly Father will treat each of you unless you forgive your brother from your heart.'

4. In Acts 7:60, Stephen's prayer for his persecutors as they stoned him reflected the words of Jesus on the Cross: 'Lord, do not hold this sin against them.'

5. Ephesians 2:14-18. The apostle Paul speaks of how both Jew and Gentile, through the work of Christ on the cross, despite the centuries of division and hostility between them, can find peace with God and with each other, v. 14, 'For he himself is our peace, who has made the two one, and has destroyed the barrier, the dividing wall of hostility, by abolishing in his flesh the law with its commandments and regulations.'

6. Ephesians 4:32, 'Be kind and compassionate to one another, forgiving each other, just as in Christ God forgave you.'

7. 1 John 4 speaks of the atoning sacrifice of Christ on the cross and its implications for our attitude and relationship to others:

   v. 10-11, 'This is love, not that we loved God, but that he loved us and sent his Son as an atoning sacrifice for our sins. Dear friends, since God so loved us, we also ought to love one another.'

   v. 19-21, 'We love Him, because He first loved us. If anyone says, "I love God," yet hates his brother, he is a liar. For anyone who does not love his brother, whom he has seen, cannot love God, whom he has not seen. And he has given us this command: Whoever loves God must also love his brother.'

Paisley ignores the teaching of these passages and bases his demand for repentance on the part of the offender before the Christian offers forgiveness on an incorrect deduction from Luke 17:3-4, in which Jesus emphasises the need for forgiveness. Jesus says, 'If your brother sins, rebuke him, and if he repents, forgive him. If he sins against you seven times in a day, and seven times comes back to you and says, "I repent," forgive him.' Revd Donald Ker, lecturer in New Testament at Edgehill Theological College, Belfast, suggests that to argue, as Paisley does, a negative inference – 'no forgiveness to the unrepenting man' – from the positive statement of Jesus – 'if he repents, forgive him' – is simply not logical and runs contrary to all the other teaching of Jesus.[72]

The significance of this hardly needs to be underlined, for Paisley's preaching has unquestionably affected many people's opinions. Most of us will acknowledge the difficulty of forgiving others – C.S. Lewis once commented that everyone says forgiveness is a lovely idea until they have something to forgive! – but it has become quite common in Northern Ireland to find people who actually believe that it is wrong to forgive one's opponents or enemies, unless, as Paisley insists, they declare their repentance. Preaching on the outworking of God's forgiveness in one's life, the need for forgiveness of one's enemies and reconciliation in Christ of those who previously were at war with each other is, in Paisley's view, part of the apostasy afflicting the country: 'Christ did not come to reconcile man to man. It was not the purpose of His Coming. This word "Reconciliation", one of the most glorious words of Gospel Truth, has been debased by the devil, and taken up by ecumenical clergymen, blind leaders of the blind that they are. If the blind lead the blind both will fall into the ditch of apostasy, and so they have.'[73]

The methods employed in this battle against apostasy also need to be scrutinised. Marches, picketing of buildings and interrupting worship have already been noted. Other methods may also have been attempted. Jim Sands was an eighteen year old when he was employed for six to seven months in 1977 in the office at Martyrs' Memorial Church. One of his duties was to collate material on ministers involved in ecumenical activities. Local organisers in different parts of the country would scan the papers for news about ministers or laity who had contact with the Roman Catholic Church and send in this information to the office where it would be carefully collated and filed. Sands attended Bethany Free Presbyterian Church in Portadown at the time, and after his period in the office at Martyrs' he was the local co-ordinator for the Portadown area until 1982. But his duties did not stop at collecting the information! He was also responsible for arranging ways and means of being a nuisance to these ministers. One method that was commonly used was making phone-calls at all hours of the day and night. The caller might let the minister know what he thought about his association with Catholics; or might call in the early hours of the morning asking for a taxi or Chinese take-out. Sands says, 'In the time I was involved there must have been hundreds of phone-calls to different ministers and lay people seen as pro-ecumenical.'[74] Eric Gallagher reports having received many abusive and nuisance phone-calls like this. I myself followed Gallagher's cousin, Ernest Gallagher – a former president of the Methodist Church in Ireland who had been a missionary in India for twenty-three years – as the minister living in the manse at Edgehill Theological College. Ernest had died in February 1984, but for some months the phone would ring in the early hours of the morning and the caller would ask for Mr Gallagher. I told him Mr Gallagher was not in as he was now in heaven. Was this kind of activity authorised and supported by the presbytery of the Free Presbyterian Church of Ulster, and by the moderator himself? Sands insists it was. In addition, daubing paint on church walls or cars, slashing the tyres of cars and jostling or pushing people were all regarded as permissible in 'fighting for the Protestant faith, stopping the spread of Rome'.

These characteristics of Paisley's 'battle against apostasy', as they unfold, reveal the ingredients of what might justifiably be described as a very dangerous cocktail. He insists he is leading a God-inspired and God-directed battle; he claims that all his teaching is biblically based; he urges his followers to pray for divine assistance in the fight. His whole campaign is conducted in such a manner that none should have any reason to doubt the infallibility of his leadership. And yet this religious warfare omits the very core of the Christian gospel: Christ's command to love one's neighbour and forgive one's enemies, and replaces it with a supposed divine mission to oppose 'every enemy of the Lord' and to take with a pinch of salt any talk of 'not hating the sinner but the sin'. While not questioning the sincerity of his desire to follow and serve Christ, his strange and unorthodox grasp of the core of the Christian gospel surely puts a question mark over his ability to lead any campaign against apostasy.

God is a Separatist

James L.M. Haire (1909-1985), a former moderator of the General Assembly and principal of Union Theological College, a jovial, saintly and scholarly man, whom Paisley once accused of trying to knock him down by driving too close to him, identified two situations in which the New Testament urges separation to preserve true Christian fellow-ship: persistent immorality (2 Corinthians 6:14; 7:1) and, secondly, times when we are challenged by those 'who deny that our salvation comes from God's mercy and lay emphasis on men's own merits' (Galatians 2:11-17).[75] When Paisley applied these and other scripture passages to his battle against apostasy, it resulted in a call for separation from every Protestant church. In other words, every strand of Protestantism, in his opinion, has been guilty of persistent immorality and denial of the gospel of grace. As apostasy has swept through the churches, separation is necessary: 'To those that are not Christ's; those that are not saved; those who have rejected the Son of God; those who have turned aside to apostasy and idolatry and Romanism in ecclesiastical commitments, we should adopt a rigid, staunch separation.'[76] God is presented as One who demands separation from all who preach reconciliation or engage in inter-church dialogue.

These lovey dovey fellows who are running around, tell you that God never fought. I want to tell you, God declared war on the Devil in Heaven and cleaned the Devil out of Heaven. God is a separatist. He did not say to the Devil, 'Let us dialogue, Satan. Let us have a round table conference and see what common ground we have between us.' Christ said, 'I saw Satan cast as lightning from Heaven.' A clean sweep.[77]

It is not hard to imagine the impact of this kind of preaching when it is repeated month after month, or indeed week after week, in rented halls or Free Presbyterian churches. The message is presented with urgency, as separation is seen as an immediate obligation on all who want to please God and experience salvation: 'Let me tell you this tonight, you cannot stay in apostasy and please God. You get that straight. It cannot be done. That is the Word of God. I trust you will face it, and you'll have no part nor lot with compromise, but you'll take a strong faithful uncompromising stand. If you are not saved, get saved tonight!'[78] Members of other churches who might be attending the Free Presbyterian meeting are warned of the great danger they are in by remaining in their denomination: 'If you are a Baptist in this meeting, waken up.'[79] The time of greatest emphasis on separation is usually when a church extension cause is being started or when hope is expressed that the day will come that larger and more magnificent premises are required. When Kyle Paisley retired in 1966 as pastor of the Gospel Tabernacle on the Waveney Road, Ballymena, few were surprised that the congregation decided it was the right time to join his son's Free Presbyterian Church of Ulster. The cause had dwindled over the years and Ian Paisley knew that a new impetus was required. R.J.

Beggs, his brother-in-law, was installed as the new minister, and Paisley felt that this was the time to preach separation coupled with an appeal for expansion of the cause: 'God's Word says "Come out" and that does not mean "Stay in". When God's Word says "Shun" it means to shun. Associate yourselves with the people of God and you will not be spectators, you will be actual workers in the Lord's service. Let us see a time when this building will no longer be big enough to hold us, and we will build a large building in this town of Ballymena, a testimony to what God can do for a people that will follow Him without the camp.'[80] It was a theme which was often repeated in Ballymena and eventually resulted in the fulfilment of his dream!

The need for separation is fostered by continually portraying other churches as being careless about reading the Bible or praying: 'I was talking to a man the other day, he has been thirty years on the road, and he was telling me, "This year is the first year I have started to read my Bible through." And he said, "If I had never become a Free Presbyterian, if I had stayed in the Baptist denomination I belonged to, I never would have read it through."'[81] The deadness of other churches is compared to the spiritual vitality of the one true church, which by implication seems to be the Free Presbyterian Church: 'The modern church is engaged in corpse-washing. They wash the corpses and they dress the corpses, and they set them up in the pews. That is all they can do. But the true church is engaged in resurrections. That is what the true church is engaged in.'[82] Indeed, one is frequently left with the impression that Paisley really sees his Free Presbyterian Church as the only genuine Christian church in existence. Preaching in Martyrs' Memorial on 5 February 1989, Paisley shared with the congregation a little thought he had recently had: 'The other day I sat down and I did a little calculation, and I discovered that if there were 10,000 Christians in the world, and they all, every year, won one person to Jesus Christ, that in forty to fifty years the total population of the world would be reached in conversion. That is a staggering thought, is it not?'[83] How did the figure of 10,000 Christians come into Ian Paisley's mind? Was it just a coincidence that the figure was somewhat similar to the number of Free Presbyterians in the world in 1989? The possibility that Paisley sees his followers, Free Presbyterians, as the only Christians in the world may seem incredible to some but, in effect, it is the only logical implication of his unique form of separatist theology.

Chapter Six

Free Presbyterians

Alas! alas! in how many things have I judged and acted wrong. I have been too rash and hasty in giving characters, both of places and persons. Being fond of Scripture language, I have often used a style too apostolical;... I have been too bitter in my zeal. Wild-fire has been mixed with it, and I find that I frequently wrote and spoke in my own spirit, when I thought I was writing and speaking by the assistance of the spirit of God... By these things I have hurt the blessed cause I would defend.

George Whitefield (1714-1770)[1]

NONE DISPUTE THE date or place where the Free Presbyterian Church of Ulster was first constituted – St Patrick's Day, 17 March 1951, in Killyleagh Street Mission Hall, Crossgar, County Down – but controversy has surrounded the circumstances leading to its founding. Every ten years Free Presbyterians have highlighted the Crossgar story while Presbyterians remained silent, not through any sense of guilt for what occurred but possibly to avoid public confrontation with Paisley, something he would have clearly wanted. In the forty-five years that have elapsed since 1951, Free Presbyterianism has effectively been the only source detailing and interpreting its origins, as Paisley's biographers have either failed to research the Presbyterian records of these events or have simply found they were not available to the public.

I have, however, had access to these records, the session minutes of Lissara Presbyterian Church in Crossgar and the presbytery of Down minutes. Consequently, it is now possible to consider both Presbyterian and Free Presbyterian sources and interpretations of events and to come to an informed opinion about what has understandably been a controversial matter.

A look at the years 1949 to 1951, as they affect Crossgar, provides the background to the dispute which came to a head in February and March 1951. By 1949 two events had occurred which were to influence future developments in Crossgar: the World Council of Churches had been formed at Amsterdam in 1948, and Ian Paisley had experienced the 'weekend of prayer' with John Douglas and Robert Scott which was to make him a 'fox-hunter' – in his own words, 'a seeker after those foxes that destroy the church of Jesus Christ' – at twenty-three years of age. Some would suggest that he had been attacking Protestant churches before this, but his own testimony is reliable confirmation that he now believed he had received a divine commission to challenge and root out what he perceived to be apostasy in Protestantism. Part of this battle against apostasy was the demand that Christians separate themselves from churches which he declared were 'defunct and dead and lifeless and useless'.

The drama began to unfold between 9 May 1949 and 27 June 1950 when there appears to have been some delay about the election of new members to the session of Lissara Presbyterian Church. The Lissara session minutes indicate two reasons for this: firstly, the list of names nominated for election in August 1949 was so short that the session felt the congregation would have little or no choice of candidates; secondly, when the first election was held in May 1950, some of the congregation objected that the proper procedure of reading the list of eligible voters for two Sundays prior to the election had not been followed. However, when a second election was held and the votes were counted on 27 June 1950, the result was almost the same as the previous month. The four elected as elders were George K. Gibson, W.J. Whyte, H.J. Adams and Cecil Harvey. Meanwhile, on 30 April 1950, the minister of the church, Revd W. McClure, had informed the session and church committee of his intention to retire at the end of June.

At some stage during the year Ian Paisley was invited to conduct an evangelistic mission in Crossgar. Free Presbyterian sources state: 'In 1950 Mr George K. Gibson approached the Revd Ian Paisley on behalf of the Committee of the Crossgar Mission Hall to ascertain whether he would be willing to conduct an Old Time Gospel Campaign in the town. After careful consideration and prayer, plans were eventually finalised and the date fixed for February 1951.'[2] It is not clear whether the invitation was sent after April 1950, when Gibson had already learned that Mr McClure was retiring, or indeed whether it was sent between June and November 1950, when Gibson had been elected but not yet ordained to the eldership. In any case the invitation seems somewhat strange, since Gibson could hardly have been unaware that Paisley was accusing his church of apostasy.

An election for a new minister was held in Lissara on 9 October 1950.

When the Revd Geoffrey Chart, who had shared with Paisley in the work of the National Union of Protestants and was the candidate favoured by Gibson and his friends, failed to win the required two-thirds majority vote, accusations concerning irregularities in the voting were voiced.

At meetings on 7 and 9 November the presbytery of Down appointed Revd Matthew Bailie to replace the Revd R.L. Pedlow as convener of the commission in charge of Lissara and ordained the four newly elected elders.

A month later the presbytery received letters containing allegations of illegal voting at the elections for a new minister at Lissara and decided to discuss them at their next meeting.

On New Year's Day, Lissara session unanimously agreed to grant an application from Mr William Emerson for the use of the church hall for an evangelistic campaign beginning on the first Sunday in February and lasting for four weeks; the preacher to lead the mission was not named. The Revd Matthew Bailie undertook to bring the matter to the attention of the presbytery.

A week later the presbytery of Down met to consider three major items of business: first, the allegations of illegal voting in the election for a new minister in Lissara; secondly, threats issued by George Gibson to build a reformed church in Crossgar; and thirdly, the application to use Lissara church hall for a mission. After letters and sworn evidence from George Gibson and others had been considered at length, the presbytery decided: 'That since a measure of illegality has been declared to have taken place, and although it cannot be proved that this would have materially affected the final decision, the Presbytery think it best in all the circumstances to declare the election null and void.'[3]

The presbytery then discussed Gibson's threat relating to the voting issue, 'that if this legitimate demand [a new election] is not honoured, we will build a reformed church in Crossgar, and issue an immediate call to the minister of our own choice'. It is highly unlikely that a newly ordained elder in the Presbyterian Church, out of his own thinking, praying and planning, or indeed as the result of discussions with other Lissara elders, would have considered separation from the church that had so recently ordained him. At this time, however, Ian Paisley was in almost daily contact with Gibson at his architect's office in Donegal Square, Belfast. It is known that from March 1951 Paisley used a room in Gibson's premises as 'the registered office of the Free Presbyterian Church of Ulster',[4] and the arrangement may well have been operating for some period before March. The idea of a new church in Crossgar

fitted in entirely with his separatist preaching, and the determination
to carry out such a radical step required energetic ministerial leadership. The young Paisley appears to have seen and interpreted the situation as ready-made for the extension of his influence and the
establishment of a church which he would control and dominate. And
so he encouraged Gibson to develop the conflict within Lissara Church.

No church could have taken such a threat without giving pastoral
reproof. Having decided in Gibson's favour in relation to the charge of
illegal voting, the presbytery now responded angrily to the threat of
separation: 'The Presbytery objects strongly to the threat extended to
it in the letter signed by Mr G.K. Gibson.... It has never refused to
hear the appeal of the humblest member of the church. It will not,
however, submit to threats.'

Finally, the presbytery dealt with the application of the Lissara
session to allow the use of the church hall for a mission commencing 4
February and lasting four to six weeks. This time the name of the
missioner was included: Revd Ian Paisley. The presbytery could hardly
have viewed this application in isolation from the dispute over irregularities in voting or the threat to form a new church in Crossgar. The
common strand now linking together George Gibson and his group with
the name of Ian Paisley was surely in the mind of the presbytery at this
time. According to the minutes of the presbytery, the application for
the use of the church hall was made 'in accordance with par. 254 of the
Code (1948)' which states:

No evangelistic mission in connection with a congregation of the Church,
or in premises belonging to a congregation, shall be conducted by any
person other than a minister, a licentiate, or a ruling elder of the Church,
or an Agent of the Assembly's Committee on the State of Religion, unless
and until such person shall have been expressly authorised to undertake
such work by the Presbytery of the bounds.

In other words, missioners other than Presbyterian ministers could
be granted permission 'if expressly authorised to undertake such work
by the Presbytery of the bounds'. However, it was scarcely conceivable
that any responsible body, religious or secular, would actually autho-
rise someone to castigate its beliefs, spirituality and practice, on its own
premises, for four to six weeks. The Down presbytery ruled 'that
consideration of the application to the Presbytery be deferred until such
times as the vacant pulpit is filled'.

The presbytery of Down met at Lissara on Saturday, 3 February
1951, to discuss the fact that 'notwithstanding the decision of the
Presbytery deferring consideration of the application for the use of the

Lissara Church Hall for the Ian Paisley Mission, advertisements were appearing in the Press stating that the Mission would be held in the Hall, commencing tomorrow'.[5] Summoning the members of the Lissara session – all but one, Cecil Harvey, were able to attend – the presbytery asked them if they had had anything to do with the press announcements. The minute recording the response is simple but significant: 'They replied they had nothing to do with the publication.' Whoever was responsible, the action was clearly provocative, perhaps even deliberately designed to bring about a confrontation with the Presbyterian Church.

Even the elders sympathetic to Paisley seem to have been caught in the dilemma of whether to defy the ruling of their church. While the presbytery had ascertained that none of the elders had actually been responsible for placing advertisements in the papers, they also wanted to know if the elders supported the ruling of the church which now, because of the advertisements, would have to be further explained to the congregation at worship the next day. The minutes indicate that when the question of support for the presbytery ruling was put to the members of the Lissara session, they 'answered so uncertainly that they were asked to withdraw to consider the matter among themselves'. Put to the test individually, Gibson and Adams refused to abide by the presbytery decision and were suspended 'till they should show signs of repentance'.

The above account of events from the records of Lissara session and the presbytery of Down runs contrary to the Free Presbyterian version published repeatedly in *The Revivalist* and elsewhere:

The Presbytery of Down of the Irish Presbyterian Church held a special meeting called an hour and a half before the Old Time Gospel Campaign was planned to begin in Lissara Church Hall. The Lissara Church Session, who had previously granted the Church Hall unanimously for the Old Time Gospel Campaign, were summoned to attend. The Down Presbytery, Revd Boland, Moderator, dictated to the Kirk Session that they must change their decision and directed that the Church hall be closed and that the Revd Ian R.K. Paisley and those who had gathered including many members of Lissara be kept out in the pouring rain. No gospel was to be preached in the hall.[6]

The Free Presbyterian account indicates that the mission had now been advertised to begin on Saturday, 3 February, and not as recorded in the Lissara session minutes, 'beginning on the first Sunday of February'. It gives the impression that the session only learned of the presbytery decision on Saturday, 3 February, whereas the presbytery records indicate that Lissara elders attended the presbytery meeting in early January at which the application for the use of the hall was considered. The Free Presbyterian version fails to explain that the only reason for the 3 February presbytery meeting in Lissara was the fact that some unauthorised person had advertised the mission as being held in the church hall contrary to the 8 January decision of presbytery.

In detailing events as they developed, Free Presbyterian sources paint a picture of the Presbyterian Church as acting in opposition to the Christian gospel. Pickets led by Paisley outside the church before and after the service on Sunday, 4 February, carried headings: 'Down Presbytery Bans Gospel Campaign', 'I Am Not Ashamed of the Gospel', 'Church Elders Suspended'. The pickets went into the service and were present when Bill Boland, moderator of the Down presbytery, explained the sequence of events which had led to the suspension of Gibson and Adams. *The Revivalist* interpreted this suspension as comparable to the papacy's attitude to Luther: 'This ultimatum reminded one of the "pope's bull" to the champion Luther calling him to repent on his Protestantism. Thank God he did not shirk from the pathway of truth. Thank God in 1951 the two elders in Crossgar did not deviate one inch from treading where the saints have trod.' When Boland was leaving the church, the RUC offered to escort him to his car, which required a mechanic to get it started. In the days following he received phone-calls and letters blaming him for what had happened. But today, looking back, he says: 'I feel no bitterness at all towards any of those people who were involved at that time.'[7]

On 11 March 1951 five former Lissara elders, including Gibson and Adams, issued a 'Free Presbyterian Manifesto' explaining their part in recent events and announcing the following Saturday, 17 March, as the day on which the Free Presbyterian Church of Ulster would be officially constituted in Killyleagh Street Hall.[8] They indicated that they themselves would be installed as the session of the new church; it was not necessary to mention who would install them as everyone knew it would be Paisley. This drastic step, they declared, was being taken because the Presbyterian Church, led by heretics, had forsaken Protestant doctrine and extended 'a welcoming hand to the Church of Rome'. The whole intent of the manifesto, the expressions used, the accusations of heresy, all provide glimpses of the real author behind this document. Only five months earlier, three of these elders had promised allegiance to Presbyterianism and its standards, but now they affirmed that 'clear thinking Christian people are beginning to realise that the only course to pursue is to save that which is worth saving, and like Sodom and Gomorrah, leave the rest to the flames of God's wrath and judgement'. Crossgar, they maintained, was giving a lead in establishing this new church, which was already being joined by other congregations 'now in the process of being formed'. The choice of name for the new church was explained: 'Free because it has struggled out from under the heel and tyranny of the Church which sails under the flag of Presbyterianism, but is really Unitarian; Presbyterian because in constitution, government and worship it will be identical with that of our Presbyterian forefathers.'

The presbytery of Down, which met twelve times during the crisis period from 7 November 1950 to 1 May 1951, publicly refuted the charge of apostasy and painstakingly endeavoured to correct what they perceived as a distortion of the facts which, they suggested, 'can scarcely be other than deliberate'. They challenged the signatories about their claims to be Presbyterian, citing, among other things, the decision of the new church to leave each individual to decide the nature and mode of baptism. In what appears as a last-ditch attempt to win back the five and any others who might have been considering separation, they asked them to compare what they would gain to what they would lose: 'The price will be heavy, the gain pitifully small; for they will have lost a church that at home and abroad cherishes the Gospel of Jesus Christ, commending it to a world that stands in need of God and His redemption.'[9]

Paisley's analysis of the events at Crossgar was predictable: 'The only possible response to the display of Irish Presbyterian apostasy, by faithful Presbyterians, was secession.'[10] The truth is that he had been preaching and teaching separation from apostasy in Protestant church pulpits, in mission halls, over cups of tea in people's homes, since his twentieth birthday. This was the message he delivered during 'gospel campaigns' and special services in various parts of the country, as well as on his own patch in Glentoran Street (off the Ravenhill Road). The message of Jesus, or those portions of it which fitted into his own brand of theology, was mixed up with fierce denunciations of the Roman Catholic Church, the World Council of Churches, Protestant ministers and churches. His booming voice, youthful appearance, strong deter-mination and forceful personality all combined to cast a spell over many of his audiences. That magic had a definite effect in Crossgar. All the evidence suggests that he read the situation there as one that had the potential for schism, and he succeeded in exploiting that potential.

Spells, however potent, rarely last forever. At two Lissara session meetings in October 1958, the minister, Revd Sam Finlay, indicated that former members were now seeking re-admission to the church. At the second meeting: 'Mr Finlay reported that he had interviewed others who had previously been members of Lissara communion and expressed the wish of Session that they should be welcomed as communicants again. These were Mr and Mrs John Gibson, Mr and Mrs G.K. Gibson, Misses Anna and Robina Gibson, Mr John Gibson (Junior) and Miss Margaret Gibson.'[11] George Gibson had become disenchanted with Paisley. Even though he was the architect of the new Free Presbyterian church building which was opened in Crossgar on Saturday, 16 March 1957, the power of the Paisley spell was rapidly diminishing.

The crunch came when George, now a lay preacher with the Free Presbyterians, was summoned before a Free Presbyterian court to face the charge of preaching Methodist doctrine, including its emphasis on perfect love (based on the two great commandments, Matthew 22:37-40). Ian Paisley, moderator, presided, with John Wylie and other Free Presbyterian ministers being present. He was asked to answer the charge, which he did as best as he could, but they decided that he was guilty of preaching Methodist doctrine and not biblical doctrine. The proceedings ended with Wylie praying that Gibson be 'handed over to Satan' so that his 'sinful nature may be destroyed and his spirit saved on the day of the Lord' (1 Corinthians 5:5), an action which was to be frequently repeated by Free Presbyterians in church courts and elsewhere. Hearing himself being 'delivered to Satan' by John Wylie was the end of his romance with Free Presbyterianism! Returning to Presbyterianism, he had the freedom to speak about perfect love and share in fellowship with Methodists.[12] His eldest son, Brian, a Presbyterian minister, has served as a missionary overseas and is now in Lisburn. Trevor, the younger of the two, says of his father: 'On 30 April 1979 we bade him farewell. As eternity beckoned he stepped beyond time and into a fairer land. While he had the faults inherent in humanity, I shall always remember his great generosity and kindness. There is no doubt that his Christian faith found expression in deed as well as word.'[13]

To Paisley's surprise, or so he suggests, the Irish Evangelical Church publicly condemned his founding of the Free Presbyterian Church at Crossgar. He argued that he was only doing what they had done in 1927 when they seceded in protest against the General Assembly's decision in favour of Professor Davey:

I was born the very year the Heresy Charges were laid against Professor Davey in 1926, and in the goodness of God I went to minister in that Secession Congregation which left the Irish Presbyterian Church, led by those men who had signed the Charges of Heresy against Professor Davey. In 1951 the battlelines were drawn, and in Crossgar the first congregation of the Free Presbyterian Church was established. It is my great regret, and I say it with a pain in my heart, that when that decision was taken the Irish Evangelical Church saw fit to go public and condemn our stand. I say that with great sorrow, because I preached as a student in the pulpits of that Church and found its people a loyal and Bible-loving people, but I learned that I too must walk alone.[14]

The Irish Evangelical Church could not simply remain silent. Paisley's whole campaign against apostasy in the Protestant churches was based on the 1927 analogy. Silence on the Crossgar episode by those who had been involved in 1927 would undoubtedly have been interpreted by Paisley and others as equivalent to support for his action. They saw their 1927 secession as one taken on the grounds of theology; their condemnation of Paisley's Crossgar action – and indeed his subsequent involvement in delicate congregational situations in other parts of the country – said in effect that Paisley's meddling had nothing to do with theology. They denied any parallel between the internal congregational tensions which Paisley was exploiting and what they saw as an authentic theological issue in 1927. This infuriated Paisley. He saw the Irish Evangelical Church as destroying the very basis of his campaign. Without their support he would have to rely more and more on the sheer magnetism of his personality and his skill in presenting himself as God's man for the hour of crisis. He fervently believed he *was* God's chosen leader, but he knew he would have to convince others of his anointing.

Martyrs' Memorial Church

On 22 April 1951 Paisley's Ravenhill Evangelical Mission Church was renamed the Ravenhill Free Presbyterian Church and thereby became the second church within the Free Presbyterian Church of Ulster. Moloney and Pollak suggest that he had to overcome some opposition from within his Ravenhill congregation before the new arrangements were agreed, and apparently he only succeeded on a split vote.[15] However, events were now moving fast for Paisley. Soon a clear pattern of activity characterised his life: firstly, church work in Belfast, particularly as it related to his Ravenhill church; secondly, vigourously pursuing the founding of other Free Presbyterian congregations in various part of the province; thirdly, intense political activity, the strands of which had one common thread: his cry that Protestantism – as he understood it – and the state of Northern Ireland were under threat. Time given to the three activities alternated according to circumstances and they were not perceived in his mind as unrelated. Indeed, the opposite was the case, for the fortunes or otherwise of the

Free Presbyterian Church of Ulster and Protestantism – the first being seen as the true manifestation of the second – served as a kind of barometer by which the well-being of Northern Ireland, or Ulster as Paisley preferred to call it, could be measured. Significantly the Free Presbyterian Church was the Free Presbyterian Church *of Ulster*, whereas the Presbyterian Church is the Presbyterian Church *in Ireland*. Nowhere is his perception of the bonds between church and state or theology and politics more clearly illustrated than in the positioning of biblical and national emblems on either side of the large spacious pulpit which dominates the east central point of his Martyrs' Memorial Church in Belfast: to the left of the pulpit there is a large Union Jack flag and further to the left a banner with the words 'Jesus Christ is Lord'; to the right of the pulpit there is the Ulster flag and further to the right a banner with the words 'Salvation to the Uttermost'. In each case the flag is the first emblem on either side of the pulpit.

Paisley's most dependable ally in this expanding work has been his wife Eileen, whom he married in October 1956. Eileen Cassells came from an industrious and enterprising family. Her father Thomas had originally worked for Kirk's, a grocer in Ballyhackamore in East Belfast, but took over the business when Mr. Kirk died. The name Cassells had changed from Castles during the lifetime of her grandfather Jack Castles', who had been land steward to the fforde family, landowners at Ardmore, near Lurgan.

Eileen Paisley ensured that her husband had a secure home base from which to pursue his church and political activities. Their first home was on the Beersbridge Road in East Belfast but they later moved to a larger house nearby in Cyprus Avenue. At home, away from the hectic routine which he continually set himself, Paisley could be quiet. Kyle suggests: 'My mother would probably say he was the quietest in the home.' The deep and genuine love that exists between husband and wife is very evident to their family and indeed to the casual onlooker. On Eileen's part, it is a love which has supported her husband in every area of his life. She has been an encourager in his church work, at one time writing a regular feature for women entitled 'Living Room' in *The Revivalist*. In the political arena her family quickly point to the fact that she was an elected representative before their father. Primarily, however, she saw her role as lying in the home, providing security and love for the family, and this has been appreciated. Rhonda – an artist in her own right – graphically expresses these sentiments: 'My mother, of course, has always been there. An obvious statement maybe, but the greatest compliment a child can pay. Mum is brilliant. She is fun, lively – and spits fire when she is angry!'[16]

Ravenhill Free Presbyterian Church, and later the Martyrs' Memorial Church at Ravenhill Avenue, acted as a 'flagship' for the Free Presbyterian Church of Ulster. This was the main base of the new church. It was here that most of the men who became ministers (the Free Presbyterian Church of Ulster are united with the Roman Catholic Church in denying the right of women to be ministers) first felt prompted to enquire about the ordained ministry. It was here they were trained until greater numbers and the support of an expanding church made it feasible to acquire separate premises. Increased numbers attending the church and generous financial giving were seen as evidence of God's blessing. While other Protestant churches were said to be failing in both areas, the prosperity of Ravenhill Free Presbyterian was held up as proof that Christian truth was being preached and basic Christianity practised. In April 1968 *The Revivalist*, in an article, 'The Bankruptcy of Apostasy and the Bounty of Separation', jubilantly quoted extracts from the *Portadown News* which drew attention to the soaring income at Ravenhill:

At a time when most churches are finding it difficult to make both ends meet, parochial treasurers, session clerks and circuit stewards must have learned, with understandable envy, the amount of income flooding annually into the coffers of the Free Presbyterian Church.

The Revd Ian Paisley has every right to make a song and dance about the kind of offerings that his members are making. What church wouldn't feel well off with £17,000! But to have that kind of income doubled in one year and reach the staggering total of £35,000 is quite phenomenal.[17]

This was the period following Paisley's 1966 imprisonment when media attention had been heavily focused on him and popular support for his politics and church was steadily increasing. The *Portadown News* made no mention of this, but suggested: 'Whatever we may like to read into the figures of the Ravenhill Road finances, the undeniable fact is that the people obviously like what they are getting and are willing to pay for it. Other churches please copy!' Paisley, on this occasion, was glad to agree with the secular press: 'We agree wholeheartedly with the view of the *Portadown News* columnist, that a major cause of poverty in churches is "departure from first principles". Indeed we maintain that this is the prime cause.' Protestant ministers, he asserted, had sunk to the depths of the 'papish priests' of old, sellers of indulgences, and were organising dances, parties, and stewardship dinners instead of preaching the gospel. 'These pathetic performances,' he declared, 'only serve to emphasise the fact that apostasy leads to poverty and bankruptcy, both spiritual and material.'

Paisley was to interpret the growth of his Ravenhill church and the Free Presbyterian Church in general as confirmation of this premise: that fidelity to Christ brought both spiritual and material prosperity. While he also made much of the fact that faithfulness to the gospel often led to persecution – as, for example, his period of imprisonment – his 'faithfulness brings prosperity' thesis took precedence over the 'discipleship leads to persecution' teaching, as prosperity was seen as the certain reward in this life for the uncompromising follower of Christ.

Increased giving and growing numbers at the Glentoran Street/Ravenhill Road church led first to an enlargement scheme in 1962 which increased its seating capacity by building two new side galleries and removing two rooms downstairs. Soon this too was inadequate. When Paisley was preaching 'on special subjects' – Free Presbyterian terminology for Reformation and anti-Catholic themes – he hired the Ulster Hall, but even this was proving too small to house his large Sunday evening crowds. After much prayer the session and committee of the church decided unanimously that they needed a larger church, one that could accommodate over 2,000 people. They found the site they required about 400 yards further up the Ravenhill Road, then the location of the Ardenlee Nursing Home. The extensive grounds beside the home would provide ample space for a large church building and the rooms of the nursing home could be adapted as minor halls and Sunday school rooms. They approached the home and purchased the site for £25,000. On 14 October 1967 they laid eight foundation stones 'made of Mourne granite and lettered in gold' as the first step in erecting what was then said to be the largest Protestant church in the United Kingdom.

The cost of the new building was estimated to be in the region of £122,000, but Paisley's business acumen and flamboyant style of ministry combined to make this an achievable target. He held a special service in the Ulster Hall to mark the signing of the contract by the trustees. Paisley preached that night on Proverbs 3:33: 'The Lord's curse is on the house of the wicked, but he blesses the home of the righteous.' The new church was named 'Martyrs' Memorial' in memory of Reformation and Covenanting martyrs and possibly his own much publicised periods of imprisonment in 1966 and 1969, which were interpreted in Free Presbyterian literature as his own 'martyrdom'. It was opened on 3 October 1969, and by 1974 the building fund debt had been reduced to £18,358. That same year James A. Heyburn, the general secretary of the church, told the annual meeting of the church that the total income for 1973 was £86,517. By 1990 the total had risen to £254,405.

While the high annual income of the church has been maintained, the numbers attending worship have declined dramatically in recent years. During the seventies and eighties, the church would frequently be packed to capacity, but this has changed. Congregations morning or evening are now about 300, making Martyrs' third in the list of large Free Presbyterian congregations. Ballymena tops the list with congregations approaching 600 and Magherafelt comes second with numbers around 500. This decline in numbers at Ravenhill can partly be explained by the growth of Free Presbyterian churches all over the province, inevitably leading to Free Presbyterians supporting their local church rather than travelling to the city. Martyrs' Memorial, and Free Presbyterian churches in general, have always relied on people travelling from a distance to them; they are 'gathered' rather than 'community' churches and large car parks are essential features of church sites.

What about the people who attend Martyrs' regularly? David McIlveen, minister of Sandown Free Presbyterian Church, also in the east of the city, covers the pastoral needs of the congregation as Paisley's other commitments use up all his available time. I had very much wanted to sit down with members of the congregation and ask them how they had become linked with the church and how they understood the Christian life. Unfortunately I did not have this opportunity as I was forbidden by Dr Paisley and the session from interviewing any member of the church. I obviously observed this ruling but was puzzled by it, because those who attend the prayer meetings and services clearly hold 'the Doc' in high regard. In seeking permission to talk with members, I certainly did not anticipate meeting many dissidents. Those with whom I had talked informally over the past few years were always courteous and helpful, and this continued when they learned I was a Methodist minister. Some indicated their willingness to be interviewed, but once they learned that W. J. Moore, clerk of session, had communicated the session's decision to me, everyone fell into line. Dr Paisley too was friendly on occasions. He twice refused me an interview, but he never once suggested that 'my toe will assist you through the door'. So why should a Christian church choose to put up a 'wall of silence' as regards the nature of its life and witness? Were they concerned that some 'skeletons in the cupboard' would fall out? Or are there other reasons to explain the drop in attendance at Martyrs' which I have not yet discovered?

Paisley's enthusiasm for the work at Martyrs' gives no indication of having waned over the years. Here he appears to be 'at home'. It was the Ravenhill Road congregation which gave him his first real opportunity to exercise his gift in public speaking, and he has revelled in it ever since. Each August he celebrates the anniversary of his ministry at Ravenhill and 1996 is the fiftieth. He believes he has been a faithful preacher throughout the years, as indicated in his prayer of thanksgiving on his forty-seventh anniversary: 'We thank Thee for the 47 years of Gospel preaching on this road. We thank Thee for the multitudes who have been converted. We thank Thee for churches formed and spread abroad on the face of the earth and we say "To God be the Glory, great things He hath done".'[18] Nor is there any hint that he intends retiring from the scene at Martyrs' or elsewhere because, as he assures his followers, God has promised him long life: 'I got a promise from the Lord years ago and I'm glad the Lord gave me it because every time I'm in an aeroplane and it's not going too well, I remind the Lord that He gave me this promise. You know what it is? "With long life will I satisfy you and show you my salvation." So I'm going to live a long time. And my enemies, I'm going to be around when a lot of them are gone for the Lord said, "With long life will I satisfy you"...The Free Presbyterians have prospered because they believed God.'[19]

Forward Movement

Following the inception of the Free Presbyterian Church of Ulster at Crossgar in March 1951 with congregations in that town and, by April, Ravenhill in Belfast, Ian Paisley – still only twenty-five years old – did not pause to draw breath. He continued to look for places where he might profitably apply his separatist ecclesiology. It is difficult to assess the degree to which people at this time were alert to his methods and goals. Gallagher and Worrall suggest that church leaders in these early days looked on him as a figure of amusement and underestimated his potential to influence Christian thinking: 'He was laughed at and dismissed by church leaders and politicians in his early days as an incongruous and irrelevant figure.'[20] With the advantage of hindsight it is now obvious that this failure to appreciate the appeal of his particular brand of theology and the hasty dismissal of his leadership potential were to prove costly mistakes. His influence on people's perception of the nature of God in Christ, their understanding of His mercy and love and its necessary outworking in people's lives, was to be immense.

Paisley, of course, had already dismissed contemporary church leaders as apostates, and he saw himself as embarking on the mission of a lifetime to persuade others of the rightness of his perception of the state of Christianity and the condition of the country. In County Antrim he learned of two further congregations in which internal tensions

existed: Drumreagh (Cabra) and Rasharkin Presbyterian Churches. In
Rasharkin in particular there could have been no accusation of Unitarian
or Romeward tendencies brought against the minister, the Revd A.E.S.
Stronge. It was the breakup of Stronge's marriage which provided the
opportunity for division in Rasharkin. Using these tensions to his
advantage, Paisley soon established two more small congregations. And
so his movement progressed, slowly but surely, and by 1966 thirteen
congregations had been begun. The circumstances of friction that had
existed at Lissara, Drumreagh – where an accusation of immorality had
split the congregation – and Rasharkin were not always found in other
areas, but his message of 'salvation' – as he understood it – combined
with a strong mixture of anti-Catholicism and calls for separation from
apostate Protestant churches produced results. Although new churches
were being formed, the small numerical response to his preaching in
the fifties may have lulled church leaders into a false evaluation of the
strength of his appeal. The 1961 census registered only 1,093 Free Presbyterians. Ireland, especially the north, had witnessed the emergence
of small independent Protestant churches in the past. Some had petered
out; others had remained, but their congregations were small.

The ingredient which really fuelled the Free Presbyterian Church
bandwagon was Paisley's two periods of imprisonment in 1966 and
1969, particularly the first, which he served with John Wylie and Ivan
Foster. Paisley himself acknowledges their significance: 'The best thing
that ever happened to the Free Presbyterian Church was the day that
we were put into prison. For God has let these things happen unto us
for the furtherance of the Gospel. Thank God the power of God has
been poured out upon us. And it has been worth it.'[21] Coming out of
prison he was delighted to find large numbers of people wanting to join
his Ravenhill congregation: 'The first morning I preached in the old
church this hand gave the right hand of fellowship to 200 new
members.'[22] Many accepted his interpretation of events that he had been
imprisoned like the apostle Paul 'for the sake of the Gospel'. At times
he would strenuously deny that he should be thought of as a martyr:
'Now we don't look upon ourselves as martyrs; people say we went in
to become martyrs.'[23] But there is no mistaking the implication inherent
in the volumes of words he has written on this topic. The new interest
in Paisley as a result of his 1966 imprisonment was translated in the
religious sphere – there was a political dividend too – into the creation
of twelve new churches in the eighteen-month period following his
release. Records from Free Presbyterian sources indicate a similar
pattern of events in each new development. In May 1967 *The Revivalist*

greeted the news of a new church in Londonderry with the headline 'Twentieth Congregation of Free Church Formed in Maiden City'. It reported on the events which had led to its formation:

At the beginning of April, the Revd John Wylie, assisted by the Revd Victor Burns, went to conduct a gospel campaign in Milltown Bandroom. The services were very well attended and there were capacity crowds on the Lord's Day evenings. There were fifteen people saved in the course of the campaign. On the final Friday night Mr Wylie issued a call to separation from apostasy and that very night over thirty people decided to step outside the camp with Christ. This number has since been augmented and an application to the Presbytery has been favourably received. Mr Wylie's mission, then, concluded at the end of April, with souls being saved and a good number of people desirous of commencing a Free Presbyterian witness.[24]

The twenty-first Free Presbyterian congregation was formed at Portadown a few weeks later. This time it was Ian Paisley who led the 'gospel campaign' which preceded the founding of a new congregation. A large tent had been erected, and crowds of around 500 attended. Once again the good news of Jesus was coupled with a fierce attack on other churches. *The Revivalist* reported:

Popery and apostasy in Co. Armagh received another body-blow as God mightily blessed the preaching of the Gospel in Dr Paisley's Tent Campaign in Portadown.... At its close, Dr Paisley preached on the great issues of the day, and called God's people to separate from the apostasy of the World Council of Churches. Some 130 people immediately signified their intention to sever all connections with the World Council of Churches, many of them seeing through the hypocrisy of so-called evangelicals who remain in denominations which are sold out to unity with Rome.[25]

In September 1967 the twenty-second Free Presbyterian congregation was formed at Dungannon. Again, it was the outcome of a campaign led by Paisley. Possibly the same large tent was used as had housed the large crowds in Portadown. On Sunday evenings – a suitable time to attract people from other churches – the congregations were estimated to have ranged from 1,000 to 1,200, many being unable to get into the tent. At the end of the campaign, Paisley announced the formation of a new congregation: 'The tent was packed to capacity for this service, and the whole congregation burst into acclamation when it was announced that the twenty-second congregation of the Free Presbyterian Church of Ulster would be started in Dungannon.'[26]

This new post-prison impetus continued for some time. In January 1972 Paisley opened his thirty-fourth church at Coragarry in County Monaghan, the first to be formed in the Republic of Ireland. By 1981

On board the Clyde Valley in Larne in the 1960s

Ian Paisley at Crossgar, 1951; George Gibson is second from the right

Leaving the Ulster Workers' Council headquarters following an
Action Council meeting, May 1977

The orator, July 1980

Staging one of many demonstrations outside the Presbyterian Assembly Belfast, 1982

Marching, August 1985

Snipping the wire at the Stormont security fence, April 1987

With his flock

With his wife Eileen after winning the North Antrim election in 1992

With James Molyneaux

At Drumcree, July 1995

With Tony Blair, September 1995

he had opened forty-nine churches in Ireland, as well as five small overseas churches. It was now the thirtieth anniversary of the founding of the Free Presbyterian Church of Ulster and he used the special service in Crossgar on 17 March as an occasion to rally his troops for yet greater days ahead:

I tell you, the next thirty years will be the greatest thirty years that we have ever seen in Northern Ireland, because God has given us a firm base from which to work. The Free Presbyterian Church is more capable now to fight Popery and the Ecumenical Movement and the enemies of Ulster than ever she has been before. And God is saying to this Church on its thirtieth anniversary, "Fear not little flock, it is the Father's good pleasure to give you the kingdom." If I had stood in that little Hall and told you that after thirty years we would have about fifty Churches, if I had told you that we would have spread to America, Canada and Australia, if I had told you of the magnificent buildings that we would build, of the ministers we would have, of the College we would found, of the missionaries we would suppport, and of the millions of pounds that would be raised for God's work, you would have laughed at me. If I had said, 'When I come back in thirty years I'll be the member of Parliament for North Antrim, and the member for Northern Ireland in the European Parliament,' you would have said, 'That fellow is off his head.' I want to tell you, God did it! Don't look for your answer, like some fools, on Ian Paisley.[27]

In the 1980s the Free Presbyterian Church decided to spearhead its church extension work under two departments: the 'forward movement', with Portadown minister Kenneth Elliott as convener, was to concentrate its efforts in Northern Ireland and the United Kingdom, while a 'mission board', headed up by Sandown Road (Belfast) minister David McIlveen, would be concerned with 'foreign work'. In the eighties it seemed for a period that church extension work in Northern Ireland was slowing down – there were only four new congregations formed between 1981 and 1989 – but the impetus returned in the nineties as the total of Free Presbyterian congregations rose to sixty-five. Paisley keeps reminding Free Presbyterians of the church extension methods which have paid dividends in the past: 'In areas where there are no fundamental witnesses, people should band together, and hold meetings in their own homes. When you get the people together, you will get the building.'[28]

Free Presbyterian work outside Northern Ireland has, since the sixties, been regarded as an essential part of its existence. At first they sent out and supported missionaries who were working with independent missionary societies. Then they launched out into their own missionary work and encouraged the planting of churches in other parts

of the world. By 1981 they had two churches in the USA, two in Canada
and one in Australia. With the establishment of the mission board, this
aspect of the work has clearly accelerated in the eighties and nineties,
the number increasing to twenty-seven overseas churches, located as
follows: USA: 12, Canada: 4, Germany: 1, Spain: 2, Australia: 5, and
the Republic of Ireland – designated as 'overseas work' in Free
Presbyterian structures – 3. In addition to these the 'forward movement'
has been responsible for the formation of six churches outside Northern
Ireland: England: 3, Scotland: 1, and Wales: 2. Free Presbyterian
missionaries are also working in Jamaica and Brazil and friendly contact
has been growing with separatist churches in Kenya and the Cameroon.

How then does one assess the growth of the Free Presbyterian
Church of Ulster within Northern Ireland and beyond its borders?
Census figures for Northern Ireland since 1961 reveal the following
growth in the number of those identifying themselves as Free
Presbyterians:

1961:	1,093
1971:	7,337
1981:	9,621
1991:	12,363

Its membership in relation to other churches grew as follows:

1961:	13th
1971:	8th
1981:	7th
1991:	7th

The 1991 census figures for the seven largest churches were:

Roman Catholic:	605,639
Presbyterian:	336,891
Church of Ireland:	279,280
Methodist:	59,517
Baptist:	19,484
Brethren:	12,386
Free Presbyterian:	12,363

Obviously the church is still growing, but the momentum of the
sixties has not been maintained; the last two decades suggest that either
the Free Presbyterian Church membership has peaked or the increase
in the next decade will be around the 2,000 to 3,000 mark, making it
the sixth largest church. The situation outside Northern Ireland is more
complex, as membership figures are not available. However, when I
recently visited the Oulton Broad Free Presbyterian Church near
Lowestoft in England, a church that was started in the mid-eighties, I

found a membership of between twenty to thirty. Its minister, Kyle Paisley, commented on the difference between the Free Presbyterian growth rate in England compared to Ulster: 'I think that England is a different place altogether and I don't think you can expect that the Free Presbyterians will spread over England overnight. It will just take time.' David Fletcher reported a slow growth rate in his church in Calgary, Alberta. A recent increase in numbers had brought attendances at worship to between seventy and eighty. With possibly two exceptions, the Toronto and Greenville, South Carolina, churches, the overseas churches appear to have small congregations, but their existence is important to Paisley. His separatist theology has meant that Free Presbyterianism has isolated itself from almost every other Christian church. Separatist congregations throughout the world whose orthodoxy and friendship they accept are relatively few in number. Hence the importance of endeavouring to open new churches overseas. Even though the membership of most of these churches remains small, their very existence assures the faithful Free Presbyterian membership at home that they are part of a worldwide church. This alone will guarantee their existence for the forseeable future.

Whitefield College of the Bible

Once the Free Presbyterian Church of Ulster was constituted, Paisley knew he would have to find and possibly train ministers for the new congregations. No one in the Free Presbyterian Church denies that these were hectic days, with staffing arrangements frequently being changed and discipline difficult to establish. Classes were held in the Ravenhill church, which for training purposes also became known as the Theological Hall. There were three students at the start: John Douglas, Cecil Menary and John Wylie, who had already been licensed and inducted into the Cabra church. Wylie was already forty and apparently unconvinced that he needed any training:

As a student or probationer minister John was required to attend the Theological Hall and to take the full course. All the indications are that he did not do so.... The intriguing thing is that those who attended the Hall at the time in question can remember John attending no more than a few classes ever, the first year included! It must be admitted that John was a man with a strong streak of defiance in him. He did not feel the need for college tutoring.[29]

Up to 1966 the Paisley father and son partnership bore the main responsibility for lecturing, Kyle teaching English Bible and Ian taking

systematic theology. For a brief interlude around 1955, they had had
the services of a Dr H. H. Aitchison, who lectured in church history
and practical theology, but John Douglas is puzzled as to why he
suddenly departed: 'Dr Aitchison did two years or a little longer. There
was no explanation about his eventual departure. I did not have any
clear understanding in my mind why the classes suddenly ceased.'
Despite the early difficulties arrangements were made for students to
have training in Greek New Testament, even if this meant sending some
students to Renshaws, the tutorial college in University Street, Belfast,
for preliminary tuition in Greek. By 1967 there were fifteen students
in training and the number of part-time teaching staff had been
increased: Ian Paisley lectured in church history, S.B. Cooke in
homiletics and pastoral theology, Alan Cairns in systematic theology,
and John Douglas in English Bible. On 6 October 1979 there was a new
and significant development with the opening of the Whitefield College
of the Bible at Martyrs' Memorial Church, with halls of residence
located at Cyprus Avenue. Whitefield, with John Douglas as principal,
had a dual purpose, serving as both a missionary training school and
theological college. Two years later the college moved to a large and
impressive building on a thirty-acre site at Laurencetown near Guild-
ford, County Down, which could provide both teaching and residen-
tial accommodation.

   Why did Ian Paisley choose to name his theological college after
George Whitefield, the famous evangelist who has been linked with
John Wesley and Jonathan Edwards as leaders of the eighteenth-century
evangelical revival in Britain and America? Undoubtedly Whitefield's
Calvinist theology and oratorical skills would have appealed to him.
Whitefield's evangelistic fervour had drawn thousands to hear him
preach while he was still in his twenties. His frequent trips to America
would also have interested Paisley. But here the attractiveness of
Whitefield for Paisley ends. He was not a separatist. He founded no
movement or denomination. As a Church of England minister, he was
at times critical of its clergy but he opposed any thought of separation
and encouraged a spirit of openness to members of other churches:
'There are certainly Christians among all sects and communions that
have learned the truth as it is in Christ Jesus.... Therefore, my dear
friends, learn to be more catholic, more unconfined in your notions; for
if you place the kingdom of God merely in a sect, you place it in that
in which it doth not consist.'[30] He warned against false reliance on a
form of orthodoxy: 'As the kingdom of God and true religion doth not
consist in being baptised, neither doth it consist in being orthodox in

your notions.... You may have orthodox heads and yet you may have the devil in your hearts.'[31] Above all, Whitefield had a humility which was prepared to recognise his mistakes, indeed serious mistakes, which could prove detrimental to the kingdom of God, and he was prepared to apologise, even to his opponents. How often has Paisley displayed this spirit?

Life at Whitefield appears to be fairly demanding. Breakfast at 7.30 is followed by twenty-five minutes of 'house duties' before quiet time at 8.15 and class devotions at 9.00. Lectures, Monday to Friday, commence at 10.00 and continue through each day – Fridays excepted – to 5.00. Students for the ministry are required to do a four-year course, taking subjects similar to those of any other theological college, the main difference being that the interpretation and approach to each subject is inevitably influenced by Paisley's separatist theology.

In 1990 the peace and tranquility of Whitefield was rocked by the discovery that some ministerial students had been cheating in examinations, not just once but on a number of occasions. The matter was covered by local newspapers and was taken seriously by the Free Presbyterian Church presbytery, who interviewed the students first at Martyrs' Memorial Church and later at Whitefield College, where they were placed in separate rooms to reduce the chance of conspiring together to give the same story to the presbytery. The outcome of the investigation was threefold: firstly, the guilty students were asked to confess and give assurances of their repentance; secondly, they were each disciplined according to the measure of their cheating (some had to resit examinations, others had to repeat the year, and some were excluded from the sacrament of the Lord's Supper for a period); thirdly, ministry and missionary students, who had already been examined by their local session and presbytery regarding their suitability for training in the college, were now required to sign an 'examination declaration':

1. As a student in Bible College I undertake not to be dishonest in any way. This will extend to examinations where I will not be dishonest in gaining or giving information.

2. I further promise before God that I will not utter any exclamation in an examination, including the most innocent of remarks. I will ask no questions of nor give explanations to any other student.

3. I will not move any place name without proper permission.

4. I will not use an unmarked examination Bible as a study Bible and further

undertake not to mark any words in these Bibles with pen or pencil.

5. I promise before God to report on any student, even my nearest friend, should that person be guilty of any misdemeanour during examinations.

None of those who had cheated were expelled, and all are now Free Presbyterian ministers.

Mervyn Cotton, a former student at the college who left the Free Presbyterian Church for reasons unconnected with the cheating crisis and set up the Reformed Free Presbyterian Church of Ulster, feels that in light of the Free Presbyterian attitude to alleged misdemeanours in other churches, the offenders should have been rejected as students for the ministry. 'Now if the Free Presbyterian Church of Ulster can condemn the sin in other places, then let them come out and condemn without reservation the sin that is found in the Whitefield College of the Bible and dismiss those ministers that are rascals in the sight of God and in the sight of men.'[32]

World Congress of Fundamentalists

While Paisley and his father had had a number of links with individual 'separatist fundamentalists' in Britain and America, they had never openly aligned themselves with any organised group of fundamentalists. Ian's 1963 decision to apply for membership of the International Council of Christian Churches was therefore a significant step in bringing him into association with other fundamentalists. Possibly at this stage he felt that the Free Presbyterian Church of Ulster was sufficiently well established to create closer links with other like-minded churches. Individual congregations made up a significant part of the membership of the International Council of Christian Churches, so the size of the Free Presbyterian Church of Ulster should not have been the deciding factor preventing him from seeking association before 1963. The International Council of Christian Churches had been formed in Amsterdam in 1948 by Carl McIntire, an American Bible Presbyterian Church pastor, as a protest against the aims and objectives of the World Council of Churches. Delegates of fifty-eight churches from twenty-nine countries had come to the first assembly, and by the twelfth world congress in 1988, McIntire could boast of a membership of 490 churches from 100 countries. When the Free Presbyterian Church of Ulster joined, it was the eighty-fourth constituent church body in the council and *The Revivalist* reported: 'The Free Presbyterian Church...is proud to be the only constituent member of the Council in Ireland.'[33]

By 1976, however, Paisley had withdrawn from the International Council of Christian Churches and he and Dr Bob Jones had formed a smaller rival body, the World Congress of Fundamentalists. As co-chairmen Paisley and Jones have controlled the congress without fear of any rival ever since. Paisley may have broken away from the International Council of Christian Churches because he was beginning to find fault with his fellow fundamentalists. During the 1970s he certainly criticised both their methods and views publicly. Some American fundamentalists in particular were ridiculed:

I go to the USA quite often and I see great churches which were founded by great fighters, but today the fight is out of those churches and they have substituted for the simple gospel preaching a whole series of gimmicks. How sad it is. They have substituted for the old-time prayer meeting a whole series of publicity stunts. Men falling from aeroplanes and parachuting down into the church grounds to gather a crowd. An offer that if you bring someone to church you will get a goldfish. Yes, that is what fundamentalism has come to in some of the great churches that were founded by God's men a generation ago.[34]

Nor did his criticisms remain mere generalisations. He was prepared to do battle with his erstwhile friends, and they in turn did not shrink from doing battle with him. Sometimes, as with Jack Glass of Glasgow, he would take high moral ground and feign a reluctance to retaliate while subtly attacking his opponent's ministry:

We have the instance of Jack Glass. He sees through a glass darkly, and when he sees through the glass darkly he excommunicates all who do not see eye to eye with him. If he thinks I am going to waste my time answering the strange allegations hurled at me continually in the *Scottish Protestant View*, he has another thing coming to him.... I shall not be wasting my time or my ammunition upon those petty people who feel it is their job to hinder the work of God.[35]

On the other hand, perhaps Paisley left the International Council of Christian Churches because McIntire's strong personality was depriving him of the limelight. Although Paisley had been elected to the executive committee in 1968, by 1976 he may have known that he would never be able to manouevre McIntire out of his leadership role. McIlveen dismisses any thoughts of a power struggle between Paisley and McIntire and suggests that the Free Presbyterian Church of Ulster left because people were joining for the wrong reasons: 'As time went on we began to appreciate that the organisation itself was probably too big to maintain control or to maintain an influence over. People were coming in purely and simply for monetary reasons, not for spiritual reasons.'[36]

Whatever the reasons for the split, the new arrangement gave Paisley and Jones the influence and platform they both wanted. The Jones family line has maintained a close link with Paisley throughout most of his ministry. They have been mutually supportive and helpful to each other: Paisley has been a frequent speaker at Bible conferences in the Bob Jones University, Greenville, South Carolina, and Jones has shared in most of the important occasions marking the rise of the Free Presbyterian Church. Of course, Bob Jones University awarded Paisley his doctorate, which was much appreciated after two earlier attempts with other colleges had misfired. This supportive role is especially evident in the lavish praise they heap on each other. Opening the new amphitorium at the university in 1976, Bob Jones junior described Paisley in glowing terms:

He is a man most distinguished both in the ministry and in the political life of his strife-torn country, a theologian, a teacher of theology, the founder and pastor of the greatest church in all of Europe, the Moderator of the Free Presbyterian Church of Ulster with many churches and new churches being added almost monthly, a man whom God has brought from a prison cell where for convictions sake he, like the apostle Paul, had time to write words of admonishment in his great commentary on one of Paul's books, suffering indeed for conscience's sake. Out of the prison cell he now sits in the Parliament of Westminster, a man whose heart is as big as his body and whose love goes out like his voice when he stands under the anointing of the spirit of God to open the Book and to lift up the Lord Jesus Christ.[37]

Perhaps the greatest similarity between the two men lies in the divine foreknowledge that each claims to possess regarding the eternal punishments and rewards which await humankind. In March 1982 United States Secretary of State Alexander Haig refused Paisley permission to enter the country. In response, Bob Jones junior, whose father had died in 1968, publicly announced he would pray for God's retribution on Haig: 'I am going to pray that God will get rid of that man.' At a chapel service in Bob Jones University, he described Haig as 'a monster in human flesh and a demon-possessed instrument to destroy America'. Perhaps, however, he experienced an element of self-doubt in the efficacy of his own prayers, for he called on the students to join him in these prayers: 'I hope you'll pray that the Lord will smite him, hip and thigh, bone and marrow, heart and lungs and all there is to him, that he will destroy him quickly and utterly.'[38]

Other Features and Structures

The Articles of Faith (reproduced in full in Appendix A) include a number of features which are distinctive of Free Presbyterianism.

Article 1, on 'The Absolute Authority and Divine Verbal Inspiration' of scripture, refers to the King James Authorised Version of 1611, the only translation permitted in Free Presbyterian churches. Other versions are not even regarded as new translations but as 'New Bibles' which form 'the Devil's strategy to destroy the Old Bible by a flood of counter-feits'.[39]

The explanation for this rigid stance lies in a distrust of the manuscripts found after 1611 which have sometimes been used by trans-lators when preparing revised English texts. Since one manuscript, *Codex Vaticanus,* was discovered in the Vatican Library at Rome, and another, *Codex Sinaiticus*, was found in a monastery in Sinai, these Roman Catholic and Orthodox associations mean that any possibility of having a genuine and reliable Bible has been eliminated. In contrast, it is argued, the Authorised Version was based on translations prepared at the time of the Reformation and has been instrumental in bringing about such miracles as the Reformation, the eighteenth-century evangelical revival, the birth of modern missions, and the great nineteenth-century revivals. No reference is made to the advice of John Wycliffe (1330–1384), the English reformer sometimes described as the 'Morning Star of the Reformation': 'Christ and his apostles taught the people in that tongue that was best known to them. Why should men not do so now?'

Baptism in the Free Presbyterian Church is distinctive in that it allows freedom of choice between the practice of baptising infants of believers or delaying the moment of baptism until adulthood and following the practice of believers' baptism. The reason given for this approach is that 'bitter controversy raging around the ordinance of Christian Baptism has divided the Body of Christ when that Body should have been united in Christian love'. This position is similar to the practice of the Church of North India, a uniting church of the 1960s which brought together churches from the Baptist, Anglican, Brethren, Disciples, Reformed and Methodist traditions. Without realising it, Paisley was in effect doing the same thing, though on a smaller scale, for he was trying to accommodate both Baptist – he himself came from the Baptist tradition – and Presbyterian practices. By accepting both baptismal practices, Paisley must have known he was distancing himself from Presbyterian discipline and ignoring the directions of the Westminster Confession of Faith which he professes to follow. It is strange that he should condemn Presbyterians for departing from the confession when he himself has so consistently disregarded it. In all my visits to Free Presbyterian churches, I never once witnessed the baptism of infants and I understand that it is seldom practised.

The sacrament of the Lord's Supper is observed monthly, or sometimes weekly, in the Free Presbyterian Church. Those who observe it weekly are closer in this regard to John Calvin's preferred custom in Geneva. In practice, however, the sacrament often seems to be a 'second service', following on after a great exodus of people have left the morning or evening service. This is, however, not dissimilar to what happens in a number of Protestant churches.

In terms of presbytery structures, continuity in office has been a particular characteristic of the Free Presbyterian Church, Ian Paisley having been moderator from the beginnings in Crossgar and John Douglas having been clerk since 1970. People like Mervyn Cotton complain that this unchanging state of affairs is not healthy for the church: 'I find it incredible to imagine how every year a group of men can vote in the same Moderator, the same deputy Moderator, the same Clerk of Presbytery, the same minute Clerk. And so we could go on down through all the offices of Presbytery.' How far this reflects feeling within the church is difficult to measure. Certainly I am not aware of any great wave of resentment. Douglas himself regards the election of Paisley as moderator each year as perfectly understandable: 'Presbytery elects him and it's due to his personal influence.... Of course in the history of the Church he has been to the fore in many things, especially in holding missions. He practically held missions in every church that we have if we look back far enough in time to the beginning of individual congregations.' Eric Smyth also defends Paisley's right to continue as moderator: 'Some people think that Ian Paisley is the boss. They say, "He's always Moderator!" He's the Moderator because people want him to be Moderator. At the Presbytery meetings Dr Paisley has stood down and said, "Look, if there's somebody else wants to take this position, please put them up. I don't mind. I've plenty to do." Nobody has done it!' But Douglas cannot forsee this kind of arrangement continuing after Paisley's death: 'It may well be that when his time on earth is at an end that the Church may routinely adopt the position of giving a Moderator a limited period in office. I'm only hazarding a guess, for who can predict what lies in the future.'

On average each church is represented by about three or four elders, bringing the total membership of presbytery to around 300. Of these it is estimated that 250 would attend monthly – a satisfactory record by any standards.

Church choirs do not exist in Free Presbyterianism, for reasons which possibly go back to the difficulties faced by both Ian and his father in their relationships with choirs. However, soloists and family group instrumentalists and singers occasionally assist in the worship. By far the most noted of their singers is Magherafelt minister and Mid-Ulster MP William McCrea, whose fame as a gospel singer is recognised beyond Ireland, particularly in the United States.

One of the first things a stranger will notice on entering a Free Presbyterian church is that the women and girls are wearing some form of head covering – hats for women and sometimes berets for girls. There are a few places where the practice is not uniformly observed, but this is usually outside Northern Ireland; at Oulton Broad, for example, most of the ladies are hatless. Thus most Free Presbyterians follow the literal teaching of 1 Corinthians 11:2-16, believing that the custom advocated by the apostle Paul in the first century is applicable for all time. Indeed, Michael Barrett, professor at Bob Jones University and assistant minister in the Greenville, South Carolina, Free Presbyterian Church, declares: 'Failure to comply with the requirement not only constitutes apparent rebellion against God's order, but it degrades the woman herself.'[40] The practice is intrinsically linked, he suggests, with the subordinate role and function of women in relation to men: 'If women exercise their right to worship without a covering upon their heads, they disgrace their head, man.' In Free Presbyterian thinking, therefore, this authoritative position for men is understood as built into God's initial purpose in creation: 'In God's order, man has a position of authority over the woman. This is true not only in the marriage relationship, but in the relationship everywhere.' The same reasoning prohibits women from becoming elders or preachers, though I have some difficulty in understanding how the rule on preaching was never applied to Isabella Paisley, Ian's mother.

William McCrea attributes his conversion to Mrs Paisley's preaching:

On the fourteenth of September 1969, I was invited by a friend to attend a Sunday night service at Magherafelt Free Presbyterian Church. I had heard much talk about this church but had never been before. I agreed to attend this service which was conducted by Dr Paisley's late mother. It was an experience I will never forget. I had never been in such a place before, it was just an old tin hall; and as they were putting on an extension, the roof was tied down with tarpaulin. As it was a very windy night this had to be held down with ropes. We had to sit on bales of straw, but it was a meeting I will never forget. I heard the gospel preached for the first time in my life. Mrs Paisley spoke on 'Hell', and the Lord really spoke to my heart that night. At the end of the service I knelt down at a bale of straw and asked the Lord Jesus Christ into my heart.[41]

Did Isabella Paisley have some role as a roving evangelist and preacher? John Douglas's comment on the Free Presbyterian attitude to the part which a woman can take in worship may partly explain the dilemma: 'We don't go as far as the Brethren and say, "Women have no ministry." A lady can give a testimony in the service or pray in the service. A lady missionary can come and take a service and will do so from time to time.'

While a variety of practice exists in Free Presbyterian circles as regards the various Christian festivals, it is fair to say that they are generally reluctant to celebrate Christmas, Easter or Pentecost in similar fashion to other Christian churches. At Christmas time there may be a few Free Presbyterian churches which have a carol service, but it is not common. Christmas Day service is never held. There is very little written on Free Presbyterian attitudes to Christian festivals, but one rare article, '5 Reasons why Christians Should not Observe "Christmas"', states, 'The Bible does not reveal the date of Christ's birth – not even the month is given; nor do we have biblical precedent for observing such a day. The Galatians were soundly rebuked for observing days.'[42] The writer goes on to suggest that observing Christmas would bring Christians into fellowship with unbelievers. 'For God's people to participate in this Babylonish holiday is to be "unequally yoked with unbelievers" who also celebrate the birthday of Christ.'

Despite this advice, Free Presbyterians enjoy their Christmas dinners. In 1977 Ian Paisley and some others faced charges relating to disturbances in Ballymena during the May strike. When the December court hearing was postponed until the following February, Paisley joked, 'At least I can have Christmas dinner at home!'[43] Groups at Martyrs' Memorial would on occasions go out together for a Christmas dinner, and Paisley himself uses the season of Christmas as a time to give presents to workers in the church. However, the spiritual preparation of the season of Lent is not observed, and the same is true of Holy Week, including Good Friday. On Easter Sunday some ministers might preach on the theme of the Resurrection, but again it is not common. The festival of Pentecost is not observed at all.

Free Prebyterians are adamant that there is no structural link between the Free Presbyterian Church and the moderator's Democratic Unionist Party. Kyle Paisley explains:

I couldn't say for definite that all the ministers of the Free Presbyterian Church were members of the DUP. Or all the elders in the Free Presbyterian Church were members of the DUP. Quite a lot of them would be. But it's not because there's an integral link between the DUP and the Free Presbyterian Church. There's a link in the sense that the Moderator of the Church is Leader of the DUP, but there's not an integral link, or any rule which says if you're a minister of the Free Presbyterian Church you have to be a DUP supporter.

While there are no structural links, the fact remains that at election times Free Presbyterians pray openly for DUP candidates. As elections approach, Paisley makes no apology for emphasising the perils facing the country and the need for people to make every effort to destroy the devil's subtle plans. No one needs to think too long to know which party he believes will defend Ulster and stand up for God! News is given on how a group of people are working hard for the local candidate or some other candidate, and the implication is that a few more enthusiastic helpers would make all the difference in getting the candidate elected. People are invited to wait behind after the service for a time of prayer to intercede for God's intervention 'at this critical time'. These times of prayer are exclusively devoted to praying that God will defeat their opponents and bring victory to DUP candidates. Kyle acknowledges that this happens:

That would be because a lot of people back home would feel that the DUP would be the party to defend Ulster when it came to a crisis. So it is in one sense party political but in another sense it's for the sake of the country that they're praying.... I would pray for a candidate first of all because he's a believer; secondly, because he has the interest of the country at heart; thirdly, because of his party link.

In his father's mind there is no confusion as regards which leader and which party stands for God and Ulster. Addressing the first World Congress of Fundamentalists at Edinburgh on 15 June 1976, he declared:

When I first fought in North Antrim, we had in our country large groups of people – the Reformed Presbyterian, the Brethren, and other groups – who never voted. I am glad to tell you that today they are voting. They cast their votes because they know that it is essential that a Christian, not one of the devil's crowd, represent them in the parliamentary arena. At our last Convention elections there were more born-again people elected than ever were elected before in the history of Northern Ireland. It is good to see Fundamentalists getting into the political arena and taking their stand right down the line for God's truth and God's righteousness.[44]

Paisley's theological separatism also extends to the area of education. Speaking at the Edinburgh fundamentalist conference, he also set out his manifesto on education: 'The government is interfering more and more in our personal lives. Here in Britain we have interference in our educational system. We are not blessed with Christian schools, as you are in the United States of America; and I feel that as Fundamentalists in this country we need to get into Christian education. We have failed in this matter. Our children who attend a Fundamentalist church on Sunday have to spend weekdays under the tutelage of evolution teachers, under teachers who repudiate Jesus Christ and deny the Bible.'[45] By the 1980s Paisley had introduced his idea into Northern Ireland, and to date there are five small Free Presbyterian schools, each providing primary level education and some attempting to cover the secondary level requirements. But it has been a costly venture because government regulations for funding church schools have not been met and the Free Presbyterian Church has had to finance each entire project: staffing arrangements, buildings and maintenance.

So what does the future hold for the Free Presbyterian Church of Ulster? The question has obviously been on Ian Paisley's mind, and he sees no reason why he should conceal his personal hopes for the future. The same day in 1981 that he shared with the Crossgar congregation his prophecy that the next thirty years would be the greatest they have ever witnessed, he also dropped a hint as to how this would happen: 'John Hume said to me, one day in Europe, "When you die, your Church will die." I replied, "You are a fool. When I die, God will send some young Joshua to lead us into the promised land. That is what will happen." I said, "It is nothing to do with me. It is to do with Almighty God."'

Chapter Seven

The Road to Stormont 1946–1970

IAN PAISLEY HAS always been a political animal. Finlay Holmes tells of an occasion in 1954 when he was travelling by train and ferry from Belfast to London via Larne – Stranraer. Changing at Stranraer he happened to meet Paisley, who was very friendly, and so the two of them chatted together for rest of the journey. Paisley indicated he was going to London for a meeting of the National Union of Protestants and would be returning that evening to Belfast. As Holmes had made similar arrangements, they agreed to meet on the train for the return journey. In the evening, before Paisley appeared, Holmes met an old friend, Joe Lyttle, who had been a major in the army, captain of cricket at Trinity College, Dublin, and was at that time teaching classics at Campbell College, Belfast. As Lyttle was not altogether 'gospel greedy' by reputation, Holmes was a little apprehensive as to how he and Paisley would get on together on the journey back. He need not have worried. Lyttle and Paisley soon discovered they shared a mutual interest in politics, particularly unionist politics. At one stage on the journey, Holmes managed to get a brief word with Lyttle on his own.

'You know who that is, of course?' Holmes enquired of Lyttle, and then went on to explain about Paisley's notoriety over recent events in Crossgar and elsewhere.

'No, I thought he was another Presbyterian minister like yourself!' said Lyttle. And then he added, 'But I'll tell you what he is, he's a first class Unionist politician *manqué*!' The last that Holmes saw of Lyttle and Paisley was of the two of them speeding off together in a taxi from the 'old' LMS railway station at York Street, Belfast – and they were still talking politics.

This consuming interest in politics is, however, shaped and controlled by Paisley's unique brand of separatist fundamentalist theology. It is his theological convictions which dominate his perspective on life. While politics have taken up a large amount of his time and his appetite for the political scene has not diminished in the slightest, at the end of the day it is only the instrument through which he seeks

to implement his theological beliefs and goals. His analysis of the
Northern Ireland conflict in an article, 'Who is Our Enemy?', published
in the *Protestant Telegraph* on 15 June 1974, just after the Ulster
Workers' Council Strike which brought down the power-sharing executive headed by Brian Faulkner, is, in a sense, timeless in its explanation of his perception of the relationship between theology and politics:

There are those who mistakenly analyse the Ulster situation in terms of
social and economic factors, in terms of politics, or philosophies. These
theories and analyses collapse because they ignore, deliberately or otherwise, the main key, and to us the most obvious factor: Protestantism versus
popery. The war in Ulster is a war of survival between the opposing forces
of Truth and Error, and the principles of the Reformation are as relevant
today in Ulster as they were in Europe in the sixteenth century.[1]

Approaching his seventieth birthday, he expressed this priority and
supremacy of theology over politics in another way: 'I'd give up politics
before the pulpit.'[2]

These twin interests in theology and politics found an outlet a few
weeks after his appointment as minister of Ravenhill Evangelical
Mission Church. Paisley began to channel his energies into establishing
an Irish base for the National Union of Protestants, an organisation set
up in England in 1942 to combat what were perceived as high church
and Roman Catholic tendencies in the Church of England. Paisley was
elected treasurer and Norman Porter, a Baptist pastor, secretary of the
Irish branch. Before long, anxious to focus the movement on issues
considered more relevant to the local situation, the two men secured
the agreement of the parent organisation that the Irish branch should
be autonomous. Concerns that dominated the movement had one thing
in common – protecting and maintaining Protestant interests or, as some
might perceive it, 'Protestant supremacy'. They called for vigilance in
a number of areas: maintenance of the Protestant monarchy and
Constitution, the danger of Catholics buying up Protestant properties
or occupying jobs vacated by Protestants, and 'over-generous' government grants to Catholic schools and institutions. Ever since the setting
up of the Northern Ireland state, Protestants generally had been sensitive to anything which might confirm their conviction that 'Home Rule
was Rome Rule' and they never felt there was any shortage of evidence
to support their argument. For example, the controversy in the Republic
over the 1950 'Mother and Child Bill' was seen as substantiating their
case against the kind of undue interference by the Roman Catholic
Church hierarchy which would ensue if partition were ever abandoned.
Dr Noel Browne, then minister of health in the Republic's Coalition

government, had introduced a scheme which, among other things, would provide free maternity care and education in child-bearing. The hierarchy intervened on 10 October by writing to Mr Costello, the taoiseach, suggesting that the state was not competent to deal with matters they believed were more the business of the church, namely, questions relating to sexual relationships, chastity and marriage; secondly, they objected to the proposed extension of the state medical service. When Dr Browne refused to withdraw his bill, he had to resign from office. Other instances, in which it was alleged that colporteurs in the Republic had been assaulted, were also cited as examples of the kind of intolerance which Protestants could expect in an all-Ireland republic.

These were the kind of cases to which the National Union of Protestants and other organisations drew attention, but Protestants, with a few exceptions, generally appeared to be either unaware or unapologetic about intolerance or injustice on their own doorstep. Dennis P. Barritt, a former company secretary to a linen firm, and Charles F. Carter, professor of applied economics at the Queen's University of Belfast until 1959, when he moved to the chair of political economy at Manchester University, were two of these exceptions. Their 1962 publication, *The Northern Ireland Problem*, was unusual in that two distinguished Protestants were actually daring to raise questions about Protestant injustices, albeit within the context of examining possible shortcomings in both sections of the Northern Ireland community.[3] One of the injustices highlighted had to do with the local government electoral arrangements, especially as they applied to Londonderry. In examining charges of 'gerrymandering', they pointed out that Protestants constituted about 41 per cent of the voting age population in the city and yet held a twelve to eight majority on the corporation. Apart from the different rules which qualified a person to vote in local government elections – a basic property qualification for 'husbands and spouses' which considerably reduced the number of voters eligible in comparison to voters in parliamentary elections – Unionists had redrawn the electoral wards in the city in such a manner that they secured a majority in two of the wards, North and Waterside, thereby giving them a working majority on the corporation.[4]

Barritt and Carter also examined charges of discrimination in employment, drawing attention to the results of their research into the religious affiliation of those appointed to the higher grades of the civil service in 1959:[5]

Grade	Protestant	Catholic	% Protestant
Permanent Secretaries	7		100
Second & Asst. Secretaries	36	2	95
Principals	103	4	96
Deputy & Asst. Principals	199	17	92
Staff Officers	349	23	94
All persons covered	694	46	94

It was acknowledged that this imbalance in Protestant/Catholic employment was not evident in the 'imperial' civil service where the proportion of Catholics employed in all grades of these services varied: 33 per cent in the Inland Revenue, 33-40 per cent in Customs and Excise, and 50-55 per cent in the Post Office.

Questions of gerrymandering in local government elections and inequality in employment opportunities were far from Ian Paisley's mind. The wrongs he perceived in Northern Ireland society, in his opinion, were quite the reverse, for it was Ulster's Protestant heritage, he declared, that was being threatened by the government's attitude of capitulation towards the Roman Catholic Church. In August 1955 he railed against the £300,000 funding of a Roman Catholic Boys' Training School by the Northern Ireland Ministry of Home Affairs: 'We also understand that a Roman Catholic Chapel is included in the plans approved. This is yet another act of base betrayal by our Unionist Government, and constitutes a subsidising of the enemies of Ulster, and is beyond the bounds of reason. It is surely time our Government was called to give an account of their stewardship.'[6]

Paisley's separatist theology and domineering personality inevitably had repercussions in the area of personal relationships. Most of these rows centred around his attitude to other members of the Orange Order, which was later to prove a major handicap in his bid for ultimate political power. The problem first surfaced when, subsequent to the formation of the Free Presbyterian Church of Ulster, the Grand Lodge of Ireland received a request that its ministers be recognised as eligible to hold the post of clerical chaplain. The Grand Lodge had always had a list of churches whose ministers were recognised as eligible for election as chaplains, and the Free Presbyterian Church of Ulster was simply asking that its name be added to the list. Paisley had already proven himself a popular speaker among many rank and file Orangemen, but his charge of apostasy against Protestant churches and his outspoken attacks on their ministers, including Orangemen, were felt by some to hit at the heart of 'brotherly kindness and charity' which every member is expected to possess before being accepted.[7] Understandably, the Grand Lodge felt obliged to enquire if Free Presbyterian Church of Ulster ministers were prepared to be in full Christian fellowship with other clerical chaplains in the order. Would they recognise them as 'brothers in Christ' and show them the respect which, they maintained, presently existed? No reply to this enquiry was ever received, and so the matter lapsed. I am told that a similar application from the Free Presbyterian Church of Ulster was received two or three years ago, and the same procedures were followed, with the same result.[8]

The issue of brotherly love surfaced in a more personal way in 1958 when Paisley rounded on the Revd Warren Porter, chaplain of the Mountpottinger Lodge. Porter had been a minister in the Irish Evangelical Church before joining Irish Presbyterianism and regarded himself as a friend of Paisley, but to his surprise he found himself accused in *The Revivalist* of being a 'time-server' who 'like Lot... began pitching his tent towards Sodom before he went to reside in the Sodom of Irish Presbyterian apostasy'.[9] Porter challenged Paisley about the article and asked him if he was prepared to face the charge of 'unbrotherly conduct' within the lodge. Paisley refused to discuss the matter that night and subsequently transferred to a Shankill Road (Belfast) Lodge before leaving the order altogether in 1962. The confrontation with Warren Porter had not been his first with other Orangemen. In 1950 both he and Norman Porter had lambasted the Belfast Corporation transport committee, and in particular its chairman, Senator Joseph Cunningham, for permitting the advertising of alcoholic drinks on its buses and trams. Cunningham also happened to be the Belfast County Grand Master and was not impressed with the manner in which Paisley had presented his case. Summoned before a rather stormy meeting of the county Grand Lodge, they were unrepentant and only narrowly avoided being expelled.

Norman Porter himself was another casualty in the list of broken relationships between Paisley and his colleagues. Ian had lodged with Norman's parents when he was a student at the Reformed Presbyterian Theological Hall and this alone should have been good reason for cementing the relationship between the two men. Clifford Smyth in *Ian Paisley, Voice of Protestant Ulster*, suggests two reasons why the friendship disintegrated.[10] Apparently at some stage Paisley invited Porter to be a minister in his developing Free Presbyterian Church, and it was Porter's refusal which led to repercussions throughout the National Union of Protestants. The explanation appears very plausible because it is known that in the early fifties Paisley approached quite a number

of people in the hope that they would become Free Presbyterian ministers. By this time Porter not only disagreed with Paisley's extreme
separatism but, according to Smyth, 'harboured reservations about Ian
Paisley's authoritarian personality and his arbitrary way of doing things'.

The vice-president of the National Union of Protestants, Eric
Borland, an Orangeman and Presbyterian minister from Bangor, also
broke his links with Paisley. The Revd Martin Smyth, at present the
Official Unionist MP for South Belfast and grand master of the Orange
Order, has described how, after the split at Crossgar, Borland
challenged Paisley about his attitude to other Presbyterian ministers.

At the committee meeting they were discussing these things and Borland
challenged Paisley: 'Am I hearing you right, Ian? You're saying that if any
of us would have any trouble you would come down to try to capitalise on
that trouble to build up your cause?' And Paisley said he would. Then says
Eric, 'Any of us in the ministry can have differences of opinion with our
congregations at any time and for any reason, but I have to say I can no
longer work with you if that's your attitude to brother ministers.'[11]

In the autumn of 1956 Paisley and others were instrumental in the
formation of Ulster Protestant Action, viewed by commentators of this
period as a potentially militant response to the anticipated IRA
campaign which in fact materialised by the end of the year. Outright
condemnation of the campaign by the Roman Catholic Church
hierarchy did little to alleviate Protestant fears, but swift government
reaction on both sides of the border – including the introduction of
internment – and the absence of substantial nationalist support largely
restricted the campaign to the border areas of Fermanagh, Tyrone and
Derry. Ulster Protestant Action (UPA), the name of the new organisation, would have brought chilling reminders of the paramilitary organisation of the same name which existed in the troubled decade of the
twenties. Also involved with Paisley in the UPA were people whose
names were to become familiar in the life of the province: a young
lawyer, Desmond Boal, who played a large part in drawing up its constitution; Johnny McQuade, a former British army Chindit from the
Shankill Road; and Billy Spence, a timekeeper in Belfast Corporation's
transport department, who, along with his brother, Gusty, was later
associated with the Ulster Volunteer Force of the mid-1960s. It was
this group, with its largely working–class anti-establishment orientation,
which provided Paisley with his second experience of life 'on the
hustings' when they decided to support the candidature of Albert Duff,
superintendent of an independent gospel mission in the Sandy Row area
of Belfast, in contesting the Stormont parliamentary seat of Iveagh

against the sitting member, Brian Maginess, the attorney-general. Paisley's first foray into the election scene had been in 1949 when he succesfully managed a campaign for Tommy Cole, already Unionist MP at Westminster for East Belfast, who was standing for the Dock division in the Stormont elections of that year. Cole's opponent on that occasion had been Hugh Downey, a Catholic barman from West Belfast who was campaigning on a Labour ticket, but Paisley ignored the social issues and centred it on the questions of religion and the constitution. This time it was Unionist against Unionist, Maginess representing the Ulster Unionist Party and Duff standing as an Independent Unionist. This did not deter Paisley from introducing a sectarian side to the contest! Maginess's Protestant credentials, it was suggested, were suspect because he was married to a Catholic! Unionism, he concluded, was failing to protect its heritage.

Fortunately for Maginess, Lord Brookeborough, the prime minister, came to the rescue and reminded audiences of his own impeccable unionist credentials. The fact that he, Brookeborough, was supporting Maginess as the Ulster Unionist Party candidate was presented as proof that Maginess would never betray Ulster, and this was sufficient to convince the electorate that he should be returned.

These experiences had whetted Paisley's political appetite and brought him into contact with the cut and thrust of Irish electioneering. He enjoyed the excitement of the hustings, and he enjoyed the intro- duction into the corridors of power which it all brought. His own reminiscences of these early political encounters reveal the new sense of status he believed he had found:

I first came to Belfast in 1946 to become the minister of the congregation that I still pastor, and shortly after that I took a leading hand in organising a Branch of the National Union of Protestants which was a very strong Protestant organisation, having its base in London. One of the leading members of the Council of Reference of that organisation was Dr James Lyttle MP who was the MP for County Down. At that time he sat as an Independent Unionist. So through that contact I went to Stormont, and I was introduced to many of the members of the House by Mr Norman Porter who was himself an Independent Unionist, and by a Mr Thomas Cole who eventually became the MP for Dock. I happened to be his election agent when he won that seat in Dock.[12]

Even at this early stage he was beginning to make his mark on the local political scene. He was forcefully articulating his own particular interpretation of the link between constitutional questions and the well- being of Protestantism. He believed that it represented the traditional

Unionist position and he was determined to convince others that he was right. The next decade would give the first indication of his success in spreading this religio-political gospel.

O'Neill Must Go!

The world of the late fifties and early sixties was much the better for the five remaining years of the life of a rather portly, warm-hearted Italian, Angelo Roncalli, better known as John XXIII. Little did the College of Cardinals realise when they elected him pope in October 1958 that this little man would in a short space of time win the hearts of millions both within the Catholic communion and outside it. More importantly but not unrelated to this, he would set in motion by his convoking of the Second Vatican Council (1962-1965), the ecclesiastical machinery which would effectively transform the Catholic Church, particularly in its relationships with other Christian communions. Born of peasant farmers, Roncalli had been a Vatican diplomat for most of his priesthood, spending a large part of it representing his church in countries where it formed a minority communion in comparison to other larger churches, particularly the Orthodox Church. The experience had enriched his life and made him more open to others, a fact which was quickly discerned by most.

The impact that he made on the Christian and non-Christian world and the spirit of optimism that the deliberations of the council initiated formed part of the world scene when Captain Terence O'Neill succeeded Lord Brookeborough as prime minister of Northern Ireland on 25 March 1963. O'Neill was not unaffected by this thawing of relationships between Catholics and Protestants, and the first sign of the new line he would take was, strangely enough, on the occasion of the pontiff's death, 3 June 1963. O'Neill sent and published a letter of condolence to Cardinal Conway at Armagh, an action apparently unprecedented at that time. In similar vein the lord mayor of Belfast had the Union flag over the City Hall flown at half mast.

O'Neill was proud of the fact that his family roots were deep in European and Irish history. In his autobiography he explains: 'According to Burke's Peerage, the O'Neill family is the oldest traceable family left in Europe, but unfortunately, and for the record, we are only descended from this ancient lineage through the female line.... There are, however, very few families in these islands who can produce an unbroken descent through the male line, not least our Royal family.'[13] Most of his male ancestors had been either clergymen or politicians, his father and grandfather both at some stage being Unionist MPs for Mid-

Antrim at Westminster. His father had drilled the Unionist Volunteers in the Ballymena area and had loyally supported Edward Carson and the Ulster Unionists. Tragically his father was killed in action in the First World War, the first MP to be killed in the war, when young Terence was only three months old. O'Neill himself enlisted with his brother in the Irish Guards in the Second World War. His 'Ulster Unionist' pedigree, therefore, was unparalleled – indeed, the legend connected with the Red Hand of Ulster which forms part of the Northern Ireland coat of arms is based on the O'Neill family history – but few were to remember this when he tried to introduce change in Unionist perceptions and to bring Unionism, however late in the day, into the twentieth century. O'Neill later acknowledged the gargantuan task he had set himself: 'It is one thing for Mr Macmillan to talk of a wind of change blowing on another continent; but a very different matter when you have to initiate the change yourself and try to drag behind you a reactionary and reluctant party which has been in power since 1921.'[14]

O'Neill's letter to the Cardinal and the fact that he had it published was a clear indication that he wanted to be known as a prime minister who was concerned about the feelings and needs of every section of the Northern Ireland community. However, both the letter and the lord mayor's action of flying the Union Jack at half mast infuriated Paisley, who responded by calling a special rally at the Ulster Hall under the auspices of the National Union of Protestants which he now entirely controlled. He described O'Neill, and the Protestant church leaders who had also sent condolences, as 'the Iscariots of Ulster' and assured his audience that 'this Romish man of sin is now in Hell'.[15] Then he led his supporters in an impromptu march to the City Hall to protest against the lowering of the Union Jack. His action was illegal because the required forty-eight hours prior notice to the police had not been given, and he was summoned to appear in court on 25 July. This was his second court appearance, the first being in 1957 when he was summonsed for making a public disturbance in Donaghadee, County Down. He attempted to make capital out of the situation by packing the courthouse with his supporters and handling his own defence. He was fined £10 and given a week to either pay or go to jail for two months. Much to his annoyance someone paid the fine and deprived him of his apparent wish to be known as a martyr for 'Protestantism and Ulster'.

In the autumn of 1964 Paisley was again incensed by the flying of a flag, this time a small Irish tricolour, which was displayed by Sinn Féin in a window of their election headquarters in Divis Street in West Belfast. A Westminster election had been called and four candidates were contesting the West Belfast seat: Billy Boyd, Northern Ireland Labour Party; Harry Diamond, Republican Labour; Liam McMillen, Sinn Féin; and Jim Kilfedder, Unionist. With so many candidates to split the vote, there was the possibility that if Unionist voters rallied to the polls, Kilfedder could win. The flying of the tricolour in itself was not illegal, but it could be banned if the police considered that it could lead to a breach of the peace. On other occasions the police had been content to take no action; Paisley, however, was determined that the flag should be removed! At an Ulster Hall rally on Sunday, 27 September, he threatened to march on Divis Street and remove the offending flag himself if the police did not take action. Gerry Adams, a teenager at the time and now Sinn Féin president, tells how the incident aroused the curiosity of his schoolmates:

In 1964 when carefree and sleepy-headed I noticed on the way to school a tricolour displayed in a shop in Divis Street, just down from Percy Street opposite St Comgall's School. That evening a character, better known now than then, by name of Paisley, threatened to march on Divis Street and remove the offending flag. Our curiosity, further aroused by a warning from our Christian Brother teachers to go straight home and not dilly-dally in Divis Street, led dozens of us to gather and peer into the window of what we were to discover was a Sinn Féin election office. Further encouragement was supplied by the RUC who sledge-hammered their way into the premises and seized the flag. It was with some satisfaction, therefore, the following day that we witnessed a large crowd replacing it, an occasion for a most defiant rendering of *Amhrán na bhFian* and the subject of some schoolboy speculation upon what would happen next.[16]

   The riots that followed have been described as the worst that the city had experienced for thirty years. Because the police had acted, Paisley had called off his march to Divis Street and held a victory rally instead at the City Hall. But the threat to take action himself had set in train a sequence of events which did nothing to improve relationships between the two communities, Catholic and Protestant, nationalist and loyalist. Michael Farrell's account of the riots state that the situation had deteriorated so much by the Friday night that 350 RUC wearing military helmets and backed by armoured cars were called in to deal with the situation. Fifty civilians were taken to hospital, but no figures of injuries to the police – as there must have been – are recorded. The rioting even spead to Dublin where about a thousand demonstrators marched to the British embassy and stoned the gardaí protecting it.[17]

The week's events obviously had a significant effect on Adams, who soon found himself folding election manifestos; even though Liam McMillen lost his deposit and Jim Kilfedder won the seat, his political consciousness had been stirred.

In the build up and aftermath of the Divis Street riots there was some awakening of national consciousness and a few of us began to query, with candid curiosity, the state of the nation. We were puzzled by our description in official forms as British subjects and wondered as we passed the customs posts on our way to Bun Beag for a summer in the Gaeltacht what actually the border was. We were beginning to get a sense of our essential Irishness, and events on the Falls Road served to whet our political appetites.

One can speculate that at some point, in his teens or later, Adams would have developed a fair degree of political awareness. He came from a Republican family and at some stage he would almost inevitably have been forced to examine his national identity. But the factor that is debatable is the nature of the convictions he would have eventually developed. Our experiences often influence the kind of convictions we form. In the light of Adams's own statement of the effect the riots had in relation to the awakening of his political consciousness, it is fair to assume that the unpleasant events of that week in early October did little to build up any measure of confidence in either the police or the state in which he lived. His earliest memories of the Protestant/Unionist community were significantly of a man called Paisley who 'threatened to march on Divis Street and remove the offending flag'. Experiences like this, and the accompanying violence, had all the potential for creating a retaliatory response.

Terence O'Neill was prepared to take political risks to further his conciliation policy, and the visit of the Republic's taoiseach, Sean Lemass, on 14 January 1965 was one of them. Arrangements for the visit had been made by civil servants whom he trusted and whom, it must be said, served him well. The wisdom or otherwise of his decision to keep his cabinet colleagues in the dark about his plans has long been debated. It is unlikely that cabinet approval would have been given had it been consulted – his predecessor had always insisted that the Republic would have to drop its territorial claims to Northern Ireland implicit in Articles Two and Three of its Constitution – so O'Neill had to weigh up the possible benefits that would accrue from such a visit against the inevitable sense of distrust that cabinet members would feel at being excluded from prior consultation.

Paisley's response to the visit was predictable. The following day he and his colleagues staged a protest at Stormont carrying placards suggesting O'Neill's complicity in betraying the country: 'No Mass, No Lemass', 'Down with the Lundys', and 'IRA Murderer Welcomed at Stormont'. Paisley challenged O'Neill to test the support for his policy by calling an election: 'By breaking your word and by acting without consulting the elected representatives of the Protestants of our country, you have adopted the tactics of a dictator and forfeited your right to be Prime Minister. We challenge you to go to the country on this issue. Surely the people have a right to a say in this grave departure from the stand of your predecessors in office.'[18]

The following month O'Neill accepted Lemass's invitation to Dublin, and Paisley stepped up his campaign further by leading a protest march on 25 February from the City Hall to the Unionist Party headquarters in Glengall Street, Belfast. I was an observer at this demonstration, which packed every inch of ground outside the Unionist offices, and will never forget the intense feeling of hostility – combining both anti-Catholicism and anti-O'Neillism, the latter because O'Neill refused to engage in the former – which swept the crowd that night as Paisley spoke. Paisley's skill in whipping up deeply held prejudices and making people believe that these same prejudices were actually divinely held rights was very evident. He attacked O'Neill for initiating the cross-border talks. Frequently inaccurate in his historical references, he warned his audience that the glorious heritage of Ulster's Protestantism was being betrayed and called on them to stand fast in the hour of crisis: 'We will stand where our fathers stood. We are the people who have a great and glorious heritage. We will not be moved.'[19] Placards carried by his supporters had the same message: 'O'Neill Welcomed in Dublin by Ulster's Would-be Destroyer', 'No Welcome for him in Sandy Row', and 'King William Crossed the Boyne to Save Us – O'Neill Crossed it to Sell Us'. Was O'Neill beginning to feel the pressure of Paisley's persistent abuse? Both the Grand Lodge and the Ulster Unionist Council gave him a vote of confidence, but he must have reflected on the size of the task that lay ahead of him. The disappointment he expressed in the low measure of support received from Protestant clergy for his cross-border initiatives may indicate the sense of isolation which he was increasingly experiencing: 'With a few shining exceptions, the Protestant clergy were too frightened to give a welcome to the meeting in case they offended some of their flock.'[20]

Paisley was not prepared for an election challenge in November 1965 when O'Neill responded to his suggestion and sought the people's approval of his cross-border policies. He freely canvassed support from both Catholic and Protestant homes and was proud of the fact that here too he was breaking new ground in the pattern of Northern Ireland politics: 'In both I had a tremendous reception. No previous Prime Minister of Northern Ireland had canvassed in Catholic houses for Unionist votes.'[21] But he may have been too optimistic about his party's manifesto, overlooking the fact that he had a long way to go, especially in the area of civil rights, if he was to effectively transform the nature of Northern Ireland society: 'Our manifesto could have stood inspection in any country in the world; for the first time it had no sectarian overtones or undertones.' When the election results came through, O'Neill was delighted: 'We swept the country to a degree which surprised everyone.' But it was the last Stormont election he would enjoy with Paisley remaining on the sidelines. Soon he too would be going to the people for endorsement of his manifesto, which would contain, however thinly disguised, his particular uncompromising anti-Catholic and anti-Republican version of Unionism.

The years 1966-1970 were some of the most momentous and significant years in Northern Ireland's history, and few would dispute the fact that it was the figure of Ian Paisley, more than any other, who dominated its events. Throughout this period Northern Ireland gradually witnessed a breakdown in law and order and, at the same time, the rise of Paisley's political fortunes and popularity. Any serious assessment of him during this period must consider whether or not he contributed to this gradual decline in law and order and, secondly, if it was this breakdown in law and order which led to his growing popularity. Paisley's continuing campaign against O'Neill, which soon led to the premier's resignation, and his election as Bannside MP at Stormont in 1970 are central to this investigation. However, they can only be considered in relation to three other features: the emergence of the Ulster Volunteer Force (UVF) in 1966, reviving the title of the Volunteer Force established in 1912 under Edward Carson to fight Home Rule; the Northern Ireland Civil Rights Association (NICRA) formed in February 1967; and the December 1969 IRA split into the Provisional and Official IRA.

Paisley's three months imprisonment in 1966 for unwillingness to be bound over to keep the peace following disturbances outside the Presbyterian General Assembly in June brought an upsurge of interest in his church and his politics. The whole year was a high point for him. Earlier in the year he had attacked the government's refusal to ban Republican parades marking the fiftieth anniversary of the 1916 Easter Rising in Dublin. Paisley claimed: 'Over Easter the soil of Ulster was desecrated by the rebels.'[22] He took two significant new steps to bolster up his campaign against O'Neill and simultaneously further his own political career now that he had decided some day in the future to throw his hat into the ring and stand for Parliament: firstly, he established a fortnightly newspaper, the *Protestant Telegraph*; secondly, he formed the Ulster Constitution Defence Committee (UCDC), which would control a very active counter-demonstration force, the Ulster Protestant Volunteers (UPV).

Like *The Revivalist*, his church magazine first published in 1955, the *Protestant Telegraph* carried a number of religiously orientated items, particularly anti-Catholic propaganda, but the main stories concentrated on perceived political perils which Paisley felt were facing the province. He had been concerned about unfavourable editorial comments in the *Belfast Telegraph* - which clearly sought to influence public opinion in favour of O'Neill – so he now used his own paper to hit back at its proprietors, the Thompson organisation, and its journalists. An article entitled 'Probing His Mind', published in one of the earliest issues, poked fun at Martin Wallace, political editor of the *Belfast Telegraph*:

I had the privilege the other evening of meeting the eminent journalist, Mr Warpedin Mallace, and I took the opportunity to ask him a few questions: 'Mr Mallace, I suppose you consider yourself to be Ulster's most forward looking newspaper columnist?' 'Well, things being the way they are in the province,' he said, leaning forward with that earnest-my-mind look which sent such a rosy ecumenical glow over his cherubic features that it caused his yellow and gold rimmed spectacles to steam up, 'I consider it to be my bounden duty as a liberal, intellectual know-all to present the truth as I would like it to be. After all, with a mind like mine' (it is not for nothing that his colleagues call him Big-Head) 'I am equipped to present a fair and balanced analysis of the situation, acceptable to all, from Cardinal Conway down.' 'But Mr Mallace, are your articles and viewpoints not a little one-sided? I mean, despite the fact that you are such a good, Border-abolishing, home-loving ecumenic, could you not spare a little good-will to the... ah... so-called extremists of the North? I will not mention any names, as I have heard it brings on your billious attacks, and I do not want Ulster to miss, even for a little while, your warped, I mean your worthy column.'[23]

From the outset the paper announced it would strain every nerve in combating the treachery and betrayal which it alleged afflicted the province and it expected its readers to do the same:

To the task of combating the combined forces of Tyranny in our Province, this paper has dedicated itself. Not with tongue in cheek, nor with kid gloves will we fight this battle. Giving no quarter and begging for none, we enter the conflict confident that the God of battles will enable us to defend the Right. We invite every true and faithful Protestant to make this paper their paper, and so ensure for the coming generation the same liberties which our fathers bequeathed to us.

And continuing in the same militant mood which claimed to have divine approval, it declared: 'As Christ died to make men holy we shall fight to make men free while God is marching on.'[24]

Noel Doherty, Paisley's printer for both the *Protestant Telegraph* and *The Revivalist,* assisted for a time in creating another propaganda structure, the Ulster Constitution Defence Committee and its subsidiary, the Ulster Protestant Volunteers. The UCDC had a membership of twelve and acted as the executive body for the UPV. Ian Paisley was chairman and Doherty secretary. The UPV was organised into divisions which could be formed in any area once a nucleus of twelve members had been accepted and constituted by the UCDC. Roman Catholics, or anyone who had ever been a Roman Catholic, were not eligible for membership. Nor were serving members of the RUC. Members wore red, white and blue sashes, paraded with flags and bands and, as Clifford Smyth has suggested, 'provided Paisley with an alternative loyalist institution to Orangeism'.[25] The constitution of the UCDC and UPV described it as 'one united society of Protestant patriots' who were 'pledged by all lawful methods to uphold and maintain the Constitution of Northern Ireland as an integral part of the United Kingdom as long as the United Kingdom maintains a Protestant monarchy and the terms of the Revolution Settlement'.[26] However, while members were warned that anyone 'associated with, or giving support, to any subversive or lawless activities whatsoever shall be expelled from the body', the possiblility was not ruled out that the time might come when 'the authorities act contrary to the Consititution'. In such a doomsday situation it was significant that the society, to which members pledged their *first* loyalty, would take 'whatever steps it thinks fit to expose such unconstitutional acts'. Obviously, this placed great power in the hands of the chairman of the committee who was responsible for guiding the committee as to when doomsday had arrived. In such a scenario the fact that a member's first loyalty was to the society and, by implication, to Paisley, the potential for absolute personal power was not excluded. The Cameron Commission, appointed in March 1969 to investigate the causes of civil disturbances in Northern Ireland in the previous six months, appeared to anticipate such a possibility when it pointed out that 'the Rules contain no provisions as to who is to decide when "the authorities act contrary to the Constitution"', but then added: 'it is plain that policy is wholly in the hands of the Ulster Constitution Defence

Committee which has a membership of twelve and is a self-perpetu-
ating body. The Chairman is Dr Paisley.'[27]

The same year, 1966, also saw the formation of the Ulster Volunteer
Force by the Spence brothers, Billy and Gusty. Billy had formerly been
closely involved with Paisley in the running of the Ulster Protestant
Association, but following its break-up the Spences and other loyalist
militants had been led to adopt violent methods to attain their political
goals.[28] One of their methods was that of killing Catholics and
Republicans, irrespective of whether or not the two categories were
found in the same person. The first shootings in the campaign at this
early stage culminated in the death of Peter Ward, one of four Catholic
barmen who had called at the Malvern Arms off the Lower Shankill
Road, Belfast, in the early hours of Sunday morning, 26 June. Shocking
as these early killings were, they were soon to fade in people's memories
as the tally of murders committed by both loyalist and Republican
paramilitaries mounted during the twenty-five years of violence.

When the Spences and others formed the UVF, they chose to use
the name of the organisation that had been drawn up under the leadership of Edward Carson and the Ulster Unionist Council in the face of
the likely introduction of Home Rule by the Westminster Parliament.
The nature of the perceived threat to the existence of Northern Ireland
which now led them to secretly organise and use violent methods may
bear a relationship to Paisley's vociferous protests about the government's betrayal of Northern Ireland's Protestant and unionist heritage,
and his speeches and sermons reminding people of actions taken in the
past to protect this heritage. How would his supporters have understood his sermon, 'No Surrender', based on Daniel 3:18, preached in
the Ulster Hall in 1964 on the occasion of the fiftieth anniversary of
the Larne gun-running?[29] Strange as it may seem, Paisley compared
Daniel's non-violent resistance against Babylonian paganism to Colonel
Crawford's call to arm Orangemen during the Home Rule crisis:

Let's just look in this context at the Ulster gun-runners. They jeopardised
everything for Ulster. We could not speak highly enough of Ulster's great
leader, but unfortunately the spirit of Lord Carson among the leaders of
our land is almost dead. May God send us a revival of the spirit of Lord
Carson. When Colonel Crawford suggested to the leaders of the Orange
Society of the day that they should arm the Orangemen, the leaders almost
passed away with fright. Yes, and many of them in our day are of the same
kind. Then part of the Ulster Unionist Council resigned when the decision
was made to bring in the guns. Many in Church and State are acting
similarly in this day of crisis. They are afraid to face the issue so they take
the easy way and simply run away.

He went on to remind the congregation of how Edward Carson had supported Crawford, and suggested: 'It is men of Lord Carson's stamp that are needed today – men who will put their hand to the plough and not look back.' How far can this kind of rhetoric, often repeated, be regarded as language which others would interpret as they saw fit?

A piece published in the *Protestant Telegraph* in May 1966, entitled 'O'Neill the Bridge-Builder', included a cartoon depicting O'Neill's welcome to Lemass at Stormont in January 1965. 'Welcome on your secret visit, Sean,' O'Neill is saying as he clasps Lemass's hand; to which the taoiseach replies, 'I love you, Terry.' But tucked in Lemass's pocket is a scroll entitled 'Sinn Féin Oath'. Tim Pat Coogan has rightly highlighted the potential for incitement contained in the occasional publication of this fabricated oath:

These Protestant robbers and brutes, these unbelievers of our faith, will be driven like the swine they are into the sea by fire, the knife or the poison cup until we of the Catholic Faith and avowed supporters of all Sinn Féin action and principles clear these heretics from our land.... At any cost we must work in secret, using any method of deception to gain our ends, towards the destruction of all Protestants and the advancement of the priesthood and the Catholic Faith until the Pope is complete ruler of the whole world.... We must strike at every opportunity, using all methods of causing ill-feeling within the Protestant ranks and in their business. The employment of any means will be blessed by our earthly fathers, the priests, and thrice blessed by His Holiness the Pope. So shall we of the Roman Catholic Church and faith destroy with smiles and thanksgiving to our Holy Father the Pope all who reject our beliefs.[30]

The document must have had wide circulation as it was later included in a British army manual distributed to soldiers stationed in Northern Ireland; it was withdrawn only after Coogan published it in the *Irish Press*.

What effect would Paisley's references to the courage of gun-runners in 1914 and the circulation of false information like the bogus Sinn Féin oath have had on his supporters? There is no suggestion that his remarks were necessarily intended to stimulate impressionable people to unlawful acts, but it may be that they had that effect without his volition. The reaction of Hugh McClean, one of the UVF members charged with the Malvern Street murder, has been well documented: 'I am terribly sorry I ever heard of that man Paisley or decided to follow him. I am definitely ashamed of myself to be in such a position.' When questioned by the police about his reasons for joining the paramilitary organisation, he replied: 'I was asked did I agree with Paisley and was

I prepared to follow him. I said that I was.'[31]

In addition to McClean's statement, whose sentiments are shared by other 'loyalist' paramilitaries, there is much more substantial evidence suggesting Paisley's influence on paramilitary activity. On 17 April 1966, at a counter-demonstration in Belfast to protest against the pro-Republican parade held to mark the fiftieth anniversary of the Easter Rising, he publicly acknowledged the presence of the UVF in his welcoming speech to the crowd.[32] The following month the UVF started its vicious campaign of murder which included the Malvern Street killing at the end of June. Paisley was questioned by the police about the case and reacted by accusing them of 'diabolical malice' in attempting to associate the UCDC, UPV and himself in the murder. Indeed, there was no suggestion that Paisley was in any way directly or indirectly involved in the relevant offences. He went further by suggesting their own complicity in the crime by drinking after hours at the Malvern Arms and thereby violating the licensing laws: 'Unable with all their underhand scheming to establish their nefarious purpose, they suddenly became mute upon one of the most serious aspects of the case - the violation of the licensing laws which set the scene of the crime. It is a well known fact that the police themselves used this pub for drinking after hours.'[33]

The most disquieting incident at this time concerned Noel Doherty's involvement with the UVF in a conspiracy to provide explosives for unlawful purposes. Again interviewed by police, Paisley acknowledged that he had driven Doherty and Billy Mitchell, a Free Presbyterian Sunday school superintendent, to the house of another Free Presbyterian, Robert Murdock, in Loughgall, County Armagh, and then gone on to another meeting. He had later collected the two and brought them back to Belfast. The significance of the trip for Doherty and Mitchell was that the Loughgall venue was later proven to be one of the 'links' in the explosives conspiracy. There is no suggestion that Paisley was directly or indirectly involved in the explosives conspiracy or any other activities of those involved, but Doherty, who admitted his involvement, was sentenced to two years imprisonment. Billy Mitchell was later to become a UVF gunman and serve a life sentence for a double murder, while Robert Murdock was charged but found not guilty of involvement in the April 1969 explosions which effectively ended O'Neill's premiership.[34]

The founding of the Northern Ireland Civil Rights Association (NICRA) on 1 February 1967 could not have been totally unexpected. Martin Luther King, a Baptist pastor, had already been leading a civil rights movement in the United States for over ten years, struggling for racial equality by the method of non-violent resistance. It had started in 1955 in Montgomery, Alabama, when he opposed the existing practice of segregation on buses by organising a boycott by blacks which lasted for over a year before the Supreme Court ruled in favour of desegregation on Alabama public transportation. The civil rights legislation of 1964–1965 had been followed by the famous march from Selma to Montgomery in March 1965, aimed at publicising the obstacles experienced by blacks when registering as voters. King's address to the marchers on that occasion had been broadcast around the world: 'Man dies when he refuses to take a stand for that which is true; so we're going to stand up right here, amid horses, we're going to stand up amid tear gas, letting the world know that we are determined to be free.'[35] It was the example of this movement which inspired many of those who became involved in the civil rights campaign in Northern Ireland. The fact that some were also motivated, and perhaps primarily motivated, by Republican ideals cannot invalidate the underlying principles which inspired many in the movement.

There was obviously concern about civil rights before NICRA. The movement was not the first to identify injustice in the community. Nationalist MPs at Stormont had attempted to publicise injustices, but their protests had often been dismissed by Unionists as the expected complaints from representatives of a disgruntled community which was reluctant to acknowledge the legitimacy of the state. The Dungannon-based Campaign for Social Justice led by Con and Patricia McCluskey had been collecting data on injustices in Northern Ireland and publicising them since early 1964. There had also been stirrings of conscience, however late in the day, in the Protestant community. The 1966 conference of the Methodist Church in Ireland, held in Dublin in the second week of June, had declared: 'Any form of injustice, inequality or discrimination based on creed, race or colour is contrary to God's Will. The Conference consequently calls on all sections of the community and in particular those in positions of influence and authority to work by word and deed for the removal of all injustices from our land.'[36]

W. D. Flackes and Sydney Elliott have summarised NICRA's main aims: '"one man, one vote" in council elections; ending of "gerrymandered" electoral boundaries; machinery to prevent discrimination by public authorities and to deal with complaints; fair allocation of public housing; repeal of Special Powers Act; and disbanding of B Specials.'[37] Cathal Goulding, then IRA chief-of-staff, has claimed that it was the IRA who created NICRA: 'The IRA set up NICRA. The Army Council of the IRA set up NICRA, it and the Communist Party together.'[38] The fact that the meeting which led to the formation of the association was held in Maghera in the home of Kevin Agnew, a solicitor and leading Republican in South Derry, and that at least four of the initial eleven-man committee were Republicans, appears to substantiate Goulding's claim.

Various sources suggest that following the failure of the 1956-1962 military campaign the IRA leadership, especially those based in Dublin, were more inclined to move away from militarism and encourage Republicanism through political activity. Influenced by their Marxist philosophy of society, they envisaged an eventual coming together of the working classes from both 'loyalist' and 'nationalist' communities. The implication is that the formation of a civil rights movement was therefore just one manifestation of the new ideas percollating through the IRA.[39] However, Clifford Smyth has drawn attention to research which had access to the journals of 'more extreme republicans' and quite a different picture emerges: namely, that the new strategy which was planned after the 1957-1962 campaign was one which would be 'the perfect blending of politics and violence at the most opportune time and under the most favourable circumstances'. Having decided on the strategy, they then seized on the example of the civil rights movement in the United States as the most suitable to adapt and apply in the Northern Ireland situation.[40] This latter analysis appears closer to the truth, as it explains much of the violence that erupted at some of the civil rights' marches even when there were no counter-demonstrations planned for the same day.

This difficulty in assessing IRA strategy possibly indicates the confusion which existed within their own ranks at the time. In moving towards an unarmed strategy they had apparently sold off almost all of their guns. However, while they planned to seek reform through the civil rights campaign, and some of them aimed to provoke the violence of a state they viewed as inherently violent, it would seem that they had no real notion of what to do about the violence when it erupted.

Ian Paisley never had any sympathy for the civil rights movements in either the United States or Northern Ireland. When Martin Luther King was assassinated on 4 April 1968 at Memphis, Tennessee, the *Protestant Telegraph* commented: 'He laid great emphasis upon the brotherhood of man rather than the Kingship of Christ. He chose liberal theology rather than fundamentalism. He chose ecumenism rather than separation. He chose pacifism, looking to Gandhi as his guru and to the Pope as his friend, but his pacifism could not adequately be transmitted to his followers.' The writer preferred to concentrate more on the violence which had broken out in some of the most deprived black suburbs of American cities: 'The people that he led have now taken to riot, arson, looting and murder. The smouldering racial tensions have once again been rekindled. The Communist agitators have whipped up grief and emotion into xenophobia and uncontrollable rioting; and America is on the brink of civil war.'[41] It was this assesment of the civil rights cause in the States which determined Paisley's reaction to civil rights' marches in Northern Ireland. However, there was a strange inconsistency in his attitude to marches: while he protested loudly if his marches were re-routed or halted, he insisted that civil rights marches should be banned.

William Craig, minister of home affairs in O'Neill's government, was the minister in charge of law and order and therefore the one responsible for authorising or banning parades or marches in the province. In April 1968 Paisley targeted Craig as he had O'Neill and insisted 'Craig Must Go!'[42] Paisley accused Craig of dragging his feet in enforcing the ban on republican clubs: 'Compromise is apparently the key word in Craig's policy. But in compromising, the lives and property of citizens are in jeopardy.' He was prepared to award Craig a prize: 'Mr Craig's parliamentary career is unparalleled in Northern Ireland. For incompetence, inconsistency, and unpopularity he certainly takes the first prize.' And yet by the middle of December that year, Craig was back in favour with Paisley, and O'Neill was accused of subversion for, on 11 December, insisting on Craig's resignation. What had happened in the intervening period to change Paisley's opinion on Craig?

On 11 May thousands had attended a demonstration in Armagh organised by the UCDC and UPV in response, Paisley declared, to 'lying and blasphemous seditions'. On 1 June Paisley had led a 'Great Protestant Demonstration and Loyalist Parade' in Dungannon. When in August the Campaign for Social Justice and NICRA had announced plans to march from Coalisland to the Market Square in Dungannon, the UPV had called for a counter-demonstration at the same time and place. According to Paisley, the Unionist Party had called a special meeting in Killyman Orange Hall and decided unanimously not to oppose the march. Paisley had commented: 'A greater bunch of traitors never met in an Orange Hall before.'[43] On 24 August the NICRA marchers and the UPV counter-demonstration had been kept apart by a police cordon.

On 7 September Paisley had led a UPV march at Maghera to protest against Kevin Agnew: 'He has called the Protestants of Ulster "Orange bastards and bigots". He has called the Union Jack "the bloody ould

Union Jack". He has called for civil disobedience – the more the better.'[44] Craig had met Paisley before the march to tell him that the local Unionists objected to it, as they feared the march might provoke trouble in the town. Craig had decided to re-route the march away from Catholic areas to avoid confrontation. Paisley had responded by accusing Craig of granting police protection to the flying of the tricolour in Maghera while refusing to grant similar protection to Protestants to march through the town.

Arrangements for a NICRA march on 5 October from Duke Street on the east bank of the River Foyle to the Diamond in the centre of Derry had rested entirely in the hands of two local activists, Eamonn McCann, a left-wing member of the Labour Party, and Eamonn Melaugh, an independent radical. McCann later acknowledged that they had encouraged a government ban on the parade by a series of goading press statements. Craig had duly obliged, claiming that the march could lead to confrontation with an Apprentice Boys of Derry parade planned for the same day. McCann also said that they had planned a confronta-tion with the police, 'to provoke the police into over-reaction and thus spark off mass reaction against the authorities'.[45] The 400 who had turned up for the march included Republicans who had travelled from Belfast and a group from the Young Socialist Alliance. McCann's hopes of a riot had been fulfilled when the Young Socialists had thrown placards at the police, who responded with baton charges into the band of marchers, now surrounded on both sides. Television cameras had relayed pictures of these baton charges around the world, and overnight Northern Ireland's problems had taken centre stage in the attention of the international media. One hundred people were injured during two days of rioting which ended only after police used armoured cars and high-pressure water-hoses in an attempt to restore order. The *Belfast Telegraph* commented on the disturbances between the marchers and the police: 'Those who set out to force a way through a police cordon – even MPs who should know better – have no reason to be surprised or outraged when they find themselves in a rough house.'[46]

Paisley had been delighted with Craig's banning of the parade and had published in the *Protestant Telegraph* the full text of Craig's Stormont speech stoutly defending police actions at the march. Craig was back in favour.

Gerry Fitt, at that time Republican Labour MP for West Belfast at Westminster and one of the MPs who had been present at the 5 October march, referred to the civil rights issue in a debate on the Queen's Speech in the House of Commons on 4 November. 'The reason why we are in this position in Northern Ireland is because for forty-eight years we have been subjected to the jackboot of Unionism, and this does not only apply to the minority of Catholics, but it also applies to the ordinary working class Protestant people, who are of no use to the Unionist party machine.'[47]

On the same day Terence O'Neill, William Craig and Brian Faulkner, minister of commerce, met British prime minister Harold Wilson at Downing Street. Two days later a 'Viewpoint' article, 'Time for Cool Heads', in the *Belfast Telegraph* warned that the British government was now taking a much closer interest in the affairs of the province, with the result that internal political changes could be imposed unless the local Parliament itself took the initiative in this direction: 'Mr Wilson now leaves no doubt – even before tomorrow's Cabinet at Stormont – that he will brook no undue delay in the implementation of reforms. More telling still, he has warned that if the Unionist Party discards Captain O'Neill, or his policy, it will bring about a "very fundamental re-appraisal" of the British Government's relations.'[48]

Five days later, at a march from Craigavon Bridge to the Diamond in Derry, Paisley warned that the October civil rights march in the city was an indication that the IRA was preparing for a massive campaign, one of the worst in the history of the province. At a Remembrance Day service the next day in Tamlagh O'Crilly Lower Church, County Derry, the Church of Ireland bishop of Derry, Dr Tyndall, spoke of his fear regarding Paisley's activities and intentions: 'Did I see yesterday on Craigavon Bridge something sinister? Did I see the march of men dedicated to religious genocide? Did I see the rising of an ideological force based on cultivated hatred and invective? Did I see the sign once again of the swastika? God forbid.' But as well as sharing his concern, he appealed that people would challenge the bigotry which, he suggested, was now rampant in their midst: 'God is calling out today moderate men to demonstrate their moderation. The battalions of the bigots must be challenged by the army of those who stand for goodwill and peace – the army of the Gospel of Jesus Christ.'[49]

On 13 November, William Craig announced a month's ban on all marches in Derry. It was immediately broken by the Derry Citizens' Action Committee, who held marches on 16 and 18 November.

On 17 November the Nationalist Party adopted a policy of civil disobedience.

Supported by London, O'Neill was eventually able to persuade his cabinet to announce, on 22 November, a five-point reform programme: a new points system was to be used by local authorities in their allocation of housing; an ombudsman was to be appointed to investigate complaints; the company vote in local council elections was to be ended, but no action was yet provided for to enfranchise non-ratepayers; a promise was made to review the Special Powers Act; and a development commission was to be appointed to replace the existing Londonderry Corporation.

NICRA gave good notice of their intention to march in Armagh on 30 November, and Moloney and Pollak indicate the intensity of feeling which this particular NICRA march engendered in Paisley.[50] According to one eye-witness he became very agitated when he first heard of the NICRA proposal: 'He was furious when he heard about it. He was roaring, "No-one is going to march there. That's my city, that's where I was born. They're not going to desecrate my birthplace!"' Paisley and a local Free Presbyterian, Douglas Hutchinson, met with the police on 19 November and told them they would take 'appropriate action' if the NICRA march went ahead. They then arranged for handbills to be distributed advising that all women and children should vacate the city on 30 November. Two days before the march, UCDC posters appeared in the town centre: 'For God and Ulster. S.O.S. To all Protestant religions. Don't let the Republicans, IRA and CRA, make Armagh another Londonderry. Assemble in Armagh on Saturday 30 November.'

The police planned to keep the two sides apart by sealing off the route of the march and setting up roadblocks at 8.00 a.m. on the morning of the march. Apparently Paisley heard news of these plans when he was in the middle of a church presbytery meeting: 'The meeting broke up with an excited Paisley issuing instructions to the church elders and ministers to round up their congregations and alert UPV divisions to make their way to the centre of Armagh before the roadblocks went up. Paisley arrived with Bunting and a convoy of thirty cars at about 1.00 a.m. and they spent the night talking in small groups or sitting in their cars. Paisley told a police inspector that he planned to hold a religious meeting and did not intend to interfere with anyone.' However, the police roadblocks revealed quite a different picture: 'As hundreds of Paisleyites converged on the city, searches of cars uncovered two revolvers and 220 other weapons including bill-hooks, scythes and pipes hammered into sharp points.' Many of Paisley's supporters who had arrived during the morning were able to breach a police cordon of the city centre by knocking down a wall in an alleyway. By midday a crowd of 2,000 had assembled, some armed with sticks taken from a building site. The police told Paisley that he was now holding an unlawful assembly, but he refused to disperse. The NICRA march proceeded along its planned route and a major disturbance was only averted by a substantial police presence which kept the two sides apart. Later, on 27 January 1969, Paisley and Bunting were found guilty of taking part in an unlawful assembly at Armagh, and sentenced to three months imprisonment.

On 9 December Terence O'Neill made a television and radio broadcast to the people of Northern Ireland, later known as the 'crossroads speech' because of its contents and especially its introductory words: 'Ulster stands at the Crossroads.'[51] He declared that for the past five years he had been pursuing a policy which sought to heal the deep divisions in the community. With this objective in mind, he had maintained a firm law and order policy 'resisting those elements which seek to profit from any disturbances'. But he had also endeavoured 'to ally firmness with fairness, and to look at any underlying causes of dissension which were troubling decent and moderate people'. In this regard he wanted to assure those who had been demonstrating for civil rights that the government was totally committed to change, as was evident in the reforms already announced. The guarantee he offered that these reforms would be implemented was his own personal commitment to change: 'I would not continue to preside over an administration which would water them down or make them meaningless.' To further this objective he appealed to the civil rights leaders to 'call your people off the streets and allow an atmosphere favourable to change to develop'.

O'Neill insisted that pursuing this policy would effectively strengthen Unionism: 'Unionism armed with justice will be a stronger cause than Unionism armed merely with strength.' Far better, he suggested, that we keep our self-respect by following the path of reform rather than having a Westminster government forcing Stormont in this direction: 'What shred of self-respect would be left to us? If we allowed others to solve our problems because we had not the guts – let me use a plain word – the guts to face up to them, we would be utterly shamed.'

His references to the Westminster Parliament, echoing warnings already sounded by the *Belfast Telegraph*, were an attempt to alert the public to the legal and constitutional limitations in which the Stormont Parliament operated. He quoted the terms of the 1920 Government of Ireland Act: 'Notwithstanding the establishment of the Parliament of Northern Ireland... the supreme authority of the Parliament of the United Kingdom shall remain unaffected and undiminished over all persons, matters and things in [Northern] Ireland and every part thereof.' Time would demonstrate that Unionists were slow, or perhaps unwilling, to accept the reality of this legislation. But O'Neill had rightly informed the community of the real world in which they lived.

He spelt out the implications even further by confirming that pressure for change in Northern Ireland would come from Westminster irrespective of which party was in power. And covering every loophole, he referred to those – no names were mentioned but he obviously had Craig in mind – who were suggesting independence from Britain. After pointing out the financial and defence implications of such a proposal, he declared: 'These people are not merely extremists. They are lunatics who would set a course along a road which could only lead at the end into an all-Ireland Republic. They are not loyalists but *dis*loyalists: disloyal to Britain, disloyal to the Constitution, disloyal to the Crown, disloyal – if they are in public life – to the solemn oaths they have sworn to Her Majesty the Queen.'

O'Neill finally appealed that the people of Northern Ireland should choose what kind of future they wanted. He gave no impression that he wanted to cling to power at all costs. Should the people want to follow the path he had outlined, he was available to lead them; but if they preferred a different kind of Ulster, then someone else would have to take over the leadership: 'If you should want a separate, inward-looking, selfish and divided Ulster then you must seek for others to lead you along that road, for I cannot and will not do it.'

Craig had been resisting Harold Wilson's pressure in favour of reform in Northern Ireland, and O'Neill, encouraged by the overwhelming support he had received for his speech from right across the community, felt strong enough on 11 December to sack him from his position as minister of home affairs and appoint William Long in his place. Despite the rumblings of discontent within his cabinet and among Unionist backbenchers at Stormont, Unionist MPs, with four abstentions, now endorsed O'Neill's policies. It appeared, at least for a short period, that O'Neill had succeeded. But how prophetic was his 'crossroads speech' in the long term? The twenty-five years of community violence that soon followed and the introduction of direct rule in 1972 would seem to indicate that the people of Northern Ireland, of all backgrounds, effectively rejected O'Neill's programme of 'stepped' reform. With the exception of the Special Powers Act, all the NICRA demands have now been introduced in Northern Ireland, but not in the measured and voluntary manner that he suggested.

In the course of nine months, William Craig had shred any vestige of liberalism which he might have possessed and placed himself firmly in the camp of those opposed to change. He accused the British government of using financial pressures to 'blackmail' the Northern Ireland government to introduce reforms, which in turn he viewed as a form of appeasement to the 'enemies of Ulster'. Craig took what some have described as a 'hardline' approach, influenced perhaps by the IRA involvement in the civil rights movement. As minister of home affairs he would have been carefully briefed on this by the police. Perhaps Paisley's bellicose rantings and the sight of thousands now responding eagerly to his leadership, or a combination of both these factors, swayed Craig.

Paisley used Craig's dismissal from office as the opportunity to take another swipe at O'Neill: 'Captain O'Neill, in sacking Mr Craig, has capitulated to the Romanists and Republicans, the anarchists, the Civil Rights agitators and the Communists – the evil alliance against Ulster's Constitution.'[52] Referring to his 'crossroads speech', he once again accused the prime minister of betraying the architects of the state: 'He has in fact indicted the Unionists of the past and showed his true character as one who has more in common with the enemies of Ulster than with her true defenders.' He sought to fan the growing unease among some Unionist MPs: 'O'Neill's policy has split the Unionist Party and the Loyalist cause, and the Ulster which we need is one with a new Prime Minister who will not flirt with Lynch – the enemy of all that Ulster Loyalists hold dear. The best thing which O'Neill can do is "Go!"' A fortnight later his *Protestant Telegraph* was reassuring its readers that as 'Biblical Protestants' they were the true successors of St Patrick: 'We are following in the footsteps of St Patrick, who was a profound expositor of Scriptural Christianity and was not a Papist priest.'[53] The battle between truth and evil in which they were engaged could well mean that the youth of Ulster would have to pay the ultimate sacrifice: 'Blood has ever been the price of liberty. Historically, the blood of Ulster's youth has run till Boyne rivers flow blood red.... Today the battle is not yet won and sacrifices will have to be made. Now is the time for Ulster to prepare for the final conflict to come.... Ulster arise and acknowledge your God. NO SURRENDER. NO COMPROMISE.'

The People's Democracy (PD) four-day march from Belfast to Derry on 1 January 1969, organised by a radical left-wing group – some of whom, as Coogan has helpfully pointed out,[54] later went on to take prominent positions in Irish society, north and south – must have been regarded by Paisley as part of this 'final conflict to come'. Major Ronald Bunting warned the marchers before they set out from Belfast that they would be 'harrassed and hindered', and every account of the events that followed would suggest that he may have understated his case. Civil rights leaders and others had unsuccessfully advised the organisers against proceeding with their plans, but the march went ahead. The Cameron

Commission later likened Bunting's preparation for and execution of
the ambush at Burntollet Bridge to a paramilitary enterprise:

In Dr Paisley's Guildhall meeting in Londonderry on 3rd January Major
Bunting was appealing publicly for recruits for the Ulster Protestant
Volunteers as well as intimating arrangements for a concentration of
supporters the following morning at a spot close to Burntollet Bridge for
the avowed purpose of continuing the process of 'harrying and hindering'
the People's Democracy march, as had been his purpose since the march
left Belfast. Indeed, his wearing of the upper portion of a military uniform,
complete with badges of rank, suggests at least that he regarded himself as
taking part in a paramilitary enterprise. The ambush of the marchers at
Burntollet Bridge, the arrangements for providing missiles of all kinds at
the place, the instruction to attackers to wear white armbands – presum-
ably for no other reason than identiification in a struggle – all point to a
carefully planned and pre-arranged operation, and, of course, Major
Bunting himself was there also and took an active part in the affair.[55]

Significantly, it was not long after these events that O'Neill and his
cabinet agreed to set up an independent enquiry, the Cameron
Commission, into the causes of violence in the community since
October 1968; but the move revealed the growing dissension in the
Unionist Party. Two cabinet ministers, Brian Faulkner and William
Morgan, resigned, followed soon after by a call for O'Neill's resigna-
tion from twelve backbench Unionist MPs, including William Craig.
O'Neill responded by calling an election for 24 February, known as the
'crossroads' election, as it followed so soon after his 9 December broad-
cast.

Having challenged O'Neill at various times to test public opinion,
Paisley now entered the political arena as a candidate for the first time,
standing against O'Neill for the Bannside seat. Five other 'Protestant
Unionist' candidates, including two of his ministers, William Beattie
and John Wylie, and his 'paramilitary' counter-march organiser, Ronald
Bunting, completed his six-man team for the election. Paisley's case
against O'Neill was unchanged from the one he had been making since
1963: votes for the Protestant Unionist candidates would be votes that
would 'save Ulster from the continuation of the O'Neill sell-out' and
assist the fight against his 'policy of appeasement'. He made capital
out of his imprisonment for his counter-demonstration in Armagh on
30 November. In a Protestant Unionist television broadcast he declared:
'This is a serious election. That is why Major Ronnie Bunting and
myself have come from the prison cell – to which we will shortly return
– in order to lead the Protestant Unionists in this election.'[56] A social

dimension was added to his cause, as he called for a crash programme on housing, reduction in unemployment, improvement in wages and thereby the level of household incomes, raising of health, welfare and education standards, and a new deal in agriculture. But perhaps most significantly, despite his opposition to civil rights, he declared: 'We stand for full civil and religious liberty for all the people of Northern Ireland, particularly Roman Catholics, whose freedom from authoritarianism is of great concern to us.' Did these final throw-away words give a clue to the type of freedom he sought for Catholics?

None of the Protestant Unionist candidates were elected, but Paisley claimed that the result was 'a great vote for Protestant Unionists'. As expected, his vote in Bannside was the one which registered the greatest number for the Protestant Unionist Party:

Terence O'Neill (Unionist)	7,745
Ian Paisley (Protestant Unionist)	6,331
Michael Farrell (People's Democracy)	2,310

The election must have disappointed O'Neill, considering the substantial measure of support for Paisley in O'Neil's own constituency. When he surveyed the post-election scene, he would have felt that little had changed regarding the measure of support he could expect on the Unionist side. The contest had been a complex one for the party. Some constituencies selected candidates who supported O'Neill but others had candidates who opposed him. This meant that in some constituencies O'Neill had to field unofficial Unionist candidates who agreed with his policies. At the final count it was found that twenty-seven of the thirty-nine Unionists elected supported him, ten 'official' Unionists still opposing him and two being undecided about their allegiance. The 'official' Unionists opposing him had captured 17 per cent of the total vote, compared to the 31 per cent for pro-O'Neill 'official' Unionists. But this alarming situation was offset by a further 12.9 per cent poll for the 'unofficial' pro-O'Neill Unionists.

The final blow for O'Neill came in the most unexpected form of a series of explosions in March and April, initially thought to be the work of the IRA. The first, at the end of March, wrecked an electricity substation at Castlereagh on the outskirts of Belfast, and it was followed by others which damaged an electricity pylon at Kilmore, County Armagh, water pipelines from the Silent Valley reservoir in the Mourne mountains and water pipelines at Templepatrick, County Antrim. For ten days water rationing was introduced in Belfast. Six months later it was revealed that the explosions had in fact been the work of the UVF and not the IRA. A member of the UVF, Sammy Stevenson, who had worked in the UCDC offices and acted as Paisley's bodyguard in early 1969, was charged and sentenced. Ten others who were charged and found not guilty – Stevenson's evidence against them was considered unreliable by the court – included at least five who were members of Paisley's UPV; one, Frank Mallon, was the UCDC treasurer. Nine of the ten had registered as Free Presbyterians when they were remanded to prison.[57] When Gusty Spence was asked if Ian Paisley had any direct or indirect links with these explosions, he replied: 'I was in prison from 1966 to 1984. I would have no direct knowledge of that, but there were things in the undergrowth that he visited Donegal Pass police station and spoke to Stevenson and asked him had he said anything, or whatever, you know. Some of the people who were connected with the explosions had been members of the UCDC and UPV, which were organisations lorded over to some degree by Ian Paisley.'

An important piece of legislation was introduced before O'Neill resigned on 28 April. The issue of 'one man, one vote' – universal adult suffrage – in local government elections was at last conceded by his cabinet on 23 April. Had he been able to include this in the reform package of 22 November 1968, its reception by nationalists might have been different, but his attempt to bring as many as possible of his party with him had caused its delay. Major James Chichester-Clark, minister of agriculture, resigned, ostensibly on the grounds of the timing of the introduction of the reform. On O'Neill's resignation as premier, he was voted in as his successor, winning a contest over Brian Faulkner by one vote.

O'Neill's premiership has been analysed in different ways, some favourable, some dismissive. It has been said that he lacked the common touch and was unable to communicate with people as his rival, Brian Faulkner, clearly could. Whatever the truth of these comments, the fact remains that he had a vision for Northern Ireland which he expressed through his cross-border and cross-community links and finally in his 'crossroads' broadcast. He was unable to translate his vision into practice in the manner that he wished, but there is no evidence that anyone else occupying the premiership at this time would have had either the vision or the ability to implement change. Overshadowing everything was the figure of Ian Paisley, who was opposed to any reform. His ability to arouse and win over the loyalist/Protestant masses to his anti-Catholic/anti-Republican crusade was becoming increasingly evident and, some felt, increasingly ominous for the country.

The Last Lap

No sooner had Chichester-Clark taken office than Paisley was seeking
assurances that he would end the policy of his predecessor and restore
traditional Unionist policies. Whatever the new prime minister wrote
in the exchange of letters, it appeared to satisfy Paisley for the time
being. However, following the annual Apprentice Boys' Parade in Derry
on 12 August, serious rioting broke out in the Bogside, which lies to
the west below the ancient inner walls of the city. Most sources report
that temporary barricades and stores of petrol bombs had already been
prepared, but opinions differ on whether they were to be used in
defence against possible attack or as weapons to provoke the authorities. I was showing a German family friend around the ancient walls in
the early afternoon and witnessed the preparations that were already in
place. Whatever the analysis regarding the circumstances of the rioting
that broke out that day, all are agreed that it was the turning point
which ushered in the next twenty-five years of bitter community
violence. Rioting in Derry soon spread to Belfast, prompting the
Northern Ireland government to call for the assistance of British troops
to deal with the rapidly deteriorating situation. The first troops began
arriving on 14 August. As the army was directly under the control of
Westminster, its presence inevitably led to further limitations on the
power of the Stormont government.

Paisley saw the Londonderry riots as part of the legacy of O'Neillism.
He possibly wrote the article ('The Aftermath of O'Neillism') which
appeared in the *Protestant Telegraph* on 16 August.[58] The writer
declared: 'O'Neillism – the policy of betraying Ulster by appeasing the
rebels – is now bearing its bitter fruits. Appeasement is a sign of
weakness, and weakness falls an easy prey to the unrelenting foe of
Romanism. History has proved that any country which failed to realise
the real nature of the Roman system and to resist its encroachments
and claims fell under Rome's jackboot.' The Roman Catholic Church
was accused of acting deceitfully by pretending to seek peace in the
name of civil rights while all the time it was planning revolution against
the Crown: 'Under the guise of peace, Rome carries out an unrelenting
war for the achievement of her aims. She is a past master in hypocrisy,
duplicity, deceit and falsehood. All the time her leaders in Londonderry
were pursuing a so-called peace campaign, her actionists were preparing
for the greatest onslaught ever to be launched against the forces of the
Crown in that city. Petrol bombs were being stockpiled, ready for this
offensive.' Only four months had passed since Chichester-Clark had
taken office, but Paisley was once again calling for resignations: 'Any

Government unwilling to protect its people from such a villanous and murderous gang of thugs should resign and be immediately replaced by one whose loyalty cannot be questioned.'

By the end of the month the presbytery of the Free Presbyterian Church had also launched its own offensive. It was infuriated at Cardinal Conway's public statement suggesting that Catholic areas of West and North Belfast had been invaded by 'mobs equipped with machine guns and other firearms'. Conway claimed: 'a community that was virtually defenceless was swept by gunfire and streets of Catholic houses were set on fire.'[59] The presbytery denied the cardinal's claim and interpreted it as a cover for subversion: 'We brand Cardinal Conway's speech as one deliberately designed to condone the violence of his flock and encourage them in their dastardly campaign of murder, arson and riot.'[60] It also poured scorn on an unofficial liaison committee – its existence was supposed to have been confidential – established between Protestant church leaders and the Roman Catholic Church during the early days of the crisis: 'The Presbytery warns the Protestants of this Province not to be deceived by a peace operation launched by leading Romanists, Ecumenists, Communists and Anarchists. This is but a devil's lullaby to chloroform Protestantism in order that the rebellion in our midst might have a better chance of success.'[61]

Paisley's vision of plots being hatched by politicians and church leaders continued. Harold Wilson in particular was seen as untrust-worthy. It is widely accepted that Wilson was in fact uninformed about Irish affairs, especially at this vital juncture in its history. Indeed, at one point he even considered solving the Irish problem by evacuating all the Protestants.[62] However, there has never been any evidence that he contemplated conspiring with the papacy to destroy Protestantism. But this is how Paisley interpreted the appointment of Shirley Williams as minister of state at the Home Office in October 1969: 'It is quite evident that Mr Wilson is following closely a policy which he intends will lead to our destruction. Mrs Shirley Williams is a member of the Roman Catholic lobby at Westminster, and her first loyalty, as a devout Roman Catholic, must be to the Pope and the Roman Catholic Church. As the Pope and the Church are bent on the destruction of Ulster Protestantism, she will no doubt pursue with vigour the official policy of her Church which teaches that outside its pale there is no salvation. She will have a religious motive to spur on her efforts in this direction.'[63]

The split in the IRA which had been looming for some time occurred in December 1969 when the IRA army council voted to recognise three

Parliaments – Westminster, Dublin and Stormont. This further step in politicising the IRA was another break from the traditional abstentionism which it had practised towards Westminster and Stormont and proved too much for those who interpreted physical force Republicanism as the right policy in the circumstances of 1969. Apparently there was considerable feeling amongst some that the IRA had been practically helpless to defend Catholic areas of West Belfast during the difficult days of 14 and 15 August. Jibes were heard that the IRA had come to mean 'Irish Ran Away'.

The split in the organisation became public at the Sinn Féin Ard Fheis in Dublin in January 1970 which voted in favour of the December army council decision. Those against walked out to form the 'Provisional' IRA, determined to continue the physical force tradition of Republicanism and steer the movement away from what it considered was an extreme form of socialism whose ultimate objective was 'a totalitarian dictatorship of the left'.[64] How far does this IRA split in January 1970 expose the fallacy of warnings during the sixties of an armed threat to the existence of Northern Ireland? And how far also had talk of the government's capitulation to 'the enemies of Ulster' had the reverse effect of actually encouraging the revival of the physical force tradition? Underlying the myth – frequently heard from his supporters and sympathisers – that all of Paisley's prophecies have come true is the possibility that his militant calls for sacrifice 'till Boyne rivers flow blood red' may in fact have contributed to the fulfilment of his predictions.

O'Neill's acceptance of a life peerage meant that Paisley had another chance to win the Bannside seat at the by-election on 16 April. Another by-election in the South Antrim constituency on the same day gave him the chance to nominate William Beattie, the Dunmurry Free Presbyterian minister, for the seat. Paisley started his campaign early, and on 21 March he made a stinging attack on Chichester-Clark in a front page article, 'Galloping Major Heads for the Falls' in his *Protestant Telegraph*. Some of the Unionist constituency associations had passed votes of 'no confidence' in Clark, so Paisley declared: 'They are giving him the message loud and clear: "Get out"... So now the die is cast. He has chosen to fight. And it will be a fight to the political death – his demise as Premier.'[65] Once again Paisley felt he was in the right in repeating his calls for Chichester-Clark's resignation, just as he had been convinced he was in the right in his unrelenting campaign against O'Neill. G.R. Elton's comments on Henry VIII appear to be as applicable to Ian Paisley as they were to the strong-willed, intelligent, but rather shallow-thinking Tudor monarch: 'He had the egoist's supreme

gift, the superb conviction that right is always on his side.'[66] Paisley felt
he always had a tremendous advantage over his opponents – Christ and
truth were on his side and this would guarantee him the victory. 'From
this battle only one can survive. One victor – truth. And the vanquished?
Lies, treachery and appeasement.... Now it is truly "Christ for Ulster."'
When he won the Bannside seat and Beattie also topped the poll in
South Antrim, there was no doubt in his mind whose side God was on.
At his victory celebrations in Ballymena Town Hall, he exclaimed: 'God
has done a great thing for us, whereof we are glad.'[67]

Paisley had scored a significant victory. Even the eighty-two-year-
old Lord Brookeborough, O'Neill's predecessor as prime minister, had
been brought to the hustings in support of Bolton Minford, the
Unionist Party candidate, but to no avail. The Unionist/Protestant
people of Bannside and South Antrim were sending a clear message of
support through the ballot box for Paisley's type of Unionist politics.
He had now qualified for a seat in the local Parliament – but for how
long would it continue to exist?

Chapter Eight

Manoeuvring for Unionist Leadership
1970–1996

T HE NEW MP for Bannside wasted no time in taking full advantage of his new status. The result of the final count had only been announced in the early hours of Friday morning, 17 April 1970, but by noon the same day, the two new Protestant Unionist MPs were holding a press conference at Stormont itself. They joked that Brian Faulkner had talked about the sobering effect that Parliament would have on them, so they were in a hurry to visit the place where they were to be sobered. Paisley's message, however, was as predictable as ever. The country, he declared, was suffering from weak leadership, the Stormont prime minister, Chichester-Clark, being nothing more than a serf of the Westminster government. Showing no signs of acknowledging the constitutional limitations on the Northern Ireland Parliament, already spelt out by O'Neill and the *Belfast Telegraph*, Paisley threw down the gauntlet at the feet of the British prime minister in what he must have known was a battle he was bound to lose: 'Harold Wilson should keep his nose out of Northern Ireland.'[1] Bringing security back under the control of a strong Northern Ireland government, he insisted, would necessitate sweeping changes in those holding top positions in the province. His short list of those to be removed from office included: Chichester-Clark; Robert Porter, minister of home affairs; Brian Faulkner, brought in by Chichester-Clark as minister of development; Lieutenant-General Ian Freeland, army GOC and director of operations in Northern Ireland; and Arthur Young, chief constable of the RUC.

After this early declaration of war from within the precincts of the local Parliament, members might have guessed they would not have long to wait for Dr Paisley's maiden speech in the House, and they were right. Within a few days – in a committee discussion on estimates – he immediately referred to the religious basis of his campaign. Playing on the varying usages of the word 'indulgence', he began by suggesting he would follow the custom for new members making their first speech in the House and 'crave the indulgence of honourable members'. He went on: 'The word "indulgence" of course reminds me of an explosion which took place in the sixteenth century, when a very strong and able man by the name of Martin Luther caused serious trouble to many people whom I personally do not like, even at this moment.... Members would need to be informed – that was the great Protestant Reformation.' Portraying himself as the representative of the Reformation tradition, he then focused his attack on Roy Bradford, the minister of commerce, who had earlier introduced the estimates to the House: 'The Minister has acted in a very irresponsible manner by attacking a large section of the Protestant community that I happen to represent and by casting slights not only upon their integrity as citizens of this country but upon the most precious thing that a man can have – this is, his religious beliefs.' Appeals from the speaker of the House to relate his remarks to the business before them had little effect on the new Bannside MP.

A month later Paisley was drawing attention to the gun-running charges brought against two former members of the cabinet in the Republic: Charles Haughey, the former finance minister who later succeeded Jack Lynch as taoiseach in 1979, and Neil Blaney, previously minister of agriculture, who were both eventually acquitted, but Lynch had sacked the two men, as soon as the charges were made public. The comment of Bishop and Mallie on the gun-running attempts in the weeks following the August 1969 violence in Derry and Belfast reveal something of the skulduggery and bungling which appears to have characterised these particular operations: 'Government policy towards the North degenerated into the uncoordinated consideration of how they could get arms to the Catholics in the North for their self-protection without being found out. Irish officials were already operating a nudge-and-wink policy towards the smuggling of guns destined for the North.'[2] The inevitable publicity surrounding these events did little to lessen fears in the Unionist community in the north, especially at a time when the government had announced the disbanding of the Ulster Special Constabulary, a largely Protestant auxiliary police force which had had its beginnings in the unsettled security period of the early 1920s. The Ulster Special Constabulary was to be replaced by the Ulster Defence Regiment (UDR) but the move was viewed with suspicion by those who had seen the USC as the ultimate guarantor of their security. Paisley, in common with many others, seized upon the allegations against the two former cabinet ministers and declared, 'I believe the security of Northern Ireland is in grave danger.... Leading members of the Eire Government have been engaged in an attempt to take over this Province by force. The sooner we awake to this position the better.'[3]

Paisley's victory in the contest for the North Antrim seat in the 18

June Westminster general election signified the growing popularity of his political message. Although William Beattie was defeated in North Belfast, the North Antrim victory was a personal triumph for Paisley as he overturned the large majority previously held by Henry Clark, Ulster Unionist MP for the previous eleven years. Nineteen-seventy was therefore proving to be a year of political changes. In the same election a Conservative administration had replaced Labour, and Bernadette Devlin, a twenty-three-year-old psychology student at Queens University Belfast, had retained the Mid-Ulster seat she had won in a by-election the previous year. Two new political parties were also formed that year. In April the Alliance Party of Northern Ireland was formed in an attempt to provide a common political platform for Catholics and Protestants, nationalists and Unionists, and break down what was perceived as sectarianism in Ulster politics. In August the Social Democratic and Labour Party (SDLP) was formed by those previously associated with a variety of interests: the old Nationalist Party, the Republican Labour Party and the civil rights campaign. Gerry Fitt, Republican Labour MP at Westminster, became party leader.

Protestant Unionism was also about to evolve into a new party, but it continued unchanged until September 1971. At a Protestant Unionist rally in Londonderry Guildhall on 8 February 1971, Paisley continued his barrage of criticism of Chichester-Clark; the disbanding of the Ulster Special Constabulary was attacked as particularly treacherous: 'There is only one force to defend Ulster with the necessary morale and courage, and that is the "B" Specials.'[4] He accused Chichester-Clark of having promised resignation if the 'Specials' were disbanded and added: 'We are waiting for his resignation. Hurry up, James.' But Paisley gave notice that it was not just the PM's scalp he wanted, or indeed an additional one or two others; it was a major reshaping of Unionism, restoring it to its true Protestant roots, which was required: 'There are many people in this city who think that all the Protestants are dead, but I will assure them that the Protestant cause is as strong as ever. When we have done a surgical operation on the body of Unionism, and expelled from the body all the cancerous Lundys who have betrayed us, a rejuvenated and revitalised Unionism shall march onward to final victory.' The message to his supporters could not have been clearer as there was only one logical outcome from his proposed surgical operation on Unionism: Paisley himself was the one to lead Unionists and the country. The implication of all he had been saying for the past decade and longer was that he was the only leader capable of restoring Protestantism to its purity and Ulster to its former glory. Paisley himself never denied his ambition to occupy the number one political post in the province. He had only been a Stormont MP for a year, but in an interview with an *Irish Times* reporter around this time, he admitted that he 'would not shirk the duty of becoming Prime Minister of Northern Ireland if the circumstances were such that the people of this country felt I was the right man'.[5]

Chichester-Clark resigned on 20 March to be succeeded three days later by Brian Faulkner, fulfilling an ambition Faulkner had long cherished. However, he had never anticipated he would become prime minister in such troubled circumstances or indeed that he would face continual political pressure from a Free Presbyterian minister whose church and politics were becoming increasingly popular within one section of the community in spite of – or perhaps as a result of? – the continued violence and mayhem which was tearing the province apart. Paisley immediately targeted Faulkner as being already tarnished by his association with the security failures of the past: 'In his acceptance speech he gave no hint of any change in his attitude: he said there was no need for new principles or policies.'[6] Aware of the degree of respect in which Faulkner was still held, certainly by many in the unionist community and possibly by some nationalists – a respect which he had largely built up during his period as minister of commerce in the sixties – Paisley acknowledged that the new prime minister did have some gifts, but warned that these were far outweighed by certain negative qualities: 'There is no denying that Faulkner is a competent and efficient Parliamentarian, but as Prime Minister he will prove demanding and dictatorial.' Faulkner's far from perfect commitment to reform in Northern Ireland was forgotten and he was portrayed instead as a prime minister in the O'Neill mould: 'We remember him for his pushing through the reform programme, including the Housing Executive Bill. We remember him for his enthusiasm for cross-border talks. We know that he had secret talks with Cardinal Conway.... We know that Faulkner is keen on establishing greater links with the Republic.' Finally, Paisley warned that Faulkner could not be trusted as the guardian of Ulster's interests: 'His declared policies are but the sugar coating of a bitter pill, and during the next few weeks the real, the aggressive, the dictatorial Faulkner will emerge, but he could be Ulster's shortest reigning Premier, as we will not tolerate any further erosion of our standards and principles.' Paisley's prophecy about the length of Faulkner's tenure in office later proved to be correct, but for once the Free Presbyterian moderator had not been the major player in the drama surrounding the resignation of a Stormont prime minister.

The introduction of internment without trial on 9 August 1971 proved without doubt to be the main factor leading to a further escalation of violence and ultimately to Faulkner's downfall and the prorogation of the Stormont parliament in March 1972. Possibly the prime minister and his advisers had been encouraged by memories of the success of internment in the late fifties, but on that occasion it had been introduced on both sides of the border by both northern and southern governments, a similarity noticeably missing in August 1971. Apart from the wisdom or otherwise of introducing the measure in the first instance, other factors such as poor military intelligence and an imbalance in the ratio of Republicans detained in comparison to the number of loyalist detainees further contributed to a worsening situation. Within a few days 7,000 people, mostly Catholics, were reported homeless, and the number of killings in the remaining months of 1971 far outnumbered that in the months prior to 9 August. One of the most damning indictments of the measure was the propaganda weapon which it presented to the IRA, which now claimed to be the victim of an unjust and corrupt regime.

Paisley is on record as having opposed internment. Speaking in Westminster a few months later, he declared: 'Until we are prepared to look at the problem of internment, we shall go from bad to worse in this situation.'[7] He realised that his questioning of the measure was far from popular with Unionist and Conservative members of Parliament: 'I have been accused by Hon. Members on this side of wanting to open the gates of Long Kesh and to set loose the street gunmen. I want to do no such thing. I want the gunmen and the murderers to be tried properly and put away.' Either Paisley was displaying a wisdom on this occasion which was less evident among other Unionists or his opposition sprang from a fear that the net of internment might be extended at some stage to include 'loyalist' suspects. When Faulkner took office in March 1971, Paisley had suggested: 'There is no doubt that he will be contemplating internment of Protestants – a plan for which there is more than mere speculation.'

The demise of the Protestant Unionists and the formation of the Ulster Democratic Unionist Party (DUP) in September 1971 marked another stage in Ian Paisley's political pilgrimage. Again he had the assistance – at least for a time – of Desmond Boal, soon to become one of the province's leading barristers. Paisley had discussed the possibility of a wider alliance with those now representing the right wing of Unionism – William Craig, Bertie Dickinson and others closely associated with the Orange Order – but nothing materialised. He may well have had his own reservations about the benefits of working within party political structures with a number of other strong personalities, and they certainly had reservations about working with him. While a number of similarities existed between Paisley and the others, his ambitions and reputation were already well known and ruled out any possibility of any shared party allegiance at this juncture, and indeed in the future.

The word 'Protestant', which had formed such a key part of the former 'Protestant Unionist' party title, was now dropped, Clifford Smyth argued, because of 'a growing awareness that it was necessary to dilute the emphasis which the Protestant Unionist Party had placed on religious issues, and in particular Paisley's coarse and unsophisticated anti-Catholicism, typified in his campaigning denunciations of the pope as "old red socks"'.[8] While Smyth's own membership of the DUP in the mid-seventies (he was forced to resign in 1976 because of his alleged association with a document linking Paisley to bogus paramilitary coup plans) makes him an authority to be respected, certainly in relation to DUP politics at this time, it has to be said that the evidence gleaned from DUP publications reveals little, if any, shift away from Paisley's anti-papal, anti-Catholic creed, which remained central to both his politics and his particular form of Christianity. Indeed, it might be argued that while Boal described the DUP as 'right wing in the sense of being strong on the constitution, but to the left on social policies', his own eventual departure from the DUP camp may have been due to the continuing prominence given to Paisley's unapologetic and unashamed anti-Catholic position. This, of course, in Paisley's mind, formed an integral element in his constitutional policy and was not unrelated to his social philosophy, since he regarded Catholicism as one of the chief causes of poverty and the social ills that poverty often brought with it.

An editorial in the *Protestant Telegraph* in December 1971, just three months after the founding of the new party, declared: 'Liberty is the very essence of Bible Protestantism. Tyranny is the very essence of Popery. Where Protestantism flourishes, Liberty flames. Where Popery reigns, Tryanny rules. As Liberty and Tyranny have no common meeting place, so Protestantism and Popery cannot be reconciled. Those who assert otherwise only show up their own abysmal ignorance.'[9] Paisley applied this message in political terms to signify – in a front page article in the same issue – 'Protestant No to a United Ireland'. In what might be interpreted as a response to Harold Wilson's suggestion in the House of Commons that moves toward the eventual reunification of Ireland could be the answer to current problems, he declared:

'Our fathers answered the agitators for Nationalism and Republicanism in Ireland with the short but effective answer 'Home Rule would be Rome rule'. Our answer today to all proposals for a united Ireland is fundamentally the same. Rule from Dublin would be rule from Maynooth [the seat of the Roman Catholic hierarchy in Ireland] and rule from Maynooth would be rule from Rome.

While Paisley's language was often emotive and alarmist, and some might also describe his allegations as exaggerated and frequently inaccurate, they were not always without some degree of substance. Part of Paisley's criticism was directed at the wording of Article forty-four in the 1937 Constitution of Ireland, which referred to the special place which the Roman Catholic Church held in the life of the people: 'The State recognises the special position of the Holy Catholic Apostolic and Roman Church as the guardian of the Faith professed by the great majority of the citizens.'[10] Those who drafted this wording may have thought they were merely reflecting things as they actually existed in the Republic, but they overlooked the fact, among other things, that others might interpret the special position of the Roman Catholic Church in the Republic as justification for the special position of Protestantism in Northern Ireland. The offending article was removed in 1972, but in 1971 Paisley was using it to support his argument that the Republic's Constitution was essentially sectarian. He struck a chord in the minds of northern Protestants when he warned that the special place of the Roman Catholic Church meant that Roman Catholic moral theology influenced all areas of the Irish government's thinking, both national and local.

In November 1971 Paisley announced that he had information from 'an unimpeachable source' – it is widely recognised that he had contacts in most government departments who were willing to breach the confidentiality of their office – that direct rule would be introduced in a matter of weeks.[11] It is now known that the Westminster government had been considering the suspension of the Stormont Parliament for some months, particularly at the time of the introduction of internment, but had held back in an attempt to avoid providing the IRA with what they would have regarded as yet another victory in their campaign. As the news on the grapevine became more positive, Paisley warned that such a measure could lead to disaster: 'Any change in the position or status of our Parliament, or any tampering with our Constitution by Heath or his legal experts will be seen as political intimidation. The Protestants of Ulster have been attacked militarily and politically from all sides – any further assault could bring Ulster to breaking point.'[12]

Many of his supporters would have interpreted his warnings as suggesting the need for a militant response:

Briefly we will not be giving up – our British citizenship, our Protestant heritage, our Civil and Religious Liberty, our Parliament and our Resolve. 'No Surrender' and 'Not an Inch' have been shouted in the past; now we must mean them. There must be no diminution of our status; we have taken enough; now we must say 'Thus far and no further'.

The Parliament that Carson and Craigavon established – 'for a Protestant people' – is not to be wrecked by Heath or Faulkner to satisfy the rebel demands and taunts of the IRA, Lynch or the SDLP. What has been built up in Ulster since King William chased tyrant James from Boyne waters is not to be pulled down to please Rome's cry of 'Ireland for the Pope'.

The Protestantism that made Ulster great must not be chloroformed by the ecumenical desire to solicit popery in the vain hope that peace can come of such a union. Our Protestant liberties must not be bound by the tyrants' ropes in Dublin or Westminster.

The Ulster people are prepared to protect this Province with their own blood. They are prepared to stand for their own cause. We are prepared to protect our heritage with our own lives. Ulster is at arms length from civil war – if Westminster does what its outriders threaten. The Roses and the Wilsons of this world must be told in no uncertain terms that Ulster will never surrender her blood-bought rights.[13]

On 24 March 1972, Edward Heath, the Conservative prime minister, announced the suspension of the Stormont Parliament for one year after the Faulkner government refused to accept the handing over of all security powers to Westminster, despite the implicit provision for such a hand-over in the 1920 Government of Ireland Act. It marked the end of fifty years in which successive Unionist goverments had ruled Northern Ireland and it was greeted with jubilation in Republican and Nationalist areas.

William Whitelaw was appointed the first secretary of state and he made it clear from the beginning that he wanted to initiate a period of political dialogue. Paisley now performed one of the most remarkable U-turns of his political life. Since his first hint in December 1971 that the British government might be considering the implementation of direct rule, he had virtually threatened a militant response should the plan proceed. He had previously said,'The Ulster people are prepared to protect this Province with their own blood', but once Heath had announced it he now urged calmness and restraint: 'Talk of making Ulster ungovernable by disruption and further strikes is tantamount to anarchy. The local and national economy would not survive any further strain; we must not wreck our country in the hope of restoring our parliament.'[14] Rather than advocate armed resistance to the measure, he now suggested that God was the one who would save the day for them: 'The motto of the UVF was "For God and Ulster" – we must not lose sight of the spiritual struggle by being blinded by the political. In the last resort it will be God who will save Ulster – not the arm of the flesh.' While his language was still colourful – he described William Whitelaw as a 'Political Pope' and taoiseach Jack Lynch as the 'head of a potato republic' – he encouraged peaceful and democratic methods by which to express their opposition to the new arrangements: 'We have a year to campaign for Ulster's rights.'

Paisley's decision to drop his militant approach came in the wake of Craig's formation of the Ulster Vanguard movement, which was clearly mopping up the support of the paramilitaries and others with its own style of militancy. At a rally in the Ormeau Park, Belfast, on 18 March which drew an estimated crowd of 60,000, Craig had warned that 'if and when the politicians fail us, it may be our job to liquidate the enemy'.[15]

Paisley, as we have seen, had been guilty of using similar language, but Craig's attempt to gather in loyalist support and the enthusiastic response he was receiving may have caused Paisley to change course rather than be seen to be in competition with him, or, indeed, within his camp. Also, Craig's suggestion of an independent Ulster may have convinced Paisley of the need for some 'clear blue water' between the DUP and Vanguard. At Westminster, Paisley cautioned: '...Mr Craig's UDI [Unilateral Declaration of Independence]. That is certainly not acceptable to the vast majority of loyalists. Had their opinions been sought, they would have said that they wanted to hold to the Union. It is the Union that is uppermost in their minds. I emphasise that.'[16] In fact Paisley momentarily appeared to ditch his enthusiasm for the restoration of Stormont and opt for complete integration within the United Kingdom: 'Let us be completely integrated. Let this House take its courage into its hands and control the destinies of part of the United Kingdom. In that way lies a *possible* solution, because I believe that there are Roman Catholics – in fact, a vast number of them – who would prefer to be part and parcel of the United Kingdom rather than have Stormont in its present place.'

Some loyalist paramilitaries suggest another reason for Paisley's sudden change of policy: despite his many warnings of the sacrifices people were willing to make to preserve their heritage, when actually faced with the doomsday situation, he found he could not and would not himself translate his militant rhetoric into militant action. They suggest that he often led others to consider the militant option but could never embrace it himself; as the nursery rhyme, 'The Grand Old Duke of York' expresses it, he would often lead his men up to the top of the hill and then immediately march them down again. Or as one anonymous paramilitary source quietly muttered (amended version): 'He didn't have the guts for it!' This kind of attitude would appear to characterise Paisley's approach for some time: calling for militancy but leaving it to others to carry it out. A month after the suspension of Stormont, he was once again calling for militant action, but this time it was the British army who were exhorted to do the job: 'All loyalists demand the implementation of a military policy to wipe out the IRA – NOW!'[17]

No to Power-Sharing

Escalating violence in Northern Ireland must surely have been a factor behind the Westminster government's suggestion of a devolved power-sharing administration in the province. Tragically the number of deaths directly related to the Troubles had continued to rise each year since 1969:

1969:	13
1970:	25
1971:	174
1972:	467

For some the answer was simply stronger security and the restoration of the *status quo* as it had existed prior to the prorogation of Stormont. Westminster, however, believed that, coupled with strong security measures, the situation also called for the consideration of new structures of government for the province. The first serious proposals regarding power-sharing appeared in the government White Paper *Northern Ireland Constitutional Proposals* issued on 20 March 1973. For the first time in the history of Northern Ireland people were being asked to consider the possibility of electing a Northern Ireland government which would draw its support from both sections of the community. 'It is the view of the government that the executive itself can no longer be solely based upon any single party, if that party draws its support and its elected representation virtually entirely from only one section of a divided community.'[18] The proposals also suggested that any new arrangements drawn up in Northern Ireland should be acceptable to the government in the Republic of Ireland and went as far as drafting the idea of a 'council' – similar to the proposal of a council in the 1920 Government of Ireland Act – to handle North-South relations: 'If a Council is to be set up not merely as a statutory concept, but as a useful working mechanism in north-south relations, it must operate with the consent of both majority and minority opinion in Northern Ireland, who have a right to prior consultation and involvement in the process of determining its form, functions and procedures.'[19]

From the outset Paisley opposed the proposals set out in the White Paper, suggesting that the real intention of the Westminster government was to lead the province into a United Ireland: 'It makes Ulster men and women second-class citizens in the United Kingdom, and is a half-way house to a United Ireland.'[20] He described the power-sharing proposals as 'an attempt to destroy democracy' and also a 'blow at the secrecy of the ballot-box'.[21] Once again he warned that the country was facing a crisis: 'The hour is grave. Both the Stormont and Westminster Governments by their disastrous appeasement policies have established the destructive principle that REPUBLICAN VIOLENCE PAYS.' His wrath was focused particularly on Brian Faulkner, the former Northern Ireland prime minister, who along with the SDLP, Alliance and NILP, was willing to take the White Paper proposals seriously.

A coalition of loyalist/Unionist groups opposed to the White Paper brought Paisley into a working relationship for the first time with some of his former rivals and opponents: Harry West, James Molyneaux (Unionists opposed to the White Paper); William Craig, Martin Smyth and Ernest Baird (Vanguard); and John Laird (West Belfast Loyalists). All groups in the coalition prepared carefully for the June election for the seventy-eight seats in the new Northern Ireland Assembly, and none more so than Ian Paisley. He suggested that the main issue facing the electorate was one of choosing whether they wished to remain within the United Kingdom or not, thereby implying that Faulkner and his Unionist colleagues were heading for a United Ireland: 'June 28th will be the most decisive day in Ulster's history. This Assembly election provides every elector with the opportunity to decide the destiny of the Province. The main issue is concise: is Ulster to remain within the United Kingdom? Intimidated as we are on all sides – let us show the world that in spite of threats Ulster can hold up its head and proudly and fearlessly say NO SURRENDER.'

The 72 per cent turnout at the polls indicated the high level of interest in the political alternatives facing the country. Parties favouring the White Paper proposals secured a clear majority in the seventy-eight seat assembly and also a clear majority of first preference votes:

Parties Favouring the White Paper Proposals:

Party	Seats	1st Preference votes	% Valid poll
Official Unionists	24	211,362	29.3
SDLP	19	159,773	22.1
Alliance	8	66,541	9.2
NILP	1	18,675	2.6
Total	52	456,351	63.2

Parties Against the White Paper proposals:

Party	Seats	1st Preference votes	% Valid poll
Unionists	8	61,183	8.5
DUP	8	78,228	10.8
Vanguard	7	75,759	10.5
West Belfast Loyalists	3	16,869	2.3
Total	26	232,039	32.1

Allowing for some unforeseen circumstances as well as the 'change your mind' factor when the assembly opened, Faulkner could rely on twenty-one Unionist votes while twenty-seven Unionist/loyalists were opposed to him, giving a final tally of forty-nine to twenty-seven Assembly members in favour of considering the White Paper guidelines. It was an encouraging majority at this early stage. A promising beginning, however, failed to develop over the next twelve months into new and sustainable structures of government in Northern Ireland, leading to the collapse of the power-sharing executive which took office on 1 January 1974 with Brian Faulkner as chief executive and Gerry Fitt as his deputy.

Firstly, there was an absence of a 'missionary spirit' behind the enterprise. While the *Belfast Telegraph* had been encouraging its readers to be more open to considering change in the structures of government in Northern Ireland, the written word alone was inadequate to prepare people for radical change. There were no advocates for change who could convince the public that power sharing was good government and good for the country. History suggests that changes in structures, whether political or ecclesiastical, can seldom be implemented and sustained if they are not supported by enthusiastic advocates for the reform. In this respect the odds were stacked against the experiment in power-sharing right from the start. The 'missionary spirit', which should have been an essential ingredient in the new package, was not only missing from among the supporters of the executive, but was found in abundant supply among its opponents. Paisley and Craig were prepared to travel the province addressing large gatherings and small meetings to persuade Unionists they were being betrayed and destroyed. In November 1973 Paisley insisted: 'There can be no doubt – no matter what Faulkner says to the contrary – that the Executive is not a step towards government but a move towards greater disaster; it is not a step towards proper democratic politics but an invitation to civil war; it is not the salvation of Ulster, but the heralding of a united Ireland.'[22] Many Unionists listened and believed him. His gifts as a communicator and his experience as a mob orator were now relentlessly employed in a crusade to block and thwart the successful implementation of power-sharing. And it was largely his rhetoric which eventually brought down the executive on 28 May 1974.

Another factor contributing to its failure must surely have been the unrealistic and untimely expectations regarding a Council of Ireland which northern nationalists, and the British and Irish governments, placed on the Unionist members of the executive. The concept of power-sharing was in itself a new departure for Unionism, which had accepted one-party government as of right for the past fifty years, but to expect Unionist voters to accommodate two major changes, power-sharing *and* a Council of Ireland, revealed, more than anything, the deep ignorance of each other's communities which existed among the parties negotiating the Sunningdale Agreement in December 1973. The Republic's government was keen to press ahead with the setting up of a council to provide some kind of north-south link as a focus by which northern nationalists might express their Irish identity, pending the day, as they thought, when a majority in Northern Ireland might voluntarily choose the path of reunification. They also saw the implementation of a council as a means of drawing support away from the IRA. They were prepared to press ahead with these demands, while at the same time doing little or nothing to alleviate Unionist concerns regarding the all-Ireland designs written into Articles 2 and 3 of its Constitution:

Article 2: The national territory consists of the whole island of Ireland, its islands and the territorial seas.

Article 3: Pending the re-integration of the national territory, and without prejudice to the right of the Parliament and Government established by the Constitution to exercise jurisdiction over the whole of that territory, the laws enacted by that Parliament shall have the like area and extent of application as the laws of Saorstát Éireann and the like extra-territorial effect.[23]

Garret FitzGerald, the Republic's minister of foreign affairs, recognised, to some extent, the difficulties which these articles created for Unionists. As the son of a Presbyterian mother and Catholic father who had both been involved in the 1916 Easter Rising in Dublin, he had had a life-long interest in politics and, in particular, the reconciliation of the two traditions in Ireland. Indeed, he unsuccessfully attempted to persuade the taoiseach, Liam Cosgrave, at least to express a willingness on the part of the government to re-examine the Constitution. In his autobiography he relates what happened to a draft speech he had prepared for Cosgrave to deliver on 21 June 1973 in advance of the Assembly elections on the 28 June: 'He dropped several passages, however. One of these stated our willingness to re-examine our Constitution and laws so as to identify what changes were necessary to demonstrate that we had learnt from past errors and that we were determined not to tolerate anything that gave offence to the religious minority within the state.'[24] After twenty-three years, Articles 2 and 3 still remain within the Constitution and unequivocal recognition of the state of Northern Ireland by the Republic's government has never been conceded. The best that Cosgrave could give in response to Faulkner's pleas that the Republic should scrap Articles 2 and 3 was a declaration 'that there could be no change in the status of Northern Ireland until the majority of the people of Northern Ireland desired a change in that status'.[25] Within this 'no-change' constitutional position on the part of the Republic, the successful acceptance of a Council of Ireland carrying some executive powers *and* a power-sharing executive should have been seen as an unrealistic dream by the majority of delegates at Sunningdale, but regrettably this was not the case. Bew and Gillespie have hinted that Whitelaw's presence at Sunningdale might have brought a greater sense of realism to the proceedings, as he was more familiar with the pressures Faulkner faced within the Unionist family. However, his move from the Northern Ireland Office to secretary of state for employment – to deal with pressures Heath was facing from the National Union of Mineworkers – resulted in the introduction of the less experienced Francis Pym.[26]

The cumulative effect of these factors resulted in an erosion of Faulkner's support within the Unionist Party and, eventually, among the wider traditional Unionist electorate. On 4 January 1974 he lost the support of the Ulster Unionist Council who rejected the proposals for an all-Ireland council by 427 votes to 374. His inevitable resignation as Unionist Party leader followed three days later. Harry West, elected as Faulkner's successor, now swung the entire Unionist Party machine against the Sunningdale Agreement. A month later the unexpected Westminster general election revealed a massive groundswell of Unionist opposition to the agreement when the United Ulster Unionist Council (UUUC), comprising West's UUP, Craig's Vanguard and Paisley's DUP, won 11 of the 12 seats. The executive had just taken office based on a working majority within the Stormont Assembly, but in the course of eight months that majority had disappeared and Unionist support for the principles of 'power-sharing' had largely evaporated. Paisley's support for the UUUC had all the hallmarks of a principled politician who put country above party, but he never missed the opportuniy to present himself as the one standing in the succession of those who had been instrumental in the founding of the state:

May we appeal to the loyalists to put principle before men and country before party. The greater issue is the salvation of Ulster. Support for any candidate other than those opposed to the Sunningdale surrender is support for a United Ireland by stealth and submission. 'For God and Ulster' was the motto of Carson's UVF – we who are the heirs of Carson Unionism must apply the same motto of resolution and determination.[27]

A third factor in the downfall of the power-sharing executive was the influence of the loyalist paramilitaries during the 'Ulster Workers' Council' (UWC) strike which began on 15 May 1974, following the Assembly's rejection the previous day of a motion condemning power-sharing and the Council of Ireland by 44 votes to 28. The actual announcement of the planned strike had been made by the UWC at the meeting of a 'study group' of the UUUC attended by representatives of the Ulster Defence Association (UDA) and the UVF and presided over by Paisley.[28] The co-ordinating committee which directed the strike included the three UUUC leaders: Paisley, West and Craig. Most now accept that intimidation practised by the paramilitaries was a significant feature of the strike. Gallagher and Worrall confirm this aspect of paramilitary involvement: 'That there was intimidation is unquestioned; and behind the UWC, giving the orders, stood the "Ulster Army Council" enforcing them, in some cases with proven acts of violence.'[29] Ken Bloomfield, the civil servant who served as secretary to the executive, similarily states: 'This committee [UWC] argued that it relied on the moral force of a popular mandate derived from the Westminster election. In reality it also relied very heavily on muscle: the paramilitary muscle of men in dark glasses armed with pickaxe handles and other inducements to co-operation, and the industrial muscle of loyalist cadres in essential services such as the generation and distribution of electricity and the distribution of petrol and fuel oils.'[30]

It is interesting to note the completely different attitude taken by
Nelson Mandela and the African National Congress to the use of
coercion in a political strike. It was an issue they faced from time to
time in the course of their struggle in South Africa. Mandela explains
how in 1958 and other occasions the ANC decided firmly against
employing coercive measures to further their political goals: 'We had
heated discussions about whether we ought to have relied on coercive
measures. Should we have used pickets, which generally prevent people
from entering their place of work? The hard-liners suggested that if we
had deployed pickets, the strike would have been a success. But I have
always resisted such methods. It is best to rely on the freely given
support of the people; otherwise that support is weak and fleeting. The
organisation should be a haven, not a prison.'[31]

Ian Paisley, moderator of the Free Presbyterian Church of Ulster,
was clearly quite comfortable with the idea of using coercive methods
and working with the paramilitaries. He feared that if he distanced
himself from the working-class leaders of the UWC – and it was difficult at times to distinguish who was affiliated to a paramilitary organisation and who was not – he would lose the Unionist support he had
so vigorously built up over the years. But he may also have been slightly
uncomfortable with the image it portrayed, and he absented himself for
a substantial period of the strike with the excuse that he had to go to
Canada to attend the funeral of a close friend. Paisley had built up a
reputation that he was always to be found where the action was, so he
was not playing true to form when, having associated himself with the
organisation of the strike, he then disappeared from the scene.

His working alliance with the paramilitaries begs the question of his
consistency in policy towards paramilitarism. In the previous four years
929 people had been killed, most of these as the result of paramilitary
activity from one source or the other. Paisley must have known
something of the track record of the people he was working with in the
UWC. Did he conclude that the purpose of the strike justified the
methods and personnel used? He had in the past published UDA
articles in his *Protestant Telegraph*, especially when they paid glowing
tributes to his leadership. In 1972 one such article, 'Dr Paisley – Ulster's
Voice', by the Sydenham Defence Association, had declared:

It was Paisley who awakened the loyalists of Ulster to the betrayal of
O'Neill's so-called bridge-building policies, Paisley who forced O'Neill out
of office, who spoke of no-go areas as far back as 1969, who exposed the
incompetence of Chichester-Clark, who warned that the B Specials would
be disbanded while Faulkner said they would stay. It was Paisley who told

that Direct Rule was on the way while press and politicians scorned such a suggestion. NO MAN IN ULSTER OR OUT OF ULSTER CAN POINT HIS FINGER AT IAN PAISLEY'S POLITICAL CONSISTENCY. Paisley has given the lead to Ulster's loyalists all down the line. He has always been one step ahead of the rest of Ulster's political field.... This is the stuff of which great leaders are made. 'Ulster is British' is Paisley's cry. It is in the hands of the ordinary grassroot loyalists of Ulster to fight to SAVE the union with Great Britain.[32]

Paisley clearly thought that this kind of paramilitary support was still important to him in 1974, but in March 1975 he uttered one of the clearest denunciations of paramilitary violence ever made by a Northern Ireland politician. Referring first to the IRA as 'bloodthirsty murderers' whose atrocious crimes 'reek to the highest heaven', he then expressed his surprise that people claiming to be Protestants should engage in similar violence: 'What stuns really the decent Ulster Protestant is that a section of his own community would engage under the guise of Protestantism and Loyalty in crimes just as heinous and hellish. As a Protestant leader I once again totally, utterly and unreservedly condemn these atrocious crimes and those who perpetrated them or planned to perpetrate them.'[33]

It was probably not a coincidence that his condemnation was made at a time when serious feuding had broken out between two loyalist paramilitary groups, the UDA and UVF, resulting in deaths within both groups. Some might consider that the condemnation would have been equally applicable twelve months earlier in the period before the strike.

Relationships with the paramilitaries continued to be complex with possibly only one clear, consistent strand emerging: courtship and a working relationship developed when political advantage could be gained – as in 1974 – but condemnation when that proved advantageous politically for him. For example, in September and October 1975 he was at odds with William Craig over his idea of a 'voluntary coalition' – involving the SDLP – as an emergency solution to continuing violence and political instability. Craig's proposal had been supported by the UDA, whose leader, Andy Tyrie, suggested that Paisley and West would be blamed for any further killings as they were the ones blocking the implementation of the coalition. Paisley turned on Tyrie: 'The brazen effrontery and confounded cheek of Mr Tyrie baffles description. He is the man who leads an organisation whose members in the past months have been tried in the courts and have pleaded guilty or have been found guilty of the most diabolical of crimes. They have murdered Protestants as well as Roman Catholics in the most sadistic and inhuman ways and have sought to intimidate decent people who seek to carry out their business in a proper manner.'[34] And yet less than two years later he was once again successfully courting the co-operation of this same paramilitary organisation in the United Unionist Action Council strike of May 1977, called by Ernest Baird, the new Vanguard leader, and himself.

Paisley must have been aware that a number of paramilitary leaders attended Martyrs' Memorial church - some more regularly than others - and this may have made him more open to the idea of working with them in the May 1974 strike: John McKeague was chairman of the Shankill Defence Association when he fell out with Paisley in 1969; David Payne and Tommy Herron, two other UDA leaders, also attended; and Ken Gibson, the East Belfast UVF leader, was a member of the Sunday afternoon men's Bible class.

Undoubtedly, one of the most notorious paramilitary leaders attending was William McGrath, the leader of Tara, who had identified himself with Paisley's anti-Catholicism since the fifties and sixties. He had formed Tara in 1966, incorporating within its aims and goals a strange mixture of, on the one hand, acceptance of Irish Gaelic culture and language, and, on the other hand, a demand for the outlawing of the Roman Catholic Church. In the seventies McGrath was a housefather in Kincora boys' home in East Belfast, eventually taking over complete responsibility for the home. One of Paisley's congregation, Valerie Shaw, had warned her minister of allegations that McGrath was sexually abusing the youths in his care but Paisley took no action. While there is absolutely no suggestion of any impropriety on Paisley's part, it must have been a source of some embarrassment to him when McGrath and four others were eventually jailed for these offences in December 1981. The Kincora scandal rumbled on for some time, further allegations being made that civil servants, the RUC and military intelligence were also involved, but Sir George Terry's October 1983 report declared that there was no evidence to substantiate these claims.

The working relationship between the UUUC leaders – Paisley, Craig and West – and the paramilitaries resulted in bringing life in Northern Ireland to a virtual standstill in May 1974 and is recognised as the factor which finally brought down the power-sharing executive. Perhaps unwittingly they had confirmed for paramilitaries on both sides of the community that the British government could, on occasions, be swayed by the use and threat of violence. The British army and the British government indicated throughout the strike that they were not going to move against the paramilitaries who were heavily involved in enforcing the stoppage of work. While some preferred to see the stoppage and the downfall of the executive as reflecting the democratic decision of the people in the February election, others saw in it another lesson: governments *will* listen to violent methods. The unfortunate consequence for Northern Ireland was that both paramilitary groupings assumed this to be the case. It was a recipe for a long and bitter struggle.

Rivalry with the Ulster Unionist Party

The United Ulster Unionist Council, created in 1974, lasted until May 1977, but the fragile alliance had been in danger of disintegrating long before this. At its strongest point in early 1974, it had recommended that 'the three parties have immediate consultations within themselves with the view to a setting up of a joint study group to examine in depth the possibility of joining the three parties into one strong political body'.[35] That nothing ever came of the proposal is not surprising; the other partners in the council very soon concluded that they simply could not trust Paisley. David Trimble, now Ulster Unionist Party leader but associated at that time with Craig's Vanguard Party, cites as an example the UUUC preparations to make a single submission in 1974 to the Gardiner Committee, which was investigating measures to deal with terrorism in Northern Ireland, with particular reference to civil liberties and human rights. Craig, who had been asked to look after the drafting of the submission, had delegated the responsibility to Trimble. After discussing it in detail with Craig, Trimble brought his draft to a meeting of the three leaders at Stormont.

Then along came Ian. And Ian pulled out of his jacket this draft. He said, 'This is the DUP draft!' He looked around and said, 'Harry, where's yours?'

And Harry spluttered and said, 'But I thought it was going to be a single draft!'

'Oh, no! No! No!' said Ian. 'Nothing of that sort was agreed at all!'

Trimble paused at this point to indicate as diplomatically as possible that he did not quite agree with the point that Paisley was making to West. He continued:

Harry was looking most distraught. There were only a few days left before the deadline for putting in submissions, and he was in quite some difficulty about this. So Harry went off in haste to try and get something. Bill went after him and I was left alone with Ian. Ian leaned forward and chuckled, 'Harry's in great trouble over this!'

I said, 'What do you mean?'

He said, 'Well, Harry was in the government that introduced internment and we are bringing forward proposals about the winding up of internment. Very embarrassing for Harry!'

I said, 'Not really. I'm sure it's not. Anybody can draw up something to take account of the change in circumstances. And anyway, this is part of the responsibility that comes from being in government – the fact that you get this embarrassment from time to time.'

And Ian guffawed. 'Oh, no!' he said, 'never be in government! Never be in government! Always stay in opposition! Much easier!' And he went off chuckling down the corridor.[36]

As Trimble commented, 'He upset an arrangement simply to score points over a colleague and rival.'

Paisley's attacks on colleagues and former colleagues soon multiplied. In the Constitutional Convention elected in May 1975 and wound up in March 1976, he strongly criticised Craig for his idea of a 'Voluntary Coalition' inclusive of the SDLP, and backed the UUUC report which called for a return to the 'majority rule' system. But he was very soon falling out with West's Ulster Unionists and frequently attacked them publicly in the columns of his *Protestant Telegraph*. In July 1976 Martin Smyth and Austin Ardill were nailed for talking to John Hume and Paddy Devlin of the SDLP. The UUP's decision to have nothing to do with his United Unionist Action Council strike of May 1977 against direct rule and in favour of a much tougher security policy – supported by the UDA and Ernest Baird's United Ulster Unionist Movement – was particularly annoying to him. When lack of public support and immediate government action signalled its failure, he appeared to forget his promise to quit politics if the strike was unsuccessful. Instead he turned on the UUP and suggested that their refusal to back the strike signified their willingness to put party interests before those of the country: 'Mr West evidently thinks that the Official Unionist Party is far more important than the country and seeks by falsehood to justify that position.'[37] In 1978 he declared that James Molyneaux, who in West's absence had taken over the leadership of the UUP MPs at Westminster, 'stands indicted before the Ulster people' because, as Paisley claimed, he had made a pact with the Labour government to give Roman Catholic schools 'power to vest Protestant property'.[38]

The two parties also differed on their attitude to the Peace People. While Paisley was scathing in his condemnation of them, the UUP appeared at least to sit back and see if the movement would draw away support from the IRA in republican areas. The movement had been prompted by massive public reaction to a tragic incident in West Belfast on 10 August 1976 which resulted in the deaths of three young children. Mrs Anne Maguire had been out with her three children – the youngest a six-month-old boy in his pram – when a gunman's getaway car crashed into them in the Andersonstown area. The driver had been shot dead by troops, causing the car to run out of control, mount the pavement and crush two of the children to death against a fence. The third child died the following day.[39] It was the children's aunt, Mairead Corrigan, and two others, Betty Williams and Ciaran McKeown, who founded the peace movement, declaring their methods and objectives as a 'non-violent movement towards a just and peaceful society'.[40] With cross-community support encouraging their initiative, they organised marches and rallies in Belfast, Dublin, London and throughout Northern Ireland.

Ian Paisley claims first and foremost to be a minister of Christ whom the Bible describes as the 'Prince of Peace'. Had he identified with the movement, swinging his great rhetorical gifts and boundless energy behind it, it would undoubtedly have elicited increased public support, including that of other leading public figures. This in turn would possibly have snuffed out support for paramilitary organisations on both sides of the political divide and produced the momentum necessary to reach an agreed political solution. However, the reality was that he launched one of his strongest attacks ever on those who were committed to the path of peace.

As he had mocked the efforts of Protestant church leaders who met Provisional IRA leaders at Feakle, County Clare, in December 1974 in an attempt to broker a genuine ceasefire, so too he hurled abuse at the peace movement: 'It is a controversial issue that the latest in a long line of spurious peace campaigns, this time under the auspices of the Andersonstown mothers, that many will be deceived and deluded. Yes, sincere, genuine and well-intentioned people will be caught up in a frenzy of emotion.... Certainly, there have been terrible personal tragedies, but building an organisation on someone's personal grief is exploitation and not a proper basis for a successful campaign.'[41] He accused Betty Williams of being a liar[42] and listed reasons for rejecting the movement: 'The Andersonstown women have failed on various counts to prove their sincerity. They say they want peace, "nothing else". At no time have they pledged, nor indeed will they pledge, their support for the police and army in the effort to stamp out terrorism. At no time did they promise to hand over the terrorists to the security forces. At no time did they agree to give information on the gangsters in their midst. At no time did they acknowledge that it was mothers who bred the terrorists.'[43] If he had no time for the non-sectarian Alliance Party, he had less time for the non-sectarian peace movement: 'The message of the UDUP is simple, you cannot be neutral in the Ulster War. Neutrality assists the enemy. On what side are you?'[44]

The Kingdom of the Beast

In June 1979 Paisley was elected to the European Parliament, the third Parliament he would attend as an elected member. As Stormont had been prorogued in 1972 and subsequent Stormont assemblies and conventions were relatively short-lived, it effectively meant that he was attending two Parliaments: Westminster and Strasbourg. Paisley topped the poll in 1979 and every subsequent European election:

Year	1st preference votes	% valid poll
1979	170,688	29.8
1984	230,251	33.6
1989	160,110	29.9
1994	163,246	29.1

Dr Paisley was always implacably opposed to any concept of closer European union. In the February 1963 issue of *The Revivalist*, a front page cartoon entitled 'The Common Market – The Papal Conspiracy Which Failed' depicted Harold MacMillan, the British prime minister, with a noose around his neck, being dragged towards a cliff edge by Pope John XXIII, who is saying, 'The end of Britain is in sight.' MacMillan, apprehensive and yet submissive, is saying, 'Nearer my pope to thee', but is held back because he is already bound by ropes around his ankles tied to a firm post labelled 'Bible Protestantism'. The cartoon graphically illustrates the religious basis of Paisley's opposition to the EEC. He sees it as the fulfilment of prophecy predicted in Daniel 2:1-45 and Revelation 17. The two passages, according to Paisley, need to be taken together because it is Revelation 17 which reveals that a religious as well as a political confederacy is predicted.[45] The passage in Revelation – understood by Paisley as referring to the papacy – depicts a woman, the great whore of Babylon, arrayed in purple and scarlet colour, decked with gold and precious stones and pearls, and upon her forehead a name 'MYSTERY, "BABYLON THE GREAT, THE MOTHER OF HARLOTS AND ABOMINATIONS OF THE EARTH"' (v. 5). Since the papacy - in Paisley's theology – controlled the religious confederacy which in turn ruled the political confederacy (the EEC), he has been an ardent opponent of the principles of European unity, but this has not prevented him from seeking the financial benefits which from time to time are made available to Northern Ireland due to its classification as one of Europe's poorer regions.

This particular interpretation of scripture forms the basis of Paisley's world view. It is not the great powers of the United States or Russia which hold centre stage in his understanding of God's plan for the fulfilment of prophecy: 'With all due respect to our American friends, they have no part nor lot in this particular matter of these kingdoms. These kingdoms are all geographically located around the Mediterranean area... the US President and the Russian leader might as well be snowmen tonight as far as Biblical prophecy is concerned.' The real drama, he maintains, is being acted out in Europe where Britain, as 'the only Protestant nation that is left in the EEC', has a vital role to play. The key therefore to understanding the issues facing people in Northern Ireland is to be found in his suggested interpretation of these two passages:

We are seeing now the development of the final kingdom of the beast. It is going to gain momentum. There is one thing which every Northern Ireland person better remember, the Anglo-Irish Agreement is tied into this. It is part of it, because in order to placate the South, in order to get the blessing of the European nations and America we in this Province are to be the sacrificial lamb. There is far more in the Anglo-Irish Agreement, than we are even aware of, internationally. We have been sold on the altar of political expediency in the furtherance of the kingdom of the beast.[46]

Paisely, however, is realistic enough to know that the general public are not going to understand easily or accept his views on biblical prophecy, so he also offers a secular case against the EEC or any developments toward greater European unity. He has three basic objections: 1. European unity militates against the sovereignty of Westminster as it places greater powers in the hands of legislatures and courts outside the United Kingdom. 2. Britain would be better off by having the freedom to trade with any country in the world. 3. Moves towards greater European unity have led to an increase in UK food prices and a worsening financial situation as regards its balance of payments.

The Anglo-Irish Agreement

The decision at the December 1980 summit between Margaret Thatcher, who had become British prime minister a year earlier, and Charles Haughey, the Irish taoiseach, to initiate a series of joint studies, signalled the beginning of a new relationship between Britain and the Republic of Ireland which was to lead within five years to the signing of the Anglo-Irish Agreement at Hillsborough Castle, County Down. The studies were to deal with matters of substance: security matters, economic co-operation, citizenship rights, measures to encourage mutual under-standing and, most significant of all, possible new institutional struc-tures which might give expression to – as the joint communiqué described it – 'the totality of relationships within the islands'. Paisley, suspicious of anything that might lead to a closer working relationship with the Republic, immediately interpreted the summit as the begin-ning of another doomsday situation. 'To surrender to the Haughey/Thatcher conspiracy would be to accept Rome Rule,' he declared. 'We are British and British we intend to stay. We will never give allegiance to Dublin.'[47] Lives were still being lost in the continuing tragedy of community violence, but he was quite prepared to suggest that further sacrifice might be required, as the situation was similar to that faced by Edward Carson and the Ulster loyalists in 1912: 'Every loyalist must now unite behind the Save Ulster Campaign and dedicate themselves, cost what it may, to the salvation of Northern Ireland.' Emotions were already running high in the nationalist/Republican community. The emotive appeal of the hunger-strike had been re-introduced the previous October into Irish political life by Republican prisoners at the Maze Prison who were demanding political status and the right to wear their own clothes and not the civilian-style clothes provided by the prison authorities.

Paisley's Save Ulster Campaign turned out to be another of his Grand Old Duke of York exercises. Selected representatives of the media were brought at midnight on 5 February 1981 to a County Antrim hillside to witness a disciplined group of 500 men in military formation waving what they claimed were firearms certificates. Paisley described the new group as 'the Third Force' and told the press: 'This is a small token of men who are placed to absolutely devastate any attempt by Margaret Thatcher and Charles Haughey to destroy the Union and take from us our heritage.'[48] A few days later he launched his new campaign with the signing of an 'Ulster Declaration' – based on the wording of the 1912 'Ulster Covenant' – at a rally held at the City Hall, Belfast. Endeavouring to stir up Unionist memories of

Carson's rallies held at various centres during the Home Rule Crisis of 1912-1914, Paisley organised similar rallies throughout the province, culminating in a final rally at the Carson monument in the Stormont Parliament grounds on Saturday 28 March. Estimates of the number who attended this final rally vary from 30,000 to 100,000.[49] Presenting himself as the true successor to Carson, he declared: 'Our campaign goes on – in different forms – but it goes on till our objective is obtained. What is our objective? It is the ending of the talks with Dublin. That is our goal and we will not rest till it is attained. Indeed we dare not rest for if these talks are not stopped then the British Ulster we know and love is finished. But I and my colleagues are determined that Ulster is far from finished and likewise therefore our campaign is far from finished.'[50] However, according to the *Protestant Telegraph*, the colleagues he mentioned did not include the Ulster Unionists: 'He lambasted the Official Unionists and in particular Mr Molyneaux.' While Paisley may have quoted Carson's famous words of defiance, 'We will stop at nothing if an attempt is to be made to hand the loyalists over to those whom we believe to be the enemies of our country', he should also have reflected on the image he was presenting of a divided Unionist family, a picture considerably different from Carson's clearly united Unionist movement.

The Anglo-Irish joint studies initiated by Thatcher and Haughey in December 1980 led to the establishment of an inter-governmental council on 6 November 1981 by Thatcher and FitzGerald, now leader of a coalition government which had replaced Haughey's Fianna Fáil administration the previous June. The DUP leader responded to this new development and the murder soon after of the Revd Robert Bradford, Ulster Unionist MP for South Belfast – shot dead along with a community worker, Ken Campbell, while attending to constituency business at a community centre – by calling for tougher security measures on the part of the United Kingdom government and announcing a 'Day of Action' for Monday, 23 November. Paisley planned a total stoppage of work from mid-day and announced that tractor and car cavalcades would be converging on all major towns. The day's events ended with a rally attended by 15,000 people in the centre of Newtownards, County Down. He addressed the rally with a large number of his 'Third Force' on display: 'We demand that the IRA be exterminated from Ulster. The aim of the IRA is to destroy the last vestige of Protestantism in our island home. But there is one army the Republic fears and that every other enemy of Ulster fears and that is the army of armed and resolute Protestants.'[51] Appearing to cast aside all caution about coded language, he declared: 'Here are men willing to do the job of exterminating the IRA. Recruit them under the Crown and they will do it. If you refuse, we will have no other decision to make but to do it ourselves.' Had Paisley assumed the role of commander-in-chief of the force or some office even higher and more comprehensive than this? His speech certainly seemed to suggest some allegiance – similar to the loyalty sworn by his earlier Ulster Protestant Volunteers – which superceded the citizen's duty to the Crown: 'These men are pledged to me and I am pledged to them, and by God's grace we shall devise a way, plan a strategy, and put it into operation and smash the London/Dublin talks.' As far as the moderator was concerned, God was with his men and on his side. Calling for the recruitment of a force of 100,000 men, he assured the crowd that victory would come: 'The men and women of Ulster, united with their faith in God and with their faith in their glorious cause, shall go forward to certain and definite victory.'

The 'Big Man' had once again led his men to the top of the hill but, like the UPV and others, he led them down again. Within twelve months, or even less, the 'Third Force' no longer existed. Certainly, there was no further reference to them.

The British government made yet another attempt to encourage the local Northern Ireland political parties in the direction of 'power-sharing' in its White Paper, *Northern Ireland: A Framework for Devolution*, published on 5 April 1982. It proposed the election of a seventy-eight-member assembly which would begin with a consultative and scrutiny role but then move on to explore the possibility or other-wise of 70 per cent of its members reaching agreement with the secre-tary of state – then James Prior, formerly employment secretary in the Thatcher cabinet – on the method and implementation of the devolu-tion of one or more local departments.

Prior envisaged a gradual devolution of powers involving the setting up of a local administration in which he would be responsible for the appointment of ministers. This 'rolling devolution' scheme was eventu-ally dismissed by the three largest parties: the SDLP thought it 'unworkable'; the UUP preferred closer integration within the United Kingdom; and the DUP, while favouring the devolution of powers to a local administration, were not prepared to consider 'power-sharing'.

Prior's scheme, however, highlighted one of the major differences between the two Unionist parties at this time, differences which surfaced in bitter wrangling at both Westminster and Stormont. Enoch Powell, who had been Conservative MP for Wolverhampton SW for twenty-four years, had identified himself with the Unionist cause and become Ulster Unionist MP for South Down at Westminster. But Powell interpreted the government White Paper as part of a conspiracy to detach Northern Ireland from the United Kingdom and pave the way for the eventual reunification of Ireland. In these circumstances he was less than lukewarm regarding the proposals for devolving local powers to departments in Northern Ireland and argued instead for complete integration within the United Kingdom. Jim Molyneaux, UUP party leader, was also inclined to favour this position. While Paisley himself had, on occasions, desired greater integration within the UK and suggested that Roman Catholics would far rather have this than a local Stormont administration, he now directed some of his strongest criticism at both Powell and Molyneaux, describing the former as 'an Englishman' and a 'foreigner and Anglo-Catholic'.[52] Clifford Smyth explains the surprise that many Unionists felt at Paisley's attack on Powell:

Paisley's rejection of Powell brought to the surface undercurrents of resentment, anti-intellectualism, and a tendency to isolationism. The paradoxes in Paisley's position were nearly as complex as the man himself. Here was the advocate of Democratic Unionism treating the leading parliamentarian of his generation to a vial of the DUP leader's vitriol, and the defender of traditional Unionism heaping ingratitude on an English politician who had chosen, not only to bear the same personal risks and dangers as Ulster politicians, but to advocate the cause of the Union with all the passion and integrity at his command.[53]

Paisley reacted swiftly to the Irish government's announcement in March 1983 that they were acceding to the request from the SDLP to set up an all-Ireland forum to allow Irish constitutional parties both north and south – those that accepted the decision of the ballot-box – the opportunity to spell out their views on the best methods of achieving their goal of a 'new Ireland'. The initiative had come from John Hume, who had become SDLP leader after Gerry Fitt's resignation from the party in 1979. Hume had mixed motives: on the one hand he wanted the Irish parties to indicate how they could pursue their goal of Irish unity without over-riding the interests and identity of northern Protestants, but he also wanted, along with the Irish government, to further the electoral interests of his party against the growing popularity of Sinn Féin, which had gained 10 per cent of the votes cast in the 1982 Assembly election.

The decision to talk about Irish constitutional politics was interpreted by Dr Paisley as equivalent to a declaration of war on Ulster Protestants: 'You think you will trample down one million people, but

I have news for you – we will trample you down. You have declared war on us. We will resist that to the death.'[54] He launched a ferocious attack on Garret FitzGerald, the taoiseach, and Peter Barry, his foreign minister: 'I indict the FitzGerald regime of being as full of hatred of the Protestants of Ulster as the IRA. Peter Barry fingers every Ulster Protestant as a barrier to peace. In other words, he sets up the whole Protestant population for targeting by the IRA.' He made fun of FitzGerald's attempts to get the Irish people to re-examine their Constitution, suggesting that while he masqueraded as a liberal, in reality he was leader of 'one of the worst sectarian governments which Dublin ever produced'.

The report of the New Ireland Forum, as it became known, was published in May 1984 after twelve months' deliberations. Not surprisingly, while also referring to the options of a federal Ireland or a system of joint authority, it stated its preference for a unitary thirty-two county state as the solution to the Irish problem. While neither Unionist Party had agreed to present their ideas to the Forum, submissions had been received from the churches, trade unions and other bodies. Sections of paragraph 5 of the report indicate a sensitivity to the aspirations of both nationalist and Unionist communities, as well as stating unequivocally its repudiation of any group which might choose coercive methods to impose its will on others:

2. Attempts from any quarter to impose a particular solution through violence must be rejected along with the proponents of such methods. It must be recognised that the new Ireland which the Forum seeks can come about only through agreement and must have a democratic basis.

3. Agreement means that the political arrangements for a new and sovereign Ireland would have to be freely negotiated and agreed to by the people of the North and by the people of the South.

4. The validity of both the Nationalist and Unionist identities in Ireland and the democratic rights of every citizen on this island must be accepted; both of these identities must have equally satisfactory, secure and durable, political, administrative and symbolic expression and protection.

5. Lasting stability can be found only in the context of new structures in which no tradition will be allowed to dominate the other, in which there will be equal rights and opportunities for all, and in which there will be provision for formal and effective guarantees for the protection of individual human rights and of the communal and cultural rights of both Nationalists and Unionists.[55]

The Irish government benefited considerably from the Forum report in that it now had carefully drafted material representing the views of Irish nationalists which it could use in discussions with the British government. It was inevitable that terminology from the report would later find its way into the Anglo-Irish Agreement.

Unionists appeared surprised by the signing of the agreement on 15 November 1985. Despite the customary alarm bells which Paisley had been ringing now for forty years, neither the DUP nor the UUP appeared ready for the news of the Hillsborough agreement. It may be that Irish neutrality during the Falklands War in 1982 – which certainly brought a temporary chill to Anglo-Irish relations – and the IRA attempt to assassinate the entire British cabinet by bombing the Grand Hotel in Brighton on 12 October 1984, might have lulled them into thinking that nothing significant was being proposed which could give them cause for concern. But the signposts to developing Anglo-Irish contacts had been openly displayed since the recommendation for joint studies had been made in December 1980 and the Intergovernmental Council set up in November 1981. Some further development should not have been unexpected in November 1986.

Mrs Thatcher's chief concern was the question of security. She was acutely aware that the IRA campaign could only be contained and repulsed if the Republic's government were fully committed to closer co-operation in security matters. She needed the confidence of the Irish government to achieve this. The Irish government, on the other hand, were interested to furthering the principles and goals spelt out in the Forum report. From time to time, therefore, their representatives would propose joint authority, community policing, joint courts, changes in the RUC and UDR, and a greater say over economic and social matters in Northern Ireland, even though they were unable to offer any change in the Republic's territorial claim over the north, enshrined in Articles 2 and 3 of their constitution. If Mrs Thatcher is to be believed – and I can find no reason to doubt her word – she frequently had to square up to FitzGerald's pressure on these matters. She describes one such meeting in Milan on 29 June 1985: 'At this point Dr FitzGerald became very agitated. He declared that unless the minority in Northern Ireland could be turned against the IRA, Sinn Féin would gain the upper hand in the North and provoke a civil war which would drag the Republic down as well, with Colonel Gaddafi providing millions to help this happen. A sensible point was being exaggerated to the point of absurdity.'[56]

Could the Unionists have been involved in these negotiations or consulted regarding their views? It is known that John Hume was kept fully informed by the Irish government at various stages of the talks, not surprisingly as Hume had largely inspired and drafted the Forum report. Would it then have been more even-handed if Thatcher had been in contact with the Unionists? This imbalance regarding the involvement of representatives from one community and not the other has often been pointed out by political analysts, but it fails to recognise the fact that Thatcher knew that Unionist approval would be withheld – had they been consulted – and opted to progress toward the signing of the agreement in the hope that it would improve security in Northern Ireland. At no time did she imagine that there was any real threat to Northern Ireland's position in the United Kingdom, which Unionists were determined to maintain. She believed this was clearly spelt out in Article 1 of the agreement:

The two governments

[a] affirm that any change in the status of Northern Ireland would only come about with the consent of a majority of the people of Northern Ireland;

[b] recognise that the present wish of a majority of the people of Northern Ireland is for no change in the status of Northern Ireland;

[c] declare that, if in the future a majority of the people of Northern Ireland clearly wish for and formally consent to the establishment of a united Ireland, they will introduce and support in the respective Parliaments legislation to give effect to that wish.[57]

She also felt that Article 2's carefully worded reference to the establishment of an Inter-governmental Conference – a development from the previous Inter-governmental Council in that it would now have a permanent secretariat based at Maryfield, County Down – made it clear that no change in sovereignty was involved: 'There is no derogation from the sovereignty of either the United Kingdom Government or the Irish Government, and each retains responsibility for the decisions and administration of government within its own jurisdiction.' Charles Haughey, then opposition leader in Dáil Éireann, appeared to agree with Thatcher's analysis for he severely criticised this aspect of the agreement, arguing that its acceptance of British sovereignty over a part of the national territory was contrary to the Constitution: 'For the first time the legitimacy of partition has been recognised by the Republic; the British guarantee to the Unionists has been reinforced by the Irish Government; and the Government are also endorsing the British military and political presence in Ireland. The Irish Government are saying to the world that Northern Ireland is legitimately part of the British State, that Northern Ireland is no longer part of national territory.'[58] Unionists disagreed, however, for they interpreted the areas of concern designated for the Conference as infringing the sovereignty of the Westminster Parliament. On the other hand, nationalists and Republicans were encouraged by Article 5 (a) to believe that their tradition had been given a new legitimacy since it was agreed the Conference would consider measures to 'recognise and accommodate the rights and identities of the two traditions in Northern Ireland, to protect human rights and to prevent discrimination'. It further stated: 'Matters to be considered in this area include measures to foster the cultural heritage of both traditions, changes in electoral arrangements, the use of flags and emblems [and] the avoidance of economic and social discrimination.'[59]

The UUP and DUP united in opposition to the agreement. Neither party could run the risk of ignoring the other at this juncture and for some time a united front was presented to the Unionist public. The first demonstration of that unity was at a massive rally at the City Hall, Belfast, on Saturday, 23 November, attended by a crowd estimated in the region of 100,000 to 200,000. The rally marked the beginning of a 'Belfast Says No' campaign, and Unionist MPs at Westminster pledged they would resign their seats and force by-elections if the agreement was not changed. Ratification of the agreement in both the Dáil – 88 votes to 75 – and Westminster – 473 to 47 – resulted in the carrying out of this threat, but it misfired slightly when the SDLP wrested the Newry and Armagh seat from the UUP, thereby bringing one of their leading spokespeople, Seamus Mallon, to Westminster.

The signing of the Anglo-Irish Agreement moved Ian Paisley to launch one of the bitterest attacks of his ministerial and political life. Margaret Thatcher was the chief target of his attack. We have already noted that leading worship in his Martyrs' Memorial Church in Belfast the Sunday after the signing of the agreement, he prayed: 'We hand this woman, Margaret Thatcher, over to the Devil that she might learn not to blaspheme.' He accused Thatcher – as he had accused many others down through the years – of declaring war on the Ulster people:

Mrs Thatcher has declared war upon the Ulster people. She has reaffirmed that come what may she will implement the destruction of the Union through the Anglo-Irish act of treachery. Without consulting a million Protestant people she signed this part of Her Majesty's territory over to a joint Government machinery between London and Dublin. A foreign power, an alien power, has now the same rights in regard to administration and in regard to the operation of Government in Northern Ireland as the British Government.[60]

Her actions, he declared, were all part of a plot to destroy Protestantism:

The Protestantism of Ulster is an embarrassment to her. The old way of thinking that the Bible is true, that men need to be changed by the power of the Holy Word, that there is a separation demanded between God's people and those that live for the devil and sin, she does not like. She thinks she will change it. So she takes Ulster and puts Ulster into a marriage bond with the Republic in order to destroy the identity of the Ulster Protestant people. She is saying to us, 'Where is the Lord thy God? I have got the Army. I have got the Police. I have got the authority. I have got the Parliament. I have got the backing of the world. I have the great American nation behind me. You defiant little remnant of people you do as I say. Where is the Lord thy God?'[61]

Paisley prophesied that God was going to deal with Margaret Thatcher:

I have news for the Prime Minister. God is in Heaven.... The day of glory for Margaret Thatcher is over. The day when she was hailed as a woman of strength is over. The day when she was hailed in the robes of glory has passed. The robing of this woman is going to be the robes of shame, for God will take her in hand.

Perhaps it was just careful political footwork which prompted Thatcher, in the midst of this kind of abuse, to invite both Molyneaux and Paisley to Downing Street on Tuesday, 25 February 1986, for a lengthy chat about the Anglo–Irish Agreement and possible ways in which both men might be consulted on a number of matters – including security – in the future. Or perhaps her action also revealed a compassionate side to her nature which refused to bear malice against Paisley for the terrible things he had said about her. Certainly the television news coverage of the two men as they came out of Number 10 that evening showed that they were impressed by her sincerity. But for some unexplained reason when they returned to Belfast and met with their colleagues, they reverted to their earlier position of unqualified hostility.

Sadly, or so it appears, not all of the reactions to the Anglo–Irish Agreement with which Paisley was associated took the form of constitutional protest. In November 1986 he and Peter Robinson took part in the launch of Ulster Resistance, an organisation said to comprise nine battalions and whose hallmark was a red beret. Questions were raised about the nature of the links between Ulster Resistance and the DUP after a major arms find in County Armagh in November 1988, the discovery of five red berets and the arrest of a former DUP District

Council candidate. In April 1989 three alleged Ulster Resistance members, including one of its founders, were detained by police in Paris with a South African diplomat and an arms dealer.[62]

Judas and his Successor

Better relationships between the DUP and UUP were short-lived. It was not long before Paisley and his colleagues were wrangling with the Ulster Unionists, either because they simply disagreed with their policies or because they wanted to win more votes in local council or Westminster elections. Most DUP members who were either dabbling in local politics or aspiring to walk the corridors of influence at Westminster were very much in the same mould as their leader – they seldom had any long-term political strategy, preferring to react quickly to a problem as they confronted it, and in handling differences with others the characteristic short fuse appeared to operate. The stories of scuffles involving DUP members, particularly in local council chambers, are legion. Paisley's obstructionist tactics and his ejection from every parliament or assembly/convention he attended was an example which DUP councillors appeared to want to emulate at the local level.

The DUP were soon targeting their rivals in various parts of the province. In June 1989 Ulster Unionists on Fermanagh District Council were accused of operating some kind of power-sharing arrangement with the SDLP because they had voted for the SDLP candidate in the contest for the vice-chairman's position. Joe Dodds of Fermanagh DUP complained: 'After this fiasco how can anyone expect us to have any dealings whatever with representatives of a party who wheel and deal and openly flirt with republicans?'[63] Three months later Reg Empey, Ulster Unionist lord mayor of Belfast, was criticised for his plans to invite an Antrim GAA team to a reception at the City Hall.[64] And in January 1990, John Taylor, Ulster Unionist MP for Strangford and a member of the Castlereagh District Council – who had had his jawbone shattered as the result of an assassination attempt by the 'Official' IRA in 1972 – was reprimanded by the DUP for passing on to his colleagues on the council an Ulster Unionist Parliamentary Party decision to change slightly the practice of boycotting government ministers. After the signing of the Anglo-Irish Agreement in November 1985 – as part of their protest against it – both the DUP and UUP had decided to introduce a total boycott of government ministers. However, the policy had already been compromised by both Paisley and Molyneaux because they had entered into talks about talks since 1987 with Tom King, the secretary of state, and his successor, Peter Brooke, in an attempt to find out if the government were open to consider an alternative to the agreement.

The UUP – four years on – were simply suggesting a slight relax-ation of the arrangement at District Council level: they would continue to register their opposition to the Anglo-Irish Agreement by not accepting social invitations from Northern Ireland Office ministers and by not extending invitations to NIO ministers to attend local councils or their activities; however, they would relax the boycott a little and allow the raising of important local issues with NIO ministers. The *New Protestant Telegraph* declared: 'The writing is on the wall for Mr Taylor and he knows it,' and promised him a stiff challenge from the DUP at the next general election.[65]

Molyneaux and Paisley's talks about talks with King and Brooke eventually led to inter-party talks involving the main 'constitutional' parties and the British and Irish governments from April to July 1991 and April to November 1992. Unionist opposition to the Anglo-Irish Agreement meant that the talks could only take place during specified gaps in the Anglo-Irish Inter-governmental Conference meetings, and, at times, the Unionists may have participated in the understanding that the Anglo-Irish Agreement had been temporarily suspended. The talks had three strands, each of which looked at a particular set of relation-ships within the two islands: Strand One considered relationships within Northern Ireland; Strand Two looked at north-south relation-ships; and Strand Three dealt with relationships between the UK and the Republic and involved only the two sovereign governments.

Not surprisingly, some Unionists were uncomfortable about the idea that their representatives were talking at Stormont and elsewhere with representatives of the Irish government. Many within the two Unionist parties, and none more so than Paisley, had themselves strenuously opposed O'Neill's 'hands across the border' policy in the sixties; almost thirty years on they were in fact giving confirmation to the very policy he had initiated, but from a much weaker position than his. O'Neill had welcomed Lemass and Lynch as prime minister of a Unionist govern-ment at Stormont. This local power-base had now been suspended and Unionist leaders were negotiating as party political leaders in the hope of agreeing a devolved administration and north-south structures accept-able across the Northern Ireland community. But Paisley never reminded anyone about his track record of hounding O'Neill for doing the very thing he was now doing; instead he sold it to the Unionist public that he was once again following in the tradition of their great forefathers

Carson and Craigavon: 'Historically Unionists wished to create a good neighbourly relationship with the country and people with whom they share this island. Our Unionist forefathers contended, as I do, that a sound basis should be established for friendly relationships with the South. No one would be more pleased than I if in this generation we could realise the objective for which Carson and Craigavon struggled.'[66] Like O'Neill, he wanted Articles 2 and 3 of the Republic's Constitution removed: 'I have been encouraged in the past few months [by] how many influential political figures in the Irish Republic have expressed their desire or willingness, or both, to remove one of the barriers to improving the relationship between us, namely, the claim to our territory contained in Articles Two and Three of the Constitution of the Irish Republic.' Such an action by the Republic – and both Unionist parties and the Alliance had been asking for it – he was convinced would usher in a new day for Ireland: 'If the claim is removed then a genuine and meaningful relationship can be established. The only basis for that must be that no part of this island has any design against another part.'

But Paisley was very uncomfortable with the whole process and found that he had to reassure his flock at Martyrs' Memorial, and the faithful in various parts of the country, that he was frequently scoring victories against the Republic's ministers. Even before he refused to go to Dublin, one of the venues for the Strand Two talks, UUP delegates found they were spending a lot of their time and energy in simply trying to keep Paisley at the negotiating table. David Trimble explains:

During those inter-party talks in 1992 we had to spend half our energies in keeping Ian on-board and keeping him on some consistent line. And we were only spending the other half of our energies in presenting a Unionist case to the British and Irish Governments, and the SDLP, and the Alliance. And that was a terribly debilitating thing. In the end it was impossible to keep the show on the road the whole way because Ian lost his nerve over spending the week in Dublin, which had been previously agreed, although he denies it.

No significant agreement resulted from the talks but they could hardly be dismissed as having been entirely fruitless. The fact that north-south contacts had been re-established on an official level was worthwhile and was bound to contribute eventually to better relationships on the island.

The Downing Street Declaration, launched by the British and Irish prime ministers at a press conference at Downing Street on Wednesday, 15 December 1993, was the next major political initiative. Both prime ministers affirmed that they were attempting to address the single most urgent issue facing the people of Ireland, north and south, namely, 'to remove the causes of conflict, to overcome the legacy of history and to heal the divisions which have resulted'. And they made separate statements on behalf of their governments in the hope of facilitating progress towards an agreement acceptable to the people of Northern Ireland, the people of Ireland, and the British government. Many of these statements were a reiteration of guarantees and intentions already given. John Major, who had succeeded Margaret Thatcher as prime minister in November 1990, reaffirmed that the British government would 'uphold the democratic wish of a greater number of the people of Northern Ireland on the issue of whether they prefer to support the Union or a sovereign united Ireland'. Significantly, he declared that Britain had 'no selfish strategic or economic interest in Northern Ireland', a statement that was construed in different ways by different people. He further stated that the British government wanted to 'encourage, facilitate and enable' the representatives of both traditions in Ireland to reach an agreement by peaceful means, and did not rule out the possibility that such an agreement might be 'agreed structures for the island as a whole, including a united Ireland'. While Albert Reynolds, the taoiseach, whom Paisley had described in March 1992 as 'a Haughey Mark II',[67] spoke of the democratic right of self-determination by the people of Ireland as a whole, he insisted that this must always be 'subject to the agreement and consent of a majority of the people of Northern Ireland'. Reynolds declared that any new constitutional agreement would include the following rights: 'the right of free political thought; the right to freedom and expression of religion; the right to pursue democratically national and political aspirations; the right to seek political change by peaceful and legitimate means; the right to live wherever one chooses without hindrance; the right to equal opportunity in all social and economic activity, regardless of class, creed, sex or colour'.

Paisley was convinced that the declaration was the result of a secret deal which John Major and Albert Reynolds had done with the IRA: 'The declaration which you and Albert Reynolds signed and made public today is not between you and him alone. It's a tripartite agreement between Reynolds, the IRA and you. You have sold Ulster to buy off the fiendish republican scum.'[68] He described Reynolds as the 'would-be destroyer of this part of Her Majesty's dominions'.[69] This accusation of a deal with the IRA was to rumble on for some time and would be made again, with great intensity, at the time of the IRA ceasefire. Meanwhile he found himself being contradicted by Jim Molyneaux, who, while not enthusiastic about everything in the declaration, denied that it was a sell-out: 'Ulster Unionists have sought to persuade Prime Minister Major and others not to embark on unattainable or undemocratic objectives. We are not perplexed by the results of our endeavours. Bluntly, there is no sell-out.'[70]

Had a deal been struck with the IRA? Eamonn Mallie and David McKittrick, in *The Fight for Peace*, indicate that contacts with the IRA had been opened as early as 1990 and had been sanctioned by Margaret Thatcher.[71] To what extent were these merely 'channels of communication', to what extent 'negotiations'? If previous government contacts with paramilitaries are any satisfactory guideline (for example, December 1974 – March 1975, which included the brief ceasefire), then the former would appear to be nearer to the truth. And I am inclined to accept Coogan's use of Martin Mansergh's comment (as political adviser to Reynolds on northern affairs he should have been well informed): 'The only deal was the one laid out in paragraph ten of the Downing Street Declaration.'[72] Paragraph 10 reads:

The British and Irish Governments reiterate that the achievement of peace must involve a permanent end to the use of, or support of, paramilitary violence. They confirm that, in these circumstances, democratically mandated parties which establish a commitment to exclusively peaceful methods and which have shown that they abide by the democratic process, are free to participate fully in democratic politics and to join in dialogue in due course between the Governments and the political parties on the way ahead.

This paragraph would later become more significant after the ceasefires when the question of decommissioning of weapons before or alongside talks would be the main point of controversy. However, if Mansergh is correct that this paragraph was the main point agreed between the two governments and the paramilitaries on both sides of the community divide – for 'channels of communication' had been opened with loyalist paramilitaries also – what objection could Paisley have had to its conclusion? Regrettably, he jumped to conclusions, but this time his normally well-informed sources appear to have failed him. His rival, Molyneaux, fared better, as the Church of Ireland archbishop of Armagh, Robin Eames – whom Reynolds consulted about the text of the declaration – made sure that Molyneaux had ample opportunity to review the text.[73]

The DUP leader was still smarting from Jim Molyneaux's indirect but public reprimand regarding his claim that the declaration had been a 'sell-out'. By 31 May 1994 he could contain his fury no longer and accused Molyneaux of being a 'Judas Iscariot': 'Yes, he's a Judas Iscariot in the betrayal he's carrying on at the present time.... The Unionist community are angry about two things. Number one, Whitehall surrender. Number two, the leader of the Official Unionist Party being in the pocket of both the Prime Ministers.'[74] The media – not slow to spot a good story – were soon quizzing Molyneaux on his reaction to this latest public disclosure of Paisley's true feelings toward the UUP and its leader. Molyneaux's reply indicated that he was more concerned about the effect the remark would have on Unionism rather than any personal rebuff he might have felt: 'The general public will be dismayed by Mr Paisley's outburst, clearly signalling a shattering of unity within the ranks of all who wish to remain within the UK.'[75]

Molyneaux has said very little since about the incident. His charitable explanation of Paisley's outburst is that the DUP leader was looking for publicity. When I interviewed him before he himself stepped down as UUP leader, he indicated that this kind of tactic to draw media attention was not his style of leadership: 'The party secretary on one occasion during an election went to the editor of a very well known newspaper – which shall be nameless – to complain that I wasn't getting as much coverage as the other party leaders. The editor said, "Yes, I know that, but he's a dull dog! Can you not gee him up and persuade him to launch a vicious attack on another party leader and then we'll give him headlines!"'[76]

Martin Smyth, a close colleague of Molyneaux for many years, hints that the UUP leader may have been hurt by Paisley's attack:

The fact that Ian called Jim Molyneaux 'Judas Iscariot' caught the headlines. It did irreparable harm to Ian Paisley. It didn't do harm to Jim Molyneaux. And Jim, in his own pawky humour a few weeks later when he was called another name, was asked by a media person, 'Were you hurt?'

He replied, 'I was.' And that's the first time that Jim has ever said he was hurt to anybody.

And the interviewer said, "What do you mean? How were you hurt?'

'Well,' he said, 'a few weeks ago I was a Biblical character; now I'm just a failed politician!'[77]

The IRA announced a 'complete cessation of military operations' on Wednesday, 31 August 1995. Seven weeks later on 13 October, the Combined Loyalist Military Command ended their campaign of violence, expressing the hope that it would be a permanent ceasefire.

The IRA had always been told that it was a war they could not win and they had replied that it was also a war they could not lose. Over three thousand people had lost their lives since 1969, most of them as the result of paramilitary violence. But a new element had been introduced by the 'loyalist' paramilitaries in the nineties – the targeting of Sinn Féin councillors and other party workers and their families. There had been evidence of this at earlier stages of the conflict but never to the same degree as occurred in the years prior to the Provisional IRA cease-fire announcement. There is in fact some likelihood that during the seventies the 'Republican' and 'loyalist' paramilitaries may have had some strange unwritten agreement not to target the officers of opposing organisations. It was quite legitimate, therefore, according to the code, for the IRA to slaughter members of the army, police and civilian population, and for the 'loyalist' paramilitaries to murder innocent Catholics, but a 'hands-off' policy may have been operating regarding the 'officer class' in both Republican and loyalist organisations.

I attended a meeting in 1977 in the Four Courts in Dublin to discuss with Sean McEntee, senior counsel, and Andy Tyrie, commander of the UDA, the case relating to Freddie Parkinson, a member of the UDA from the Woodvale area of Belfast who was charged with attempting to firebomb Dublin. I was utterly opposed to any 'firebombing' attempt, but as a minister in Dublin at the time I had visited Parkinson while he was in Mountjoy Prison because I knew that he would have been been completely isolated from contact with others during the remand period. He had asked me to take an interest in his case. I was quite surprised to find Tyrie arriving for the meeting at the Four Courts without any apparent concern for his security within the building or outside it. This was just one example which suggested the existence of some kind of understanding between the rival paramilitary groups. It was also the case that loyalist paramilitaries on the run, like the IRA, found safe sanctuary during the seventies in the Republic of Ireland.

On the announcement of the IRA ceasefire, Ian Paisley again accused John Major of having made 'secret concessions' to the organisation. After a meeting with the prime minister, Molyneaux denied the existence of a deal. He said that the fact that a 'permanent ceasefire' had not been mentioned in the IRA statement 'meant no secret deal was done nor did I ever suspect that it was'.[78] Paisley was not satisfied and went with Peter Robinson and William McCrea to see Major on 6 September. The ten-minute confrontation possibly took even Paisley by surprise! The prime minister's first words to him were to enquire if he trusted his word. When Paisley said, 'No!' he was ushered out of the room. According to Paisley's account of the brief encounter, Mr

Major ordered him: 'Get out of this room. Never come back until you're
prepared to say I speak the truth and do not tell lies.'[79] Seldom one not
to have the last word, Paisley replied: 'You are the first Prime Minister
that ever asked a political opponent in this room or outside this room,
that if he doesn't swear that he believes in your truthfulness, then you
will not listen to him.' Following the confrontation, 'Viewpoint' in the
Belfast Telegraph had words of reproof for both Major and Paisley. Of
the DUP leader it said: 'Mr Paisley's brand of protest politics is ill-
suited to the moment. At a time when unionism needs influential
friends, he helped create a situation which is likely to alienate international opinion and further raise tension on the streets of Ulster.'[80]

The Joint Declaration of December 1993 had included the suggestion that the Irish government would 'make their own arrangements
within their jurisdiction to enable democratic parties to consult together
and share in dialogue about the future'. It was specific about the type
of consultation the taoiseach had in mind: 'The Taoiseach's intention
is that these arrangements could include the establishment, in consultation with other parties, of a Forum for Peace and Reconciliation to
make recommendations on ways in which agreement and trust between
both traditions in Ireland can be promoted and established.' Following
the IRA ceasefire the plan for the Forum went into operation and it
met for the first time on 28 October 1994. Despite the statement that
the arrangements for the Forum would be 'within their jurisdiction',
the participants declared their wish for Unionist participation. John
Hume declared: 'The Unionist people will fully realise that we mean
what we say. It is agreement we are looking for, not victories, not
defeats. And agreement threatens no-one.'[81] Unionists, however, were
suspicious. Two UUP councillors travelled down to Dublin to hand in
a letter of protest. They suggested that the whole exercise was not really
designed to further the cause of peace but to bring Sinn Féin into the
political process. DUP party secretary, Nigel Dodds, was more scathing,
suggesting that those taking part were 'helping to give political
respectability to the apologists for murder'.

The lack of any devolved administration in Northern Ireland or any
acceptable expression – especially for the nationalist community – of
north-south relations meant that documents on both subjects continued
to be churned out by the British government or by both the Irish and
British governments acting in tandem. This really was the background
to the document *Frameworks for the Future* issued on 22 February 1995.
Patrick Mayhew, secretary of state, tried to explain it all as a follow-on
from the 1992 inter-party talks when the participants apparently had
asked the two governments to set out what kind of settlement they

envisaged would solve the continuing deadlock. The outcome – whatever its origins – was the publication of two sets of proposals for discussion: one, drawn up by both governments and dealing with north-south relations, was called *A Framework for Agreement*, and the other, drawn up by the British government and dealing with proposals for a devolved government, was entitled, *A Framework for Accountable Government in Northern Ireland*. In the area of north-south relations there appeared to be something new, namely paragraph 21, which declared: 'As part of an agreement... the Irish Government will introduce and support proposals for change in the Irish Constitution to implement the commitments in the Joint Declaration. These changes in the Irish Constitution will... be such that no territorial claim of right to jurisdiction over Northern Ireland contrary to the will of a majority of its people is asserted.' This reference to the possible removal of Articles 2 and 3 from the Republic's Constitution was what Unionists, including Paisley, had been concerned about for decades, but they hardly saw the words in print because the same statement referred to a north-south body with elected representatives from the proposed ninety-member assembly in the north and from Dáil Éireann which would possibly have 'executive functions' (par. 28): 'Both Governments expect that significant responsibilities, including meaningful functions at executive level, will be a feature of such agreement.' It was this reference to executive functions for the north-south body which became paramount in Unionist thinking, and despite all denials that it amounted to joint authority, this was how it was construed. The *New Protestant Telegraph* referred to the document as 'The Plan for Ulster's Destruction' and declared: 'They have tried to pretend that it does not amount to a sell-out of the Province. All unionists recognise that this is a formula for the destruction of Northern Ireland as part of the United Kingdom.'[82] Unionists, both UUP and DUP, simply ignored the document and very soon it became yet another faded epistle

As the 1995 marching season approached, Ian Paisley was convinced that he had discovered yet another sinister Roman Catholic plot to overthrow Protestantism in Northern Ireland. Michael Ancram, parliamentary under-secretary at the Northern Ireland Office – a Scottish peer who does not use his title of earl – had been placed in charge of the Northern Ireland Office team who were meeting with representatives of Sinn Féin, led by Martin McGuinness, in an attempt to break the deadlock over the question of the decommissioning of IRA weapons before the admission of Sinn Féin to inter-party talks. The fact that both men, Ancram and McGuinness, were Roman Catholics, was proof of the conspiracy: 'Ulster is to be sold out by a leading British Roman Catholic to a senior Republican Roman Catholic. Who said the problem in Northern Ireland has nothing to do with religion? The fact is there is a major conspiracy to destroy the Protestant inheritance on this island and deny to Protestants their rights.'[83]

Two months later he was publicly accusing Jesuits in Portadown of stirring up trouble. In July Orangemen had been prevented by police and demonstrators from marching along one of their traditional routes – the Garvaghy Road in Portadown. Catholics in the Garvaghy Road area resented the signs and symbols of Orangeism and the insults they sometimes received from the supporters who accompanied the marchers. Paisley rushed to the scene as soon as he heard that problems had arisen. By the time he arrived, representatives from both opposing groups – the Orangemen and the Garvaghy Road residents – were meeting with the police in an attempt to find a solution acceptable to both sides. When Paisley discovered that one of the residents' negotiators was a Jesuit, he told the Orangemen that this was the cause of the trouble they were facing:

Let me say something tonight, could you expect anything else? Would you expect anything else when the Pope sent into Portadown a Jesuit priest to take over the public relations of his people? You can expect trouble and you will have trouble. Anywhere a Jesuit priest is there is trouble.

Some of us know our history. Some of us know who the Jesuits are, what their oath is and what their aim is. Their aim is the extermination of heresy and we to them are the heretics. They have not changed their objectives.[84]

Three days after his seventy-fifth birthday on 26 August 1995, Jim Molyneaux stepped down from the leadership of the Ulster Unionist Party – a position he had held for sixteen years. Under O'Neill, and then Faulkner, Unionism had shown a degree of flexibility towards accommodating the rights and aspirations of the nationalist/Republican community. But for various reasons the Unionist population had decided to reject their 'olive-branch' approach and had discarded both men and their supporters and reverted very much to traditional Unionist conceptions of democracy, which in the Northern Ireland context meant one-party majority rule. Their rejection of O'Neill and Faulkner meant paying a price, for with the dismissal of both men they also lost their chance of a devolved administration at Stormont, and no other acceptable alternative has emerged in the twenty-two years since the collapse of the power-sharing executive. Molyneaux had been leader in the period following the rejection of this more moderate Unionism. He saw his task as one of rebuilding the party along traditional lines while at the same time making it an acceptable and convincing force for arguing the Unionist case at Westminster. He had a difficult task. The country was caught up in the most vicious IRA campaign ever experienced in Northern Ireland, exacerbated by an equally sinister and cruel military 'response' from loyalist paramilitaries, and further compounded by Paisley's vociferous anti-Catholic, anti-Republican crusade to take over the leadership of Unionism.

David Trimble, a barrister, was elected Molyneaux's successor on 8 September 1995. As he must have expected, it was not long before the DUP leader was trying to make life difficult for him, but the new UUP leader appears to have outsmarted him within the first two days by calling his bluff and suggesting the merger of the two Unionist parties. He knew Paisley would reject this suggestion because Trimble was the leader of the larger party and Paisley would never play second fiddle to anyone. Paisley, however, tried to regain the initiative and called on Trimble to bring his party to the Unionist commission the DUP had set up in the hope of gathering all shades of Unionism together to draw up a report on the government's handling of the arms issue and the progress towards inter-party talks. Molyneaux, wary of Paisley's intentions, had agreed to send 'observers', but Paisley challenged Trimble to enter his carefully woven web: 'We have already the forum for unionist unity. It's here. The machinery is already set up. Why doesn't he join the machinery that is already set up?'[85] Trimble saw the trap and steered clear of Paisley's manoeuvrings, pressing ahead instead with his own calls for a new Assembly, suggesting that this was the way to break the logjam over decommissioning and all-party talks. As Trimble travelled to Dublin, London and the United States, getting to know the main players influencing the political future of Northern Ireland, he displayed an energy which was more typical of the DUP leader in his younger years. The more Paisley saw of the relatively favourable impression Trimble made on world leaders, the more anxious he became. The explosion came at his party conference on 25 November 1995. *Belfast Telegraph* reporters Mark Simpson and Vincent Kearney witnessed the occasion: 'The Ulster Unionist Party came under ferocious attack at today's DUP conference. Ian Paisley and senior colleagues lambasted David Trimble's party, mainly over their failure to work in a unionist forum.'[86] And Trimble himself was chosen by Paisley for what might be described as a severe dressing down! 'They have been busy stealing our political clothes since Mr Trimble's election to the leadership.'

In September Paisley had made clear his opposition to President Clinton's planned visit to Northern Ireland. Lobbying Republicans in Washington on the 13th, he declared: 'Bill Clinton is the man who elevated Gerry Adams and put him up as a front-line democratic leader. I don't think unionists will get anywhere with the Clinton administration.... If he visited [Ulster] there would be trouble.'[87] However, he changed his tactics somewhat when he observed the warm reception which the president received from all sections of the community on Thursday, 30 November, and was prepared to have his photograph taken with him, though Clinton significantly omitted Paisley's name when expressing appreciation for those working for mutual understanding and peace.

Paisley was not prepared to make the same compromise in relation to the Mitchell Commission appointed in December 1995 by the British and Irish governments in an attempt to bring an independent opinion to bear on the controversy over the decommissioning of arms. None of the political parties representing the paramilitary organisations had indicated their willingness to hand over arms prior to their participation in all-party talks. The international body was well chosen: George Mitchell, a former US senator and special adviser to the president on Northern Ireland matters; Harri Holkeri, a former prime minister of Finland; and, recognising the importance of someone qualified to comment on military matters, John de Chastelain, a Canadian general. Significantly, the DUP were the only political party to refuse to talk to the commission.

After seven weeks of intensive work, the commission published their findings on 24 January 1996. They recommended that all participants in all-party talks should affirm their total and absolute commitment:

1. To democratic and exclusively peaceful means of resolving political issues;

2. To the total disarmament of all paramilitary organisations;

3. To agree that such disarmament must be verifiable to the satisfaction of an independent commission;

4. To renounce for themselves, and to oppose any effort by others, to use force, or threaten to use force, to influence the course of or the outcome of all-party negotiations;

5. To agree to abide by the terms of any agreement reached in all-party negotiations and to resort to democratic and exclusively peaceful methods

in trying to alter any aspect of that outcome with which they may disagree;

6. To urge that 'punishment' killings and beatings stop and take effective steps to prevent such actions.[88]

The most crucial part of the commission's report included what they openly accepted was a compromise regarding the thorny issue of whether arms were to be handed over prior to or after all-party negotiations: 'The parties should consider an approach under which some decommissioning would take place during the process of all-party negotiations rather than before or after as the parties now urge.' This was dismissed by Paisley who saw the report as 'caving in' to the IRA: 'Any talks that took place on this basis would still be overshadowed by the spectre of the IRA gunmen. There would be no level playing field. Talks would be taking place with the IRA gun literally at the head of unionist negotiators. The arms must be handed over.'[89]

Following the publication of the findings of the Mitchell Commission, the British prime minister announced that elections would be held on 30 May to a Northern Ireland Forum, from which elected parties would appoint their representatives to multi-party talks on 10 June. Normal election procedures would not be followed on this occasion. To allow for some representation from the smaller political parties the first ten parties with the highest percentage poll were each guaranteed two seats at the Forum, irrespective of the number of seats gained in the election. Further representation at the multi-party talks would also be assured for these ten parties conditional on their acceptance of the Mitchell principles. Each party would have three front-line members with three other support members. This representation would be irrespective of the number of seats gained at the election. The following ten parties were elected to the Forum:

Party	Members elected	% valid poll
UUP	30	24.2
SDLP	21	21.4
DUP	24	18.8
Sinn Féin	17	15.5
Alliance	7	6.5
UK Unionist	3	3.7
PUP	2	3.5
UDP	2	2.2
Women's Coalition	2	1.0
Labour	2	0.8

The London Docklands bombing by the IRA on 9 February 1996, in which two people were kllled, cast a dark shadow over the progress that was being made, shattering hopes that the IRA ceasefire of August 1994 had been permanent. Further bombings continued to cast doubts on the sincerity and intention of the IRA's commitment to 'democratic and exclusively peaceful means'. It was on this basis that Sinn Féin were deemed to have excluded themselves from the multi-party talks which commenced in June. However, there was little progress during the first seven weeks of discussions save agreement on the appointment of a chairman, George Mitchell, and rules of procedure for the talks.

Drumcree 1996

While heated discussions and wrangling had started at Stormont, the issue of parades once again became a major question. As in July 1995, differences focused on the traditional Orange march on the Sunday prior to 'the Twelfth' which usually returned to Portadown along the Drumcree and Garvaghy roads after service in Drumcree parish church. The Portadown District officials of the Orange Order had refused to meet representatives of the Garvaghy residents to discuss their objections to the march because of their alleged Sinn Féin/IRA links. Orangemen regarded the residents' objections as an infringement of their rights to march on the 'Queen's highway' and as further evidence of a nationalist agenda orchestrated over recent years through an unofficial coalition of the Republic's government with nationalist and republican groups in the north. On the other hand Garvaghy Road residents expressed anger at what they perceived as the triumphalist approach of Trimble and Paisley following the compromise agreement in July 1995 which had enabled the march to proceed peacefully.

When the RUC refused permission for the march to proceed along the Garvaghy road on Sunday 7 July the Orange leaders activated well-organised contingency plans to disrupt air, road and rail traffic in many parts of the province. As in 1995, Ian Paisley, while not a member of the Orange Order, turned up at Drumcree to indicate his support. On his first visit to the scene of the stand-off he told the Orangemen that the future well-being of their children's lives was at stake: 'We do not want them under the tricolour or under Dublin. This is the seige of the whole province. And the seige of the UK because every citizen has rights and those rights cannot be surrendered. Those rights are ours. We intend to maintain them and we intend to defend them.' He assured the Orangemen that he was personally identified with them in their struggle: 'This is going to be a long hard slog. I have always laid myself on the line for Ulster. I will be with you all the way.'[89] At midnight on the Monday he was back again to speak to those on the front-line of the barbed-wire barricade that had been erected by the army: 'The pressures are on. We have the resolution, strength and determination to win through. And we will , because you can't beat the Ulster people. There's no doubt about it – if we stand together we will win.' He reminded the crowd of the widespread support in the province for their case: 'All across the province tonight there are protests here, there and everywhere. Across Ulster, people have made up their minds that this is the crisis hour, but it is also the hour in which we can win back what we have lost.'[90]

It is hard to avoid the conclusion that Ian Paisley, David Trimble and the Orange leaders must have been aware that to resist Chief Constable Sir Hugh Annesley's decision to re-route the march and to encourage the disruption of traffic in various parts of the province carried with it the potential for causing serious public disorder; certainly police intelligence were aware well in advance that paramilitaries on both sides of the community were 'putting in a lot of planning for this event.'[91] As Senator Sam McAughtry later suggested: 'Either David Trimble and Ian Paisley knew that their call for Orangemen to come out all over the north and support the Drumcree demonstration would encourage loyalist thuggery, in which case Trimble and Paisley came very close to fascism, or they didn't forsee the consequences of their call, which means that they are too lacking in judgment to be party leaders.'[92] The Church and Government Committee of the Presbyterian Church in Ireland appeared to include these leaders in their condemnation: 'Those who initiate actions in volatile situations cannot evade total responsibility for the consequences of what they begin.'[93]

The Chief Constable's change of policy on the morning of 11 July, which now directed his police force to clear the residents off the Garvaghy road and provide safe passage for the Orangemen to march along it, caused widespread consternation and disbelief among nationalists and other sections of the Northern Ireland community. SDLP MP Eddie McGrady expressed the hurt experienced by many in the nationalist community: 'The Orange card has been played yet again. In these events we see illustrated, one law for the majority community and another law for the minority community. The vicious onslaught on the residents of the Garvaghy road in peaceful protest contrasts so vividly with the kid glove approach to the thugs on the barricades, to the hooded men with their guns and cudgels.'[94] Taoiseach John Bruton interpreted the situation as one which necessitated a public statement as well as the sentiments which would be expressed through the normal diplomatic channels. He declared: 'A state cannot afford to yield to force; a state cannot afford to be inconsistent; a state – a democratic state – cannot afford to be partial in the way it applies the law, and I'm afraid we have seen all three basic canons of democracy breached in this instance.'[95]

The riots, arson and intimidation which accompanied the Orangemen's decision to resist the re-routing of their march were now duplicated on the nationalist side, and the consequences of the violence on both sides of the community were far-reaching. Of most immediate concern was the suffering inflicted: one murdered; another crushed to death; 250 injured, and 241 families forced out of their homes. There was over twenty million pounds of damage, and nationalist trust in the RUC plummeted to a new low. All these factors combined to heighten community tensions and endanger the chances of economic recovery.

The Verdict of the Ballot-Box

Publicly Ian Paisley has appeared to place more emphasis on the massive personal vote which he has consistently received in the elections for the European Parliament than on the verdict of the ballot-box when other elections are held. The 230,251 votes he received in the 1984 European election represented undoubtedly his finest hour. Prior to 1984 he had claimed to speak for Ulster Protestantism but, after this his claims had a little more substance. These European election results are significant and cannot be overlooked. Twenty-nine per cent of the voters in Northern Ireland since 1979 have consistently said that they see him as the best person to represent them at Strasbourg and Brussels. Nor is it misreading the results to suggest that 29 per cent of the voters have also voiced their acceptance of his fierce anti-Catholicism and his manner of representing Unionism in the wider European community.

The political analyst, however, inevitably asks why this large personal support for Paisley has not been translated into a similar measure of support for his party? Three areas have to be considered: Westminster general election results, Assembly election results, and district council elections. I have compared DUP and UUP election results after 1977 as the most accurate way of assessing DUP fortunes at the polls.

Westminster General Elections

Year	Party	Seats won	No. NI seats
1979	DUP	3	12
1979	UUP	6	12
1983	DUP	3	17
1983	UUP	11	17
1987	DUP	3	17
1987	UUP	9	17
1992	DUP	3	17
1992	UUP	9	17

1982 NI Assembly Election

Party	Members elected	% valid poll
DUP	21	23.0
UUP	26	29.7

1996 NI Forum Election

Party	Members elected	% valid poll
DUP	24	18.8
UUP	30	24.2

District Council Elections

Year	Party	Members elected	% valid poll
1977	DUP	74	12.7
1977	UUP	178	29.6
1981	DUP	142	26.6
1981	UUP	152	26.5
1985	DUP	142	24.3
1985	UUP	190	29.5
1989	DUP	110	17.7
1989	UUP	194	31.3
1993	DUP	103	17.3
1993	UUP	197	29.4

DUP support appears to have peaked in the years 1981-1985. This was the period of their highest poll in the district council elections and they also fared well in the 1982 Assembly election, and of course Paisley won his highest percentage first preference vote as an MEP in 1984. Since 1985, support for the DUP has declined in the district council elections, running in both 1989 and 1993 at around 17 per cent, possibly suggesting that at local council level Unionist voters have a clear preference for UUP councillors. The Westminster representation statistics are a little harder to analyse because in some constituencies the DUP or the UUP have not fielded a candidate, when there was a chance of Unionism's losing the seat altogether. But there has been no great public demand that the DUP should have the majority of Unionist MPs at Westminster, and this may explain better the continuing superiority of the UUP in this area.

Outright competition between the UUP and DUP is more than likely in a number of constituencies at the next Westminster election. The results should then indicate whether the Unionist voters' preference for the UUP at district council elections is also reflected in the contest for seats at Westminster.

Chapter Nine
A Paisley Dynasty?

We must learn to live together as brothers or perish together as fools.

Martin Luther King (1929–1968)[1]

NINETEEN SIXTY-SIX WAS a significant year for the Paisley family. In June, Ian Paisley had led his supporters in a march to the Assembly Buildings, Belfast, to protest against what he claimed was the 'Romeward' trend in the Presbyterian Church in Ireland; in the middle of July, as a result of the disturbances connected with the June protest, he and two of his colleagues were sent to prison because they refused to give assurances that they would 'keep the peace'; on his release from prison three months later he found that there had been a considerable groundswell of support both for his church and his form of protest politics; and finally, on 12 December his wife gave birth to twin boys, Kyle and Ian. If Paisley had had any uncertainties about divine confirmation on his life and ministry – and there was never any time when he appeared to doubt this confirmation – the birth of the twins would have dispelled them for ever. His Free Presbyterian Church was fifteen years old and he had by now made up his mind to stand for the Stormont Parliament. The birth of his sons meant there was every likelihood that one or both of the sons would one day take up and continue the work which he had started, just as he himself had followed his father's example and become the minister of an independent separatist church.

The twins had three older sisters: Sharon, Rhonda and Cherith, but FPCU rules excluded any of the girls from becoming ministers in their father's church, even though their grandmother had been known to preach and lead worship from time to time. The possibility therefore of one of the girls following in the father's and grandfather's footsteps as an ordained minister was nil. Nor had there been much encouragement in Ulster society for women to pursue a career in politics. Their mother's experience as a Belfast city councillor from 1967 – 1975, Assembly member 1973-1974, and convention member 1975-1976, was quite rare. Certainly women had not figured prominently in the political life of the province. Against the odds, Rhonda, like her mother, endeavoured to make progress up the political ladder, but after eight years as a Belfast city councillor – which included a spell as lady mayoress when Sammy Wilson was mayor – she packed it in as something ill-suited to her temperament. She later reflected: 'The game plan of politics frustrated me.'[2]

The birth of the twins undoubtedly strengthened the possibility of the establishment of a Paisley dynasty. Almost thirty years later, with Kyle a Free Presbyterian minister in Oulton Broad, East Anglia, and Ian one of the five Forum members for North Antrim and personal political assistant to his father, that likelihood has grown even stronger. It is plain to most that the father intends Kyle to follow him as minister of Martyrs' Memorial Church and then one day as moderator of the Free Presbyterian Church of Ulster. For the past number of years he has arranged that Kyle deputises for him during an occasional absence from Martyrs' and has also included him as one of the special preachers during conventions or times of special services. Kyle shares completely his father's extreme separatist theology but is unlike his father in his style of preaching. While his diction is clear and his sermon material at times quite forcefully presented, there is none of his father's shouting or dramatic gestures. Kyle, his wife Janice and two daughters Cara and Danielle are clearly very much loved by the small congregation at Oulton Broad and, gentleman that he is, will elicit this kind of response wherever he is minister.

There is every likelihood that Kyle will one day follow his father as minister at Martyrs' Memorial. Indeed, no one would be surprised if there was some kind of arrangement in the near future whereby both father and son were recognised as ministers of the church. There are two reasons for this happening sooner than later: firstly, the opening up of various small causes in different parts of the world means that the father is frequently absent from his own pulpit, resulting in a lack of continuity in ministry; secondly, the arrangement whereby David McIlveen acts as pastor at Martyrs' Memorial Church is bound to have its problems both for the Martyrs' church and for McIlveen's own Sandown church, not to mention McIlveen himself. A change in the arrangements whereby both father and son preached regularly and Kyle looked after the pastoral needs of the congregation could strengthen the congregation – its dwindling numbers are bound to be causing concern to the elders – and also prepare for the eventual hand-over from father to son.

Ian junior is similarly being prepared to take over his father's political mantle. As personal assistant to his father, he has had every opportunity to learn his father's version of the ABC of politics. And just as his brother Kyle has imbibed his father's theology, so it is true to say that Ian junior's political creed is a carbon copy of Paisley senior's position. The theological basis which determines the father's politics appears to wield a similar influence on the son. Ian junior, however, lacks the fiery oratory which has characterised his father's church ministry and political pilgrimage. The son is aware of this difference: 'We believe in the same things but we put them across differently. I am not a firebrand orator.'[3] Time alone will tell whether this difference between father and son will affect the son's popularity. However, whatever he lacks of his father's rhetorical skills is compensated somewhat by his enthusiasm to be involved in the political game. 'Ian is keen to take on a major political role,' is Rhonda's observation, and she makes no attempt to conceal her hope that one day her brother will be DUP leader.[4] Much of the father's political cunning and guile has been passed on to Ian junior, who admits he enjoys the 'wheeling and dealing' of politics. Other DUP notables cannot be unaware of Ian junior's presence and aspirations – not to mention the father's plans for his son! He is bound to be seen as a rival by those who have been longer in the political battlefield. This possibly was the reason for Sammy Wilson's robust response to Ian junior's attempt to interfere in the internal business of DUP councillors on Belfast city council in July 1994. Wilson, press officer for the DUP, was in the process – along with other DUP councillors – of forging a closer working relationship with UUP councillors despite the friction that had been emerging between the two parties. Ian junior, not even a member of Belfast city council, was critical of Wilson's plans. He claimed that the move would damage the DUP and 'cover up the ineptitude of the UUP'.[5] It is more than likely that Ian junior had already discussed the matter thoroughly with his father before voicing his criticisms. Wilson, however, pretended to ignore the father's hand behind the deed and rounded on the son: 'Since no senior members of the party expressed any concern about the arrangements, it seems odd that someone so junior should take it upon himself to express his opposition in public before he has used the proper party channels to have this issue debated.'[6] UUP city councillors were also clearly annoyed at Ian junior's intervention and, perhaps with Wilson's blessing, joined in the chorus of disapproval. Fred Cobain declared: 'As far as we are concerned Ian Paisley junior does not count.... If the DUP group at the City Hall is happy with the arrangement, he should mind his own business and leave them to decide what is best.'[7]

It was not the last time that Ian junior was to raise – like his father – the ire of the Ulster Unionists. In January 1996 the UUP received reports that he had urged DUP members to prepare to contest all Westminster seats at the next election. As a result the UUP let it be known that if this was the case they would consider contesting the East Belfast seat held by DUP deputy leader Peter Robinson. This in turn infuriated Robinson.[8] Within twenty-four hours Ian junior had issued a statement denying that he had ever suggested that the DUP would be fighting *all* the parliamentary seats.[9]

Election to the Westminster Parliament would effectively boost Ian junior's standing in the DUP and increase his chances of following his father as leader of the party. It is not beyond the bounds of possibility that he might contest a seat at the next general election. The very fact that he has been speaking about the party's preparing for the next election could be an indication that he is one of the names being considered. It is unlikely that the father would want him to contest a seat unless there is a reasonable chance of success, and the only seat where this is likely is the North Antrim seat which his father has represented for twenty-six years. The fact that he and his father were two of the candidates contesting North Antrim for the DUP in the 30 May Forum election suggests that he is being prepared for this seat. It is unlikely that Paisley senior will retire from politics for some years – health permitting – so it could be that the DUP leader plans to have his son nominated as a candidate for North Antrim and he himself contest another neighbouring Westminster constituency seat.

However, the key factor in the emergence of a Paisley dynasty in both church and politics is the continuation of public support for the Paisley brand of theology and politics. Paisley's Free Presbyterian Church has failed to draw in the large numbers that its founder must have wanted, but his separatist theology has unquestionably affected the opinions of considerable sections within Protestantism. While enthusiasm for examining the implications of Christ's teaching on the unity of his followers has never been strong in any part of the world, in Northern Ireland the response to the question is often one of hostility. Much of this, I would suggest, has been fuelled by Paisley's extreme anti-Catholicism which fails to recognise the Roman Catholic Church as a Christian church in need of reformation like any other church. And his theology has also affected the membership of Protestant churches in other ways: for example, his interpretation of Christ's grace and forgivenenss as 'conditional' upon repentance by the individual. As we noted earlier, it is our experience of forgiveness which requires

repentance, not the initial love of Christ which is given uncondition-
ally and is not dependent on the merit or otherwise of the one forgiven.
In similar fashion we are called to demonstrate this forgiveness of Christ
to others irrespective of their deserving or their spirit of repentance.
Paisley's teaching on hatred – that is, to take with a grain of salt those
who say, 'Do not hate the sinner but the sin' – is another significant
example of his teaching which has permeated this society.

These aspects of Paisley's theology have served to buttress the
attitudes of extreme Unionism which form the basis of his Democratic
Unionist Party. His form of anti-Catholicism encourages the rejection
of Republicanism and nationalism, including even the aspiration to
national unity. Political parties representing these viewpoints have been
portrayed as a threat to Protestantism and Unionism, irrespective of
whether or not violent methods were being employed. Attempts therefore to find a resolution to the conflicting aspirations of Unionism and
nationalism/Republicanism is beset by the difficulties thrown up by the
extreme protagonists on both sides. On the Republican side, Sinn Féin
openly declare they are subversives. They want the destruction of the
Northern Ireland state and will not be placated while it exists. On the
Unionist side, Paisleyism regards the Roman Catholic Church and
Republicanism as part of a world strategy – devised within 'the kingdom
of the beast' – to overthrow Protestantism. While substantial sections
of the public continue to pledge their support to these extreme philosophies the task of reconciliation is well nigh impossible.

How long, therefore, will public support be given to Paisleyism?
Outside Northern Ireland that support has been almost non-existent.
The Free Presbyterian Church mission congregations in other parts of
the world – with the exception of the churches in Toronto and
Greenville, South Carolina – have shown few, if any, signs of growth.
Similarly, Paisley's form of Unionism has failed to win at Westminster
the slightest degree of support even among those most likely to be
sympathetic to the Unionist position. David Wiltshire, Conservative
MP for Spelthorne, Surrey, and a member of the Northern Ireland
Select Committee, would be among those most inclined to be supportive
of the Unionist cause. He charitably accepts Paisley's strident rhetoric
as representing the strong views of his constituents. However, he is
somewhat pessimistic regarding the DUP leader's general effectiveness
in presenting the Unionist position at Westminster:

Talking from a purely Westminster political perspective and judging him
by how I guess an awful lot of other people would judge him, he is held

to be not effective; it's a good rant, but it's been heard many times before. I've heard people say in the tea room, 'There's no need to go and listen to Ian Paisley, who's speaking in a minute. You've only got to go and look at his last ten speeches and you'll read it!' Once you have that sort of reputation of being repetitive it's a pity![10]

Wiltshire sees Paisley as a negative influence against any proposals for change in Northern Ireland: 'I have a sense that Ian bit by bit has become less productive than he was and is seen more and more as a blocking mechanism to any sort of change, rather than as a positive person seeking change in a particular direction. That's very much a subjective impression, but it's one that I get increasingly the more I look at the peace process.' Donald Anderson, Labour MP for Monmouth and shadow solicitor-general, regrets that Paisley never attends the House of Commons Christian Fellowship. Anderson has taken a particular interest in Northern Ireland affairs and has endeavoured to listen and learn from its representatives. His opinion of Paisley differs little from the views of Wiltshire:

He's clearly a powerful man physically and a powerful man in his community, and a man therefore capable of doing a great deal of good in the province in terms of reconciling, bridge-building, looking to the future. I say this with some sadness. I'm not persuaded that he is really a bridge-builder. Yes, people have to understand the past, but not be imprisoned by it. Ulster needs politicians who have the courage, not just to feed the great beast of the old prejudices, but to carry it forward. I'm not convinced from what I've seen of Ian's operations, both in the House and back home, that he really steps outside the cosy limits of his own community, and therefore is not prepared to play a positive and constructive role.[11]

Will the Free Presbyterian Church last longer than the DUP? Certainly the former has been in existence longer than the latter and it is the theological basis of the former which gives both substance and impetus to the latter. And yet it is that same theological basis which may have prevented Paisley from finally dominating Unionism and which may eventually ensure the demise of the party before the church. Its extreme anti-Catholicism has shaped much of the DUP's policies and provided the missionary spirit which has won Paisley and the party the degree of public support they have received. However, his separatist theology also involves the denunciation of the existing Protestant churches and this has possibly been the factor most responsible for limiting Paisley's chances of securing total Unionist support for his party. While many Unionist voters have been prepared to overlook his scathing attacks on their churches, others have not. Suspicions about

Paisley's intentions have existed throughout his ministry and political life. For example, some have wondered if it was personal ambition which was the dynamic of all his ecclesiastical and political activity. Did he want to destroy the Protestant churches and set himself up as moderator of a new 'protestantism'? Certainly his own teaching clearly states his belief in the apostasy of Protestantism, and his leadership of a new church would be expected to follow after the decline of the existing churches. In his ambition to lead Irish Protestantism in both the ecclesiastical and the political domain, he has perhaps overreached himself and failed in both objectives

When Paisley dies his desire to lead Irish Protestantism – as he understands it – dies with him. Although the Paisley dynasty of Kyle in the Free Presbyterian Church and Ian junior in the DUP may continue, subject to their retaining the measure of public support given to their father, the political dynasty appears more vulnerable than the small church dynasty. The threat which Ian Paisley senior posed to Unionist solidarity by his desire to dominate both the ecclesiastical and political arenas will have disappeared, but so too will the distinctive DUP identity which existed during his lifetime due to his dual role as church and party leader. Ian junior's ambition to be a politician only, and not, like his father, both a 'separatist' minister and a Unionist politician, removes the obstacle which many feel has been responsible for the division within Unionism. David Wiltshire, who regards himself as a friend of Peter Robinson, anticipates this reunion of Unionism when Paisley senior leaves politics: 'I think he [Peter Robinson] would readily accept that for as long as Ian is in politics any chance of reconciliation is probably nil. But certainly, reading between the lines, I have a sense that Peter would want that reconciliation between the two branches of Unionism as soon as it is practically possible, but it won't be for a while.' If this reunion of Unionism results in the demise of the DUP, it may have consequences for Ian junior's political role. Time alone will tell if Unionist voters will want to provide the same limited support they offered his father, or possibly give him a higher measure of support. More likely, he may find one day that the Paisley era has finally ended.

One can only anticipate what the future may hold. The past, however, is a matter of history. We have witnessed in this century in Ireland a strange phenomenon. We have seen a form of anti-Catholicism which went beyond anything previously experienced. Paisley's denial of the Roman Catholic Church as a Christian church was not true of the Reformers, the evangelical tradition, the Unionist founders of the state of Northern Ireland, or their successors. His accusations of apostasy throughout Protestantism were also unique. The trust which many Unionist voters placed in the leadership of a man who combined his personal religious crusade with traditional Unionist principles was also unparalleled. And all this within a land which already had major community tensions and problems.

Paisleyism existed because people supported it. Its future existence, personified in Ian Paisley or in the dynasty which he wishes to establish, depends on the nourishment of that same support.

Notes and References

Chapter One

1. Ian Paisley, *The Preaching of Ian Paisley*, (Belfast: Martyrs' Memorial Recordings), 17 November 1985.
2. *The Preaching*, 24 November 1985.
3. *The Revivalist*, September 1967, p. 1.
4. *The Preaching*, 24 October 1986.
5. Ian Paisley, *Northern Ireland, What is the Real Situation?* p. 15.
6. *The Revivalist*, February 1984, p. 2.
7. *The Revivalist*, June 1990, p. 8.
8. Gusty Spence, interview with author, 20 October 1995.
9. *The Revivalist*, November 1988, p. 8.
10. *The Preaching*, 17 March 1991.
11. Ian Paisley, *Go Tell That Fox*, Martyrs' Memorial Recordings, undated.
12. *The Revivalist*, March 1979.
13. Rhonda Paisley, *Ian Paisley, My Father* (Basingstoke: Marshall Pickering, 1988), p. 135.
14. Ibid., p. 142.
15. Ibid., p. 4.
16. Kyle Paisley, interview with author, 15 July 1995.
17. Eric Smyth, interview with author, 26 October 1995.
18. Tommy Cecil, interview with author, 2 November 1995.
19. *The Revivalist*, October 1990, p. 3.
20. Maurice Hayes, *Minority Verdict*, (Belfast: Blackstaff Press, 1995), p. 98.
21. Rhonda Paisley, *Ian Paisley*, p. 142.

Chapter Two

1. W. D. Killen, *The Ecclesiastical History of Ireland* (London: Macmillan, 1875), p. 212.
2. J.C. Beckett, *A Short History of Ireland* (London: Hutchinson, 1958), p. 18.
3. Patrick Corish, *The Irish Catholic Experience* (Dublin: Gill and Macmillan, 1985), p. 64.
4. Finlay Holmes, *Our Irish Presbyterian Heritage* (Belfast: Publications Committte of the Presbyterian Church in Ireland, 1985), pp. 20-21.

5. Beckett, *A Short History of Ireland*, p. 86.
6. Peter Robinson, *Their Cry Was 'No Surrender'* (Dublin: Crown Publications, 1988), p. 19.
7. Patrick Corish, *The Irish Catholic Experience*, p. 123.
8. *The Works of John Wesley* (Grand Rapids, Michigan: Zondervan, undated, reproduced from the authorised edition published by the Wesleyan Conference Office in London, 1872), vol. XI, pp. 187-95.
9. John Wesley, *Explanatory Notes on the New Testament* (London: Wesleyan Methodist Bookroom, undated).
10. David Hempton, *Methodism and Politics in British Society, 1750-1850* (London: Hutchinson, 1984), p. 43.
11. Wesley, 'Of the Church' (sermon), *Works*, vol. VI, p. 397.
12. Wesley, *Works*, vol. XI, pp. 80-86.
13. Quoted in Patrick Bishop and Eamonn Mallie, *The Provisional IRA* (London: Corgi, 1987), pp. 19-20.
14. Edmund Curtis, *A History of Ireland* (London: Methuen, 1957), pp. 336-37.
15. Quoted in Finlay Holmes, *Our Irish Presbyterian Heritage*, p. 90.
16. Ibid., p. 90.
17. Quoted in Desmond Bowen, *The Protestant Crusade in Ireland, 1800-1870* (Dublin: Gill and Macmillan, 1978), p. 73.
18. William Urwick, 'A Brief Sketch of the Religious State of Ireland' (Dublin: John Robertson, 1852), in *Methodist Pamphlets, Vol. XV*, bound at St Patrick's Reformatory School, Upton, Co. Cork, undated.
19. Bowen, *Protestant*, p. 267.
20. Ibid., p. 312.
21. Corish, *The Irish Catholic Experience*, p. 194.
22. Ibid., p. 218.
23. Bowen, *The Protestant Crusade*, p. 233.
24. Holmes, *Presbyterian Heritage*, p. 123.
25. Quoted in Holmes, *Presbyterian Heritage*, p. 134.
26. *Christian Advocate*, 8 January 1886.
27. See Mary Harris, *The Catholic Church and the Establishment of the Northern Ireland State* (Cork: Cork University Press, 1994).

Chapter Three

1. R.J. Beggs, *Great is Thy Faithfulness* (Ballymena: Ballymena Free Presbyterian Church, 1978), p. 12.
2. Ian R.K. Paisley, *This is My Life*, (Belfast: Martyrs' Memorial Recordings), tape 1, undated.
3. *The Revivalist*, November 1991, p. 11.
4. E. Maloney and A. Pollak, *Paisley* (Swords, Co. Dublin: Poolbeg, 1986), p. 11.
5. Jack Henry, *A Door That God Opened* (published by the author, 1989), pp. 14-38.

6. Ian R.K. Paisley, *The Man and his Message* (Belfast: Martyrs' Memorial Publications, 1976), p. 134.
7. William McKillen, *History of Ballymena Baptist Church*, unpublished transcript.
8. Maloney and Pollak, *Paisley*, pp. 14-15.
9. Ibid., p. 15.
10. *The Revivalist*, June 1983, p. 24.
11. Quoted in Austin Fulton, *J. Ernest Davey* (Belfast: Presbyterian Church in Ireland, 1970), p. 101.
12. Ibid., p. 101.
13. Beggs, *Great is Thy Faithfulness*, p. 17.
14. Ibid., p. 7.
15. Finlay Holmes, interview with author, 8 September 1995.
16. *Ballymena: Our Town. Ian Paisley and Jack McCann in conversation with Eull Dunlop* (Ballymena: Mid-Antrim Historical Group, 1994), p. 15.
17. Paisley, *This is My Life*, tape 1.
18. Ivor Colman, interview with author, 5 December 1995.
19. *The Solemn League and Covenant, 1643.*
20. Adam Loughridge, interview with author, 9 December 1994.
21. *Reformed Presbyterian Theological Hall Committee Minutes*, 21 October 1943.
22. Sabine Wichert, *Northern Ireland Since 1945* (London: Longman, 1991), p. 41.
23. Maloney and Pollak, *Paisley*, p. 21.
24. Joseph Thompson, *Your Church is On Fire! The Story of Ravenhill Presbyterian Church* (Belfast: Ambassador Productions, undated), p. 43.
25. See chapter four.
26. Ian Paisley, *W.P. Nicholson, Tornado of the Pulpit* (Belfast: Martyrs' Memorial Publications, 1982), p. 10.
27. John Douglas, interview with author, 28 November 1994.
28. Paisley, *This is My Life*, tape 1.
29. Ibid.
30. *The Revivalist*, April 1980, pp. 9-11.
31. Gordon McMullan, interview with author, 9 October 1995.

Chapter Four

1. John Hewitt, *The Collected Poems of John Hewitt*, ed. Frank Ormsby (Belfast: Blackstaff Press).
2. *The Revivalist*, February 1986, p. 30.
3. Ibid., p. 24.
4. *The Revivalist*, February 1956, p. 1.
5. Paisley, *This is My Life*, (Belfast: Martyrs' Memorial Recordings) undated, tape 3.
6. *The Revivalist*, September 1983, p. 9.

7. *The Revivalist*, January 1989, p. 13.
8. Martyrs' Memorial Recordings, 8 October 1995.
9. *Psalms, Paraphrases and Hymns* (Belfast: Presbytery of the Free Presbyterian Church of Ulster, 1989).
10. *The Revivalist*, September 1990, p. 3.
11. *The Revivalist*, October 1983, pp. 11-12.
12. Ian R.K. Paisley, *Concise Guide to Bible Christianity and Romanism*, 1991.
13. *Letter and response* from Michael Hurley, 14 May 1992; *letter and response* from Paul Fleming, 3 July 1992.
14. Vatican Council II, *Dogmatic Constitution of the Church*, ed. Austin Flannery (Dublin: Dominican Publications, 1988), pp. 350-432.
15. *The Roman Missal*.
16. Alan Cairns, *A Prophet with Honour* (Belfast: Presbytery of the Free Presbyterian Church, undated), pp. 77-85.
17. *The Revivalist*, March 1981, p. 7.
18. Steve Bruce, *God Save Ulster! The Religion and Politics of Paisleyism* (Oxford: Oxford University Press, 1986).
19. Ibid., back cover page, carrying the quotation from *London Review of Books*.
20. Ibid., p. 35.
21. Ibid., p. 50.
22. Ian R.K. Paisley, *Antichrist*, Belfast: Martyrs' Memorial Productions, no date give but *c.* 1980.
23. Ian R.K. Paisley, *No Pope Here* (Belfast: Martyrs' Memorial Publications, 1982).
24. John M. Barkley, 'The Antichrist. A Historical Survey', lecture delivered at the public closing of the Presbyterian College, Belfast, 26 May 1967.
25. Ian R.K. Paisley, *The Massacre of St Bartholomew* (Belfast: Martyrs' Memorial Productions, 1972), p. 38.
26. Beza's speech quoted in Pierre de la Place, *Commentaires de l'Etat de la Religion et Republique sous les Roys Henri et Francois II et Charles IX*, re-edited by Buchon, in *Pantheon Litteraire* (Paris, 1836), pp. 157-67.
27. Martin Luther, *Works*, American Edition, vol. 40, pp. 231-32. Quotation in article by R. Buick Knox, 'Continuity and Controversy: Before and After Calvin and Sadoleto', in *The Journal of the United Reformed Church History Society*, vol. 4, no. 7 (October 1990), pp. 408-18.
28. Letter from John Calvin to Cardinal Sadolet in *Tracts Relating to the Reformation*, ed. Henry Beveridge, vol. I, pp. 21-68.
29. Ibid., p. 38.
30. Ibid., p. 50.
31. John Calvin, *Institutes* (James Clarke & Co., undated), vol. 11, pp. 313-14.
32. *The Revivalist*, February 1993, pp. 14-21.

33. Wesley, *Works*, vol. 6, p. 397.
34. Quoted in David Butler, *Methodists and Papists, John Wesley and the Catholic Church in the Eighteenth Century*, (London: Darton, Longman, and Todd, 1995), pp. 167-68.
35. Charles Hodge, *The Church and Its Polity* (London, Paternoster), 1879.
36. Ibid., p. 192.
37. Ibid., p. 207.
38. Ibid., p. 208.
39. Ibid., p. 208.
40. Ibid., p. 214.
41. *The Revivalist*, February 1979, p. 2.
42. *Protestant Telegraph*, 11 February 1979, p. 8.
43. *The Revivalist*, March 1979, p. 2.
44. Quoted in R. Finlay Holmes, 'Modern Roman Catholic Reaction to Luther', in *Irish Biblical Studies*, vol. 6 (January 1984), p. 2.
45. *Irish News*, 18 December 1931.
46. Quoted in N. Lossky et al., eds., *Dictionary of the Ecumenical Movement* (Geneva: WCC Publications, 1991), p. 883.
47. Vatican Council II, *Dogmatic Constitution*, pp. 452-70.
48. *Dictionary of the Ecumenical Movement*, p. 85.
49. Ibid., p. 649.
50. 'The Evangelical-Roman Catholic Dialogue on Mission, 1977-1984: A Report', *International Bulletin of Missionary Research*, vol. 10, no.1.
51. Eric Gallagher and Stanley Worrall, *Christians in Ulster, 1968-1980* (Oxford: Oxford University Press, 1982), p. 78.
52. *Violence in Ireland, A Report to the Churches* (Belfast: Christian Journals, 1976).
53. *Protestant Telegraph*, 12 August 1972, p. 5.
54. *Protestant Telegraph*, 2-15 December 1972, p. 1.
55. John C. Heenan, *Not the Whole Truth* (London: Hodder and Stoughton, 1971), p. 201.
56. *Protestant Telegraph*, 10-23 August 1974, p. 1.
57. *Protestant Telegraph*, 15 February 1975, p. 6.
58. *The Revivalist*, September 1985, p. 2.
59. *The Revivalist*, September 1988, p. 2.
60. *The Revivalist*, July/August 1988, p. 10.
61. *Protestant Telegraph*, 3 December 1988, p. 2.
62. Ian R.K. Paisley, *Irish Roman Catholic Priests Challenged and Answered* (Edinburgh: Scottish Protestant Union, 1953).
63. Paisley, *This is My Life*, tape 2.
64. *The Revivalist*, April 1985, p. 7.
65. *The Revivalist*, July 1956, p. 1.
66. J.H. Whyte, *Church and State in Modern Ireland, 1923-1979* (Dublin, Gill and Macmillan, 1980), p. 320.

67. *Irish Press*, 23 July 1979.
68. Tim Pat Coogan, *De Valera. Long Fellow, Long Shadow*, (London: Hutchinson, 1993).
69. Quotation from Gallagher and Worrall, *Christians in Ulster*, pp. 122-23.
70. *Protestant Telegraph*, 2 January 1971, p. 7.
71. Tim Pat Coogan, *The Troubles* (London: Hutchinson, 1995), p. xiii.
72. *Irish Times*, 1 September 1986, p. 1.
73. *Violence in Ireland*, p. 80.
74. Cathal B. Daly, *Price of Peace* (Belfast: Blackstaff Press, 1991).
75. Ibid., p. 69.
76. Ibid., pp. 52-53.
77. *Belfast Telegraph*, 20 December 1995.
78. Daly, *Price of Peace*, p. 78.
79. Ibid., p. 197.

Chapter Five

1. *Hymns and Psalms*, (London: Methodist Publishing House, 1983), no. 230.
2. *The Revivalist*, September 1983, p. 9.
3. Ian R.K. Paisley, *The Soul of the Question and the Question of the Soul* (Belfast: Martyrs' Memorial Publications, 1989), p. 57.
4. *The Revivalist*, November 1991, p. 6.
5. Paisley, *This is My Life*, undated, tape 4.
6. Paisley, *Go Tell That Fox*.
7. *The Revivalist*, May 1991, p. 10.
8. Paisley, *Go Tell That Fox*.
9. Paisley, *This is My Life*, tape 3.
10. Norman Goodall, *The Ecumenical Movement* (London: OUP, 1964), p. 5.
11. Ibid.
12. N. Lossky et al., *Dictionary of the Ecumenical Movement* (Geneva: WCC Publications, 1991), p. 704.
13. Ibid., p. 705.
14. W.A. Visser 't Hooft, *The Pressure of our Common Calling* (London: SCM Press, 1959), p. 27.
15. Faith and Order, Final Report (Oxford 1937), p. 160f.
16. W.A. Visser 't Hooft, *The Genesis and Formation of the World Council of Churches* (Geneva, WCC, 1982), p. 16.
17. Ibid., pp. 66-67.
18. *The Revivalist*, July/August 1981, p. 17.
19. Paisley, *Go Tell That Fox*.
20. Paisley, *The Soul of the Question*, p. 58.
21. Paisley, *This is My Life*, tape 5.

22. Ian R.K. Paisley, *Blu-Print Union with Rome* (Belfast: Martyrs' Memorial Publications, 1989), p. 31.
23. *The Revivalist*, September 1989, p. 3.
24. *The Revivalist*, December 1995, p. 2.
25. *The Revivalist*, January 1993, p. 8.
26. *The Revivalist*, February 1984.
27. *The Revivalist*, June 1968, p. 9.
28. *The Revivalist*, June 1955, p. 1.
29. *The Revivalist,* March 1956, p. 1.
30. Alan Cairns, *A Prophet with Honour* (Belfast: Presbytery of the Free Presbyterian Church), p. 159.
31. *The Revivalist*, June 1955, p. 8.
32. They were Arians, not Unitarians. This is a common popular error. Montgomery himself resisted Unitarianism in the Non-Subscribing Church.
33. R. Finlay Holmes, *Henry Cooke* (Belfast: Christian Journals, 1981), p. 119.
34. Quoted in the *Presbyterian Herald*, June 1968, p. 4.
35. A.J. Weir, interview with author, 3 October 1995.
36. Frank Pantridge, *An Unquiet Life, Memoirs of a Physician and Cardiologist* (Belfast: W.G. Baird, 1989), pp. 91-92. Leonard Small, the Scottish Moderator that year, claims in his autobiography that his wife – and I believe Lady Erskine – suffered ill-health permanently as the result of that night's experience.
37. E. Maloney and A. Pollak, *Paisley* (Swords, Co. Dublin: Poolbeg, 1986), pp. 132-33.
38. *Presbyterian Herald*, July/August 1966.
39. *Protestant Telegraph*, 30 July 1966.
40. Ian R.K. Paisley, *Romans* (Belfast: Martyrs' Memorial Publications, 1968).
41. *The Revivalist*, February 1968, p. 11.
42. *The Revivalist*, June 1968,
43. *The Revivalist*, December 1978.
44. *The Revivalist*, September 1989, p. 2.
45. *The Revivalist*, January 1989, p. 6.
46. *The Revivalist*, April 1986, pp. 2 and 11.
47. *The Revivalist*, May 1986, pp. 4-5.
48. *The Revivalist*, July/August 1986, p. 27.
49. *Protestant Telegraph*, 18 March 1967, pp. 6-7.
50. Ian R. K. Paisley, *Billy Graham and the Church of Rome* (Belfast: Martyrs' Memorial Free Presbyterian Church, 1970), Preface. Students at Bob Jones University have actually been directed *NOT* to pray for the Billy Graham organisation.
51. Ibid., p. 41.
52. *The Revivalist*, February 1981, p. 2.

53. Ibid.
54. *The Revivalist*, February 1983, p. 5.
55. *The Revivalist*, May 1991, p. 15.
56. *The Revivalist*, March 1983, pp. 10-11.
57. Paisley, *Go Tell That Fox*.
58. *The Revivalist*, February 1980, p. 7.
59. *The Revivalist*, January 1983, p. 10.
60. Cairns, *A Prophet with Honour*, p. 37.
61. *The Revivalist*, January 1980, p. 14.
62. Paisley, *Go Tell That Fox*.
63. Ibid.
64. *The Revivalist*, June 1993, p. 29.
65. Ibid.
66. Ian R. K. Paisley, 'Temptations of the Ministry', sermon, 1 August 1993.
67. *The Revivalist*, June 1993, pp. 29-30.
68. *The Revivalist*, October 1990, p. 17.
69. *The Revivalist*, March 1988, p. 3.
70. Gordon Wilson, *Marie* (London: Collins, 1990), p. 46.
71. *The Revivalist*, December, 1987, pp. 23-24.
72. Donald Ker, interview with author, 1 March 1995.
73. *The Revivalist*, December 1987, p. 24.
74. Jim Sands, interview with author, 4 October 1995.
75. James L.M. Haire, 'A United Church – is it Biblical?', *Irish Ecumenical Pamphlets*, no. 7 (Irish Council of Churches, undated).
76. *The Revivalist*, February 1981, p. 18.
77. *The Revivalist*, February 1980, p. 10.
78. *The Revivalist*, December 1986, p. 6.
79. *The Revivalist*, March 1981, p. 14.
80. *The Revivalist*, December 1991, p. 9.
81. *The Revivalist*, March 1983, p. 10.
82. *The Revivalist*, September 1989, p. 12.
83. *The Revivalist*, March 1989, p. 4.

Chapter Six

1. *The Works of George Whitefield* (London, 1771), vol. 2. p. 144, quoted in Arnold Dallimore, *George Whitefield* (Edinburgh: The Banner of Truth Trust, 1970), p. 333.
2. *The Revivalist*, September 1967, p. 2.
3. *Presbytery of Down Minutes*, 8 January 1951.
4. Henry Gilpin, interview with author, 6 October 1995.
5. *Presbytery of Down Minutes*, 3 February 1951.
6. *The Revivalist*, September 1967, pp. 2-3.
7. William Boland, interview with author, 5 October 1995.
8. *The Revivalist*, December 1967, pp. 2-3.

9. *Presbytery of Down Minutes*, 15 March 1951.
10. *The Revivalist*, March 1991, p. 6.
11. *Lissara Presbyterian Church Session Minutes*, 31 October 1958.
12. Henry Gilpin, interview.
13. Letter from Trevor Gibson to author, 28 October 1995.
14. *The Revivalist*, June 1983, pp. 30-31.
15. E. Moloney and A. Pollak, *Paisley* (Swords, Co. Dublin: Poolbeg Press, 1986), p. 40.
16. Rhonda Paisley, *Ian Paisley, My Father*, pp. 304.
17. *The Revivalist*, April 1968, p. 9.
18. *The Preaching of Ian Paisley*, Martyrs' Memorial Recordings, 1 August 1993.
19. Ian R.K. Paisley, *This is My Life*, Martyrs' Memorial Recordings, undated, tape 6.
20. Eric Gallagher and Stanley Worrall, *Christians in Ulster, 1968-1980* (Oxford: Oxford University Press, 1982), p. 24.
21. Paisley, *This is My Life*, tape 4.
22. *The Revivalist*, February 1993, p. 28.
23. Paisley, *This is My Life*, tape 4.
24. *The Revivalist*, May 1967, p.1.
25. *The Revivalist*, July-August 1967, p. 1.
26. *The Revivalist*, October 1967, p. 1.
27. *The Revivalist*, May 1981, p. 11.
28. *The Revivalist*, November 1992, p. 15.
29. Alan Cairns, A *Prophet with Honour* (Belfast: Presbytery of the Free Presbyterian Church), p. 22.
30. George Whitefield, 'The Kingdom of God', sermon preached on 13 September 1741 in Glasgow, Scotland, and quoted in *Christian History* (Spring, 1993), p. 17.
31. Ibid.
32. Mervyn Cotton, interview with author, 10 October 1995.
33. *The Revivalist*, February 1963, p. 2.
34. *The Revivalist*, May 1979, pp. 5-6.
35. Ibid.
36. David McIlveen, interview with author, 24 November 1995.
37. Paisley, *This is My Life*, tape 5.
38. *The Revivalist*, May 1982, p. 30.
39. Ian R.K. Paisley, *Why We Hold the Authorised King James' Bible and Reject Modern Versions* (British Council of Protestant Christian Churches, undated).
40. *The Revivalist*, June 1993, p. 3.
41. David Porter, *The Story of Rev. William McCrea* (London: Lakeland, 1980), p. 93.
42. *Protestant Telegraph*, 19 December 1970, p. 8.
43. *Protestant Telegraph*, 17 December 1977, p. 8.

44. Ian R.K. Paisley, *The Fundamentalist and His State* (Greenville, South Carolina: Bob Jones University Press, 1976, p. 6.
45. Ibid.

Chapter Seven

1. *Protestant Telegraph*, 15-28 June 1974.
2. *Belfast Telegraph*, 4 April 1996.
3. Denis P. Barritt and Charles F. Carter, *The Northern Ireland Problem* (Oxford: Oxford University Press, 1962).
4. Ibid., p. 120.
5. Ibid., p. 96.
6. *The Revivalist*, August 1955, p.5.
7. This attitude to others is inclusive of Roman Catholics. While Orangemen are expected to 'strenuously oppose the fatal errors and doctrines of the Church of Rome, and scrupulously avoid countenancing (by his presence or otherwise) any act or ceremony of Popish worship', they are also instructed to abstain 'from all uncharitable words, actions, or sentiments, towards their Roman Catholic brethren'. W.W. Dewar, *Why Orangeism?* (Belfast, 1958), pp. 23-24.
8. Warren Porter, interview with author, 11 October 1995.
9. E. Moloney and A. Pollak, *Paisley* (Swords, Co. Dublin: Poolbeg Press 1986), p. 53.
10. Clifford Smyth, *Ian Paisley, Voice of Protestant Ulster* (Edinburgh: Scottish Academic Press, 1987), p. 6.
11. Quoted in Moloney and Pollak, *Paisley*, p. 49.
12. *Voice of Ulster*, December 1982, p. 3.
13. Terence O'Neill, *An Autobiography of Terence O'Neill, Prime Minister of Northern Ireland, 1963-69* (London: Rupert Hart-Davis, 1972), pp. 1-2.
14. Ibid., p. 50.
15. Moloney and Pollak, *Paisley*, p. 111.
16. Gerry Adams, *Falls Memories* (Dingle, Co. Kerry: Brandon, 1993), pp. 132-34.
17. Michael Farrell, *Northern Ireland: The Orange State* (London, Pluto Press, 1980), p. 234.
18. Moloney and Pollak, *Paisley*, p. 119.
19. *Belfast Telegraph*, 26 February 1965.
20. *Terence O'Neill*, p. 75.
21. Ibid., p. 74.
22. *Protestant Telegraph*, 22 May 1966, p. 1.
23. Ibid., p. 3.
24. Ibid., p. 2.
25. Smyth, *Ian Paisley*, p. 13.
26. The Constitution and Rules of the UCDC and UPV are found in Appendix IX of *Disturbances in Northern Ireland*, Report of the

Commission Appointed by the Governor of Northern Ireland (Belfast: Her Majesty's Stationery Office, 1969), pp. 118-19.

27. Ibid., p. 88.
28. Moloney and Pollak, *Paisley*, p. 136.
29. Paisley later published this sermon in the *Protestant Telegrap*h, 11 November 1968.
30. Tim Pat Coogan, *The Troubles* (London: Hutchinson, 1995), pp. 47, 105, 111; also *Protestant Telegraph*, 23 September 1972, p. 2; also *New Protestant Telegraph*, February 1996, p. 3.
31. Moloney and Pollak, *Paisley*, p. 138.
32. Smyth, *Ian Paisley*, p. 15.
33. *Protestant Telegraph*, 11 November 1968.
34. These facts are considered in greater detail in Moloney and Pollak, *Paisley*, pp. 140-41, 185.
35. Quoted in Charles Wheeler: *Wheeler on America*, BBC, 3 March 1996.
36. *Minutes of the Conference of the Methodist Church in Ireland* (Dublin, 1966), p. 137.
37. W.D. Flackes and Sydney Elliott, *Northern Ireland. A Political Directory, 1968-1993* (Belfast: Blackstaff Press, 1994), p. 248.
38. Quoted in Coogan, *Troubles*, p. 36.
39. For example, Patrick Bishop and Eamonn Mallie, *The Provisional IRA* (London: Corgi Books, 1987), pp. 68-76 and Coogan, *Troubles*, pp. 56-57.
40. Smyth, *Ian Paisley*, p. 20.
41. *Protestant Telegraph*, 13 April 1968.
42. Ibid.
43. *Protestant Telegraph*, 21 September 1968. p. 2.
44. Ibid.
45. Quoted in Bishop and Mallie, *The Provisional IRA*, p. 75.
46. *Belfast Telegraph*, 7 October 1968.
47. *Belfast Telegraph*, 5 November 1968.
48. *Belfast Telegraph*, 6 November 1968.
49. *Belfast Telegraph*, 11 November 1968.
50. Moloney and Pollak, *Paisley*, pp. 162-64.
51. *Terence O'Neill*, pp. 145-49.
52. *Protestant Telegraph*, 14 December 1968.
53. *Protestant Telegraph*, 28 December 1968.
54. Coogan, *The Troubles*, pp. 67-70.
55. *Disturbances in Northern Ireland*, pp. 88-89.
56. *Protestant Telegraph*, 22 February 1969.
57. Moloney and Pollak, *Paisley*, p. 185.
58. *Protestant Telegraph*, 16 August 1969.
59. Quoted in Eric Gallagher and Stanley Worrall, *Christians in Ulster, 1968-1980* (Oxford: Oxford University Press, 1982), p. 51.
60. *Protestant Telegraph*, 30 August 1969.

61. Gallagher and Worrall, *Christians in Ulster*, p. 51.
62. Philip Zeigler, *Wilson, The Authorised Life of Lord Wilson of Rievaulx* (London: Weidenfield and Nicholson), p. 345.
63. *Protestant Telegraph*, 25 September 1969.
64. Quoted in Farrell, *Northern Ireland: The Orange State*, p. 270.
65. *Protestant Telegraph*, 21 March 1970.
66. G. R. Elton, ed., *The Reformation, 1520–1559* in New Cambridge Modern History (Cambridge: Cambridge University Press, 1979), vol. II, p. 230.
67. Moloney and Pollak, *Paisley*, p. 204.

Chapter Eight

1. *Protestant Telegraph*, 25 April 1970.
2. Patrick Bishop and Eamonn Mallie, *The Provisional IRA* (London: Corgi Books, 1987), p. 129.
3. *Protestant Telegraph*, 23 May 1970.
4. *Protestant Telegraph*, 27 February 1971.
5. Quoted in Clifford Smyth, *Ian Paisley, Voice of Protestant Ulster* (Edinburgh: Scottish Academic Press, 1987), p. 28.
6. *Protestant Telegraph*, 27 March 1971.
7. *Protestant Telegraph*, 19 February 1972.
8. Smyth, *Ian Paisley*, p. 30.
9. *Protestant Telegraph*, 11 December 1971.
10. *Constitution of Ireland* (Dublin: Government Publications Office, undated).
11. *Protestant Telegraph*, 13 November 1971, p. 2.
12. *Protestant Telegraph*, 4 March 1972, p. 1.
13. *Protestant Telegraph*, 18 March 1972, p. 1.
14. *Protestant Telegraph*, 1 April 1972, p. 1.
15. Quoted in Bew and Gillespie, *Northern Ireland. A Chronology of the Troubles, 1968–1993* (Dublin: Gill and Macmillan, 1993), p. 46.
16. *Protestant Telegraph*, 1 April 1972, p. 5.
17. *Protestant Telegraph*, 22 April 1972, p. 1.
18. Par. 52 quoted in Bew and Gillespie, *Northern Ireland*, p. 60.
19. Ibid., par. 111.
20. *Protestant Telegraph*, 26 May 1973, p. 1.
21. *Protestant Telegraph*, 23 June 1973, p. 1.
22. *Protestant Telegraph*, 24 November 1973, p. 1.
23. *Constitution of Ireland*, p. 4.
24. Garret FitzGerald, *All in a Life. Garret FitzGerald, an Autobiography* (Dublin: Gill and Macmillan, 1991), pp. 201–02.
25. Sunningdale Communiqué, par. 5, quoted in Bew and Gillespie, *Northern Ireland*, p. 73.
26. Ibid., p. 74.
27. *Protestant Telegraph*, 23 February 1974.

28. Fitzgerald, *Autobiography*, p. 238.
29. Eric Gallagher and Stanley Worrall, *Christians in Ulster, 1968–1980* (Oxford: Oxford University Press, 1982), pp. 90–91.
30. Ken Bloomfield, *Stormónt in Crisis, A Memoir* (Belfast: Blackstaff Press, 1994), p. 215.
31. Nelson Mandela, *Long Walk to Freedom, An Autobiography of Nelson Mandela* (London: Abacus, 1995), pp. 255–56.
32. Sydenham Defence Association, 10 June 1972, published in *Protestant Telegraph*, 1 July 1972, p. 6.
33. *Protestant Telegraph*, 29 March 1975, p. 8.
34. *Protestant Telegraph*, 4 October 1975, p. 3.
35. *Protestant Telegraph*, 15 May 1974, p. 8.
36. David Trimble, interview with author, 19 July 1995.
37. *Protestant Telegraph*, July 1977, p. 13.
38. *Protestant Telegraph*, July 1978, p. 3.
39. Bew and Gillespie, *Northern Ireland*, p. 113.
40. W. D. Flackes and Sydney Elliott, *Northern Ireland. A Political Directory, 1968–1993* (Belfast: Blackstaff Press, 19??), p. 265.
41. *Protestant Telegraph*, 21 August 1976, p. 1.
42. *Protestant Telegraph*, July 1977, p. 7.
43. *Protestant Telegraph*, 21 August 1976, p. 1.
44. *Protestant Telegraph*, 18 September 1976, p. 1.
45. *The Revivalist*, December, 1986, p. 5.
46. Ibid., p. 9.
47. *Protestant Telegraph*, 18 April 1981, p. 1.
48. Quoted in Smyth, *Ian Paisley*, p. 173.
49. Flackes and Elliott, *Northern Ireland*, p. 261 (30,000); *Protestant Telegraph* 18 April 1981 (100,000).
50. *Protestant Telegraph*, 18 April 1981.
51. *Protestant Telegraph*, 12 December 1981.
52. Smyth, *Ian Paisley*, p. 183.
53. Ibid.
54. *The Voice of Ulster*, April 1983.
55. Quoted in Anthony Kenny, *The Road to Hillsborough* (Oxford: Pergamon Press, 1986), p. 43.
56. Margaret Thatcher, *The Downing Street Years* (London: Harper Collins, 1993), p. 401.
57. Quoted in Kenny, *Road to Hillsborough*, p. 96.
58. Ibid., p. 107.
59. Quoted in Bew and Gillespie, *Northern Ireland*, p. 187.
60. *The Revivalist*, March 1986, p. 2.
61. *The Revivalist*, January 1986, p. 6.
62. Coogan, *Troubles*, p. 200.
63. *New Protestant Telegraph*, 24 June 1989, p. 3
64. *New Protestant Telegraph*, 16 September 1989, p. 3

65. *New Protestant Telegraph*, 27 January 1990, p. 3.
66. *New Protestant Telegraph*, July/August 1991, p. 5.
67. *New Protestant Telegraph*, March 1992, p. 1.
68. *Belfast Newsletter*, 16 December 1993, p. 5.
69. *Belfast Newsletter*, 17 December 1993, p. 2.
70. *Belfast Telegraph*, 7 January 1994.
71. Eamonn Mallie and David McKittrick, *The Fight for Peace* (London: Heinemann, 1996), p. 253.
72. Tim Pat Coogan, *The Troubles* (London: Hutchinson, 1995), p. 381.
73. Ibid., p. 368.
74. *Belfast Telegraph*, 31 May 1994.
75. *Belfast Telegraph*, 1 June 1994.
76. James Molyneaux, interview with author, 17 July 1995.
77. Martin Smyth, interview with author, 17 July 1995.
78. *Belfast Newsletter*, 1 September 1994. p. 2.
79. *Belfast Telegraph*, 7 September 1994, p. 3.
80. Ibid.
81. *Belfast Telegraph*, 28 October 1994, p.1.
82. *New Protestant Telegraph*, February 1995, p. 1.
83. *New Protestant Telegraph*, May 1995, p. 1.
84. *New Protestant Telegraph*, September 1995, p. 4.
85. *Belfast Telegraph*, 12 September 1995, p. 7.
86. *Belfast Telegraph*, 5 November 1995.
87. *The Irish Times*, 14 September 1995, p. 8.
88. Quoted in *Belfast Telegraph*, 24 January 1996, p. 6.
89. Ibid., p. 7.
90. *Belfast Telegraph*, 8 July 1996, p. 4.
91. *Belfast Telegraph*, 9 July 1996, p. 3.
92. *Sunday Times*, 7 July 1996, p. 1.
93. *Belfast Telegraph*, 23 July 1996, p. 9.
94. Statement of Church and Government Committee of the Presbyterian Church of Ireland, 23 July 1996.
95. *Belfast Telegraph*, 12 July 1996, p. 6.
96. *Belfast Telegraph*, 13 July 1996, p. 1.

Chapter Nine

1. Martin Luther King, speech at St Louis, 22 March 1964, printed in *St Louis Post-Dispatch*, 23 March 1964.
2. *The Sunday Times*, 14 January 1996.
3. *The Irish Times*, 17 May 1996.
4. *The Sunday Times*, 14 January 1996.
5. *Belfast Telegraph*, 27 July 1994.
6. Ibid.
7. Ibid.

8. *Belfast Telegraph*, 12 January 1996.
9. *Belfast Telegraph*, 13 January 1996.
10. David Wiltshire, interview with author, 18 July 1995.
11. Donald Anderson, interview with author, 17 July 1995.